THE MANDOLIN LESSON

FRANCES TAYLOR

Copyright © 2014 Frances Taylor

The moral right of the author has been asserted.

Apart from any fair dealing for the purposes of research or private study, or criticism or review, as permitted under the Copyright, Designs and Patents Act 1988, this publication may only be reproduced, stored or transmitted, in any form or by any means, with the prior permission in writing of the publishers, or in the case of reprographic reproduction in accordance with the terms of licences issued by the Copyright Licensing Agency. Enquiries concerning reproduction outside those terms should be sent to the publishers.

Matador
9 Priory Business Park
Kibworth Beauchamp
Leicestershire LE8 0RX, UK
Tel: (+44) 116 279 2299
Fax: (+44) 116 279 2277
Email: books@troubador.co.uk
Web: www.troubador.co.uk/matador

ISBN 978 1783062 980

British Library Cataloguing in Publication Data.
A catalogue record for this book is available from the British Library.

Typeset in Bembo by Troubador Publishing Ltd
Printed and bound in the UK by TJ International, Padstow, Cornwall

Matador is an imprint of Troubador Publishing Ltd

Grazie mille, a thousand thanks, to all my teachers and especially to my parents, Molly and Peter Taylor; my late husband, Colin Keiller; my Italian mandolin teacher, Ugo Orlandi; and Paul Marquis, who started me off on the violin and mandolin and speaking Italian.

SURREY LIBRARIES	
Askews & Holts	07-May-2014
945.092 WOR	£9.99

Introduction

What is the mandolin? Why learn the mandolin? And most importantly, is this journey for me?

The mandolin is a small half-pear-shaped stringed instrument, which is held a bit like a guitar and plucked with a piece of plastic called a plectrum. A bit simple, perhaps even a bit crude as an explanation, but I have to come up with something that makes sense when I am asked this ubiquitous question. Usually I am asked at unguarded, relaxed moments – you know the kind of thing – when I am having dinner with friends but there are some new people to meet. The new people ask me what I do and I say I am a mandolinist. Eyes glaze over. The new people say, "Oh, that's interesting. What *is* a mandolin?"

That's when it starts; my attempt to give a cool, succinct explanation. Sometimes I try the, "Oh, it's like a lute, only much smaller," routine. Sometimes it works but sometimes it doesn't, because these new people don't seem to know what a lute is either. (I was thinking Shakespeare and thought it might have made a connection!)

Really, it is all very strange, because the mandolin as we know it seems to connect to so many different genres of music and so many different cultures. Mandolins come in all shapes and sizes – some have flat backs – and most countries in the world have a plucked stringed instrument, a close or distant relative, which has a role in traditional music. Think the *bouzouki* from Greece, the *balalaika* from Russia, the *bandurria* from Spain, the *ruan* from China and the *charango* from South America – the list is just endless. At the same time, the mandolin appears in jazz, folk, pop and rock music just as easily as it does in the opera, ballet and other types of classical music.

Not only that, the mandolin seems to have a history which extends back through the entire timeline of civilisation, to the very beginning when man scraped out the tasty contents of the gourd and used the shell, stretching over it another waste product – gut – to make strings and, in turn, a kind of early mandolin.

So the answer to 'why learn the mandolin?' isn't just because I love its sound. Although I *do love* its sound, which is at times sparkly, effervescent, and at times, evocative and illusive. After all, how can eight pinging cheese-wires make such soulful, stirring music? But the answer also has to do with the oneness of the instrument – the way it can connect to so many people at so many levels.

And that brings me to my last question – is this journey for me? Or what I really meant is – is this journey for you? Well, I don't expect everyone to learn the mandolin or even music. (Although the incredibly inspiring project El Sistema, which provides free instruments and free lessons for all children in Venezuela, does bear testament to the life-enhancing power of music for everyone.) However, I have read and I do believe that feelings are the language of the soul. I also believe that music is a way of expressing those feelings and that it can communicate whether it is understood or not. In other words, you don't have to play an instrument or have any particular musical knowledge to fully enjoy music. *You* are already fluent in the language. That's right. Just in case you think I have made a typing error, I shall repeat it. *You* are already fluent in the language of music. If you are watching a film, for instance, you know immediately the mood of what is happening or about to happen by listening to the music. You know when it's tragic and you know when it is ecstatically happy, and you know all the emotions of the spectrum in between.

The thing is that this journey of mine and, if you read my book, the journey you will take, isn't really about learning the mandolin or learning about music. Yes, the mandolin is my thing. It gives me that fantastic rush of pleasure endorphins just as sport, sex or dark chocolate, does for other people. (Actually I *love* dark chocolate but I'm not much good at sport and as for sex – well, that's too much information.) You, on the other hand, probably want to do something completely different from me. Climb a mountain, a sponsored bike ride across India, improve your skiing, learn to paint or cook, learn a new skill or revisit an old skill, travel somewhere unheard of – I can't begin to list the infinite possibilities. Whatever it is though, learning something new, honing a forgotten skill, a sponsored challenge, a grand project, a little project – the process of achieving a goal or many little goals helps us to have insights about ourselves and others.

Yes, my journey is set in the beautiful land of Italy, but it could have been set anywhere. My story is not just about music or about Italy – they just combine to become a delightful coat-hanger upon which to hang the garment that is the story. The theme of my book is timeless and universal. It is about a journey that we are all on, a journey to find out about ourselves and to reconnect with who we are. In this sense, *the mandolin lesson* is not just for mandolin lovers like me – *the mandolin lesson* is for everyone.

(As a precaution, I've included a small glossary at the end for those of you who might find the odd technical term a bit confusing!)

il preludio

I look at the train ticket in my hand with awe and reverence, as if it is a Roman artefact belonging to the British Museum, which through some miracle I have been allowed to handle and inspect closely. On the orange ticket is printed 'from LONDON to PADOVA' under the title 'Outward' on the left-hand side. The destinations are reversed under the title of 'Return' on the right-hand side. At the bottom of the ticket, it states that the journey will be via 'SEALINK OR HOVERSPEED – FRENCH PORTS – PARIS / LILLE – BASEL / DELLE / VALLORBE / VERRIERES – ISELLE / CHIASSO – MILANO'. Normally, my train tickets are for the tube and printed with destinations such as Oxford Circus or Bond Street.

It seems quite incredible to me that I am about to depart from Victoria Station, London, on such a long and international train journey. It is October 1994 and the Channel Tunnel is not yet a reality. Until now, British people have been acutely aware of their island status. In order to go abroad, it is necessary to cross the sea, historically by ship and recently more frequently by air. Despite the cultural differences within our United Kingdom, it is still difficult for us to understand how people separated by language, governments and hugely contrasted cultures, are able to cross land borders, easily and quickly, in order to visit friends and relatives, go to work, undertake shopping or do many other routine activities.

Even more incredible is the fact that I am not leaving this island for a once-in-a-lifetime holiday trip or a great railway journey. I am travelling almost a thousand miles to Padua, Italy, with a special purpose: to study the mandolin. However, unlike young music students in their early twenties, I am unable to stay there for a year or two when I arrive. I have to maintain the life I already have in England, with its family and work commitments, and this means I will return almost immediately. I will spend twenty-four hours travelling on various trains (including a quick sea crossing of the English Channel).

It is now almost a quarter to nine in the morning and when I arrive at this time tomorrow morning in Padua, I will spend the entire day at the Music Conservatoire. At five o'clock in the afternoon, I shall have a few hours to wander around the nearby streets and to eat a meal in a restaurant. At about half past eight in the evening, I will catch the Venice-Paris overnight train from Padua Station to start my homeward-bound journey. After another twenty-four hours, I will arrive home in London. The whole expedition takes three days and two nights – the nights being spent in the train. I leave on Wednesday morning and arrive home early on Friday evening.

In essence, I am planning to embark upon a course of music study that will entail me attending a mandolin lesson, approximately once a month, in a foreign country. I am going to commute from England to Italy for a year, or maybe two years.

I look around at the other travellers and I notice a party of Japanese people. The young girls, small and elegantly dressed, contrast with the huge moulded plastic suitcases they wheel along the platform. I carry a small, navy blue canvas bag, which I am about to test for its potential. It is supposed to be strong and yet small and well designed to carry papers, a spare shirt and other overnight things. Instead of papers, I have my music in the large pocket section. In addition, I carry the mandolin in its case and a small handbag which, like the canvas bag, has a shoulder strap. I intend to travel as light as possible.

As I board the train and choose a shabby, worn, blue plaid seat next to the window I settle down to think. I am looking forward to thinking time on my journeys. The train bumbles slowly through Kent, sometimes described as the garden of England. The rhythmic movement of the train is disturbed unexpectedly from time to time by a jolting movement. Despite these unexpected movements and the consequential fierce noises of jarring metal, I still myself and begin to reflect on my work. I wonder exactly how all this began.

It begins with a telephone call while I am cooking pasta for the evening meal.

Just as the telephone rings, I notice that the water seems to be bubbling a little too fast for my liking.

A man's voice speaks with a strange accent that I don't recognise. I am immediately suspicious and my head races with all kinds of ideas. *Is he crazy? Drunk? A serious enquiry from abroad about my playing? Or perhaps someone I know very well playing a trick on me?*

Eventually, after some difficult moments, I understand, at least I think I understand, what he is saying. He is Ugo Orlandi (the distinguished Italian mandolinist), and he is staying in Dublin whilst undertaking a concert with an orchestra called *I*

Solisti Veneti. The day after tomorrow he is returning to Italy via a connecting flight at Heathrow Airport. He wants to meet me at the airport to have a chat and to receive, if possible, a copy of an essay I had written on the mandolin. (He knows about me and my essay from a visit he made to a mandolin factory in Naples. I had left a copy of my essay with the owner of the factory, because it concerned music written by his grandfather, Raffaele Calace.)

After I put the phone down, I return to my dinner preparations but it is difficult to focus on what I am supposed to be doing. My head is in a spin. Being a classical musician means that I belong to, what some people believe to be, a small and elite group within society. Within this category of classical musician, I belong to another very tiny group, which is almost an extinct species – the professional mandolinist! I don't like being thought of as part of an elite group, but I dislike even more being nearly extinct! Orlandi's work had for some time been an inspiration to me through his recording of the beautiful Paisiello mandolin concerto, which I absolutely *adore*. It seems unbelievable that he had just phoned and asked to meet me.

Four days before Christmas 1989, I find myself waiting at the airport for Maestro Ugo Orlandi. I have been wondering what he will look like. I am suffering from pre-Christmas stress and my mind is fragmented as I mentally try to catalogue various lists of jobs that still need doing in the ever decreasing time available. Periodically I bring my attention back to the people arriving and I realise that it will be easy to recognise Ugo since he will be carrying a mandolin case. However, when the musicians of the orchestra appear, it isn't clear at first who is carrying a mandolin case. Somehow Ugo notices me first, probably because I am looking intently for someone. He is tall, with an olive complexion, dark receding hair and a beard. He has a wicked grin and twinkling brown eyes. I have the impression that he is a little older than me. Maybe it is his greater height and broad shoulders or maybe he exudes an aura of expertise. Anyway, the mandolin case is swung over his shoulder like a pregnant tennis racket carried by a Wimbledon champion. I have never seen a mandolin case like this before.

We spend an hour together talking about the mandolin and musical life in England and Italy. I give him a copy of my essay as requested. He is encouraging and interested in my research into mandolin music, and I feel hopeful that it is the beginning of a mutually helpful working relationship.

For the second time in its 400-year-old history, the mandolin is undergoing something of a revival. The term *mandola* was first used in Florence in 1589. *Mandolino*, the Italian for mandolin, Ugo tells me, is the diminutive of *mandola*, just as *violino*, violin, is the diminutive of *viola*. In other words, the present-day mandolin is a small *mandola*. The Italians worked from the biggest instrument downwards when they chose words of description, rather than the other way around. I imagine that we shall be able to swap all sorts of useful bits of information as we each explore the libraries of Europe in search of forgotten manuscripts.

Ugo introduces me to another mandolinist, Dorina Frati. She played with Ugo in Dublin. Together, they were soloists in a performance of Vivaldi's double mandolin concerto.

Before we part, Ugo pulls a large, glossy white sheet of folded paper out of his bag and hands it to me. I read the words at the top of the sheet. '*Programma del corso straordinario di Mandolino*': Programme of the Extraordinary Mandolin Course. *Straordinario* might be better translated as special, in which case the heading would be 'Programme of the Special Mandolin Course'. Either way, it acknowledges the unusualness of this course of study. The four-sided prospectus laid out the requirements for the seven-year course, the scales and repertoire to be studied during each of the years, as well as a list of pieces from which a choice could be made for the two diploma exams. So many beautiful Italian names, some well-known to me and others unknown. Gervasio, Eterardi, Barbella, Conforto, the list was endless – all like dishes on a menu. Each name beautiful in itself for its musical sound and representing some great treasure to be cherished by the ear and sensed by the body. So often people are disparaging about the mandolin because they think it has little or no repertoire. The prospectus was an affirmation of exactly the opposite. I feel a great surge of excitement about the whole idea of the course and I think that if I had my life again, how fantastic it would be to be able to attend a course specifically designed for my instrument.

―◦―

Between Christmas and the New Year, I receive a second surprise phone call, this time from the Royal Opera House asking me to attend a rehearsal the following day for Verdi's opera *Otello*. It is a stunning and much publicised production starring big names – Placido Domingo, Katia Ricciarelli and the legendary conductor Carlos Kleiber. I am contracted for two rehearsals and three performances. OK, yes I know this definitely sounds a bit elitist, but although I may have privately fantasised about such a possibility, all the odds were heavily stacked against me, and it is the proverbial 'dream come true' experience. I am at once exhilarated and utterly amazed – there has been a big shake-up in the mandolin world to make this break possible for me. The lives of the mandolinists usually booked have taken them in different directions. I am so grateful for the opportunity it gives me to extend into a new area of professional activity. Until now, most of my work has been as a soloist, giving recitals around the country.

At the first rehearsal, I meet another mandolinist, Sue Mossop. Although mandolin courses do not exist here – they are not advertised in any prospectus – Sue managed to break new ground by becoming the exception. She was accepted as a student at Trinity College of Music and she was able to continue her mandolin studies with her previous teacher. Whilst she was able to study harmony, history of music and other shared components of her music course with her contemporaries, it must have been strange being the only mandolinist – sometimes special, sometimes isolated.

The rehearsal takes place in the Crush Bar, famously so-called because of the crush to get a drink in the interval. It exudes richness: deep red and gold, and glittering chandelier light. I am part of the off-stage band, which includes four mandolins, two guitars and an oboe. Apparently, when Giuseppe Verdi wrote the opera, he had in mind a small mandolin band. When it was first produced at La Scala, Milan, in 1887, just over one hundred years ago, the band comprised of six mandolins and *mandolas* with four guitars. They walked around the stage whilst playing. We sit hidden, between the wings, and are conducted by an assistant conductor who is kept in contact with the orchestra pit by means of headphones and a small television monitor.

The Maestro, Carlos Kleiber, takes the rehearsal himself instead of sending along an assistant. I have a healthy respect for the Maestro, knowing that some great names are difficult to work with. However, the rehearsal goes easily and at the conclusion, the Maestro compliments us on our good playing and asks if we were part of a mandolin orchestra. We tell him that we are not.

—⁂—

It is still January and I receive a letter from Ugo introducing himself and saying everything he told me during the phone call before Christmas. I realise that he had tried to prepare in advance for our meeting. The letter is headed Brescia, 29th October 1989.

I had also written a letter to Ugo, which I had handed to him personally at our first meeting. I was unhappy about my essay since it had become a bit of a disaster, and I wasn't confident that my Italian language skills were up to explaining the technical details. The essay – really a thesis of sorts – had been for a research diploma, which was not awarded to me and at the same time was discontinued as an exam.

I didn't really want to give Ugo a copy of my thesis because I felt it was somehow negated since it failed the exam, not to mention an exam which didn't exist anymore. More than anything, though, I think it showed my driving desire to find out more about music for the mandolin – music that you can't find in any shop. I just wanted to find music that I could play on the instrument whose sound I loved so much. This is the reason I found myself turning music detective and becoming interested in the libraries and museums that might harbour secret supplies of mandolin music. Sadly, as far as the essay/thesis was concerned, without any research skills I found it hard to present my argument in an academic manner. All I had wanted to do was to raise the profile of the mandolin; to share with others this small, fragile, yet enchanting and passionate instrument.

In the meantime, I enrolled on another course – a Master's degree in which I was able to specialise in the performance of mandolin music and to pursue my research into its repertoire. The course has helped me to develop the research skills I so desperately needed and I am now about halfway through this part-time study.

It is July and I receive another surprise phone call from Ugo. At about five o'clock in the afternoon, and after a gap of about six months, Ugo is explaining that he is in London to play in a concert this evening and could I come? He was playing at the Mansion House as part of the City of London Festival. Once again, my head is in a spin. I can't miss this opportunity, but I have to get a ticket and find a babysitter for my five-year-old son.

Within an hour, I am driving to the concert having arranged for a neighbour to look after my son and having booked the last ticket, a return, by telephone. I am not used to arranging my life at such short notice, but to be fair, Ugo had said that he had written to me. Another letter had obviously gone astray. Is the Italian postal service really so relaxed?

The concert consists of a number of concertos with various soloists. The playing is the most elegant that I have heard for a long time. The magnificent Baroque surroundings of the Mansion House provide a good acoustic and an ambience that is evocative of the period of the music. I am particularly enraptured with the Vivaldi double mandolin concerto, played by Ugo and his pupil, Dorina.

Afterwards, I dine with Ugo and Dorina at their hotel in Bloomsbury and we talk about mandolin music until midnight. The Masterclass, a term used in Italy to mean a music course, begins tomorrow in Venice. There is to be another one at the end of August in Brescia. I didn't find out this information previously because of the letter going astray. I am unable to leave for Venice immediately because of my domestic commitments and the Brescia dates clash with other family commitments. I also know I shall have difficulty in finding someone to look after my son since everyone will be away on holiday in August. It is impossible and I shall just have to wait patiently until next year. Dorina very kindly invites me to stay with her.

A few weeks later and another unanticipated event occurs when my mother phones and offers to look after my son. It means that suddenly I am free to attend the course in Brescia.

The Brescia course is a real turning point because although until now I have had a great desire to improve my playing, I hadn't understood precisely what I was searching for. Ugo spends time explaining posture to me. He has a different right-hand technique from mine, which, he explains, is considered more modern than the way in which I have been taught. My technique allows greater freedom for the Romantic tremolo, but his technique is more secure for greater control, security and speed in Baroque music. My wrist is arched and my forearm is just slightly touching the edge of the instrument's body. His wrist is straight and his forearm is in contact with the strings behind the bridge. My mandolin sits on my lap with the fingerboard at a forty-five degree angle to the floor. His mandolin is parallel to the floor. I feel dismayed that I have such fundamental changes to make.

At the same time, being my first solo trip to Italy – I had once visited Finland by myself for a concerto engagement – it is a heady experience. Although I have made several visits to Italy, before they were always essentially holidays, even though these holidays often included some experience connected with the mandolin. Naturally these visits were also always with other people. This time my visit is only for the purpose of improving my mandolin playing skills. I am completely on my own, which is both exciting and, at times, frightening.

The room we play in is a modern white attic room, which overlooks red tiled roofs and potted plants. The floor of the room interests me because it has the appearance of a large Lego base: hundreds of small raised circles made of a synthetic material, perhaps a type of plastic or rubber. Around the walls are enlarged photographs of Ugo and other local musicians with their instruments.

Every morning, we start at half past nine and play for two hours; the first hour being technique, exercises and explanations. The second hour is real music, which we usually play together and then individually. The playing is punctuated by advice from the Maestro. Then follows an hour of discussion about mandolin history. How many music lovers know that Scott Joplin's rags were intended for a mandolin orchestra? After a two-hour lunch break, there is another two hours of music-making: chamber music, mostly *suonato a prima vista*, played at first sight, or in other words, sight-reading. One afternoon we play music by Telemann, written originally for four violins, but serving the mandolin well because of the similar tuning and fingering. It is most enjoyable music, radiant and energising.

I am always animated when hearing new sounds; sounds I hadn't known were possible on the mandolin. Exquisite decorations; jewels crafted not in precious metals and stones, but in notes. Vibrations which are received by the ear and somehow have the power to move our souls. The neatest tremolo, the quietest *pianissimo*, the shimmer of a passage of notes played with the utmost rapidity and articulated with the greatest precision. These and many more resonate deep within me.

I return home to London and I spend hours agonising over the difference in posture and right-hand technique. I know that interpretation, the expression and shape given to music, is of the utmost importance in performance. Musicians are not merely machines churning out vast quantities of notes; their vocation and their artistry is to place these notes in time and space, so as to sculpt the sound and communicate with the listener. At the same time, I am aware that in order to achieve such eloquence, it is necessary to have an appropriate technique. It is like trying to write poetry with a limited vocabulary. In such a case, I should improve my linguistic skills. With the mandolin, I should also try to improve my technical skills – and yet changing such a fundamental aspect of my playing, whilst still trying to honour playing commitments, seemed an impossible task.

In the autumn, I perform in a concert at Waltham Abbey: I am soloist in Vivaldi's mandolin concerto. I wear a turquoise green dress enriched with a gold thread design. It contrasts sharply with the stark stone structure of the abbey's interior. Internally, I am in conflict about the two approaches to right-hand technique. On the one hand the glimpsed brilliance of my new sound is encouraging, whilst on the other hand the difficulties of making physical adjustments to posture are dispiriting.

―∾―

It is Good Friday and I have just put my shoes on to go to church, when I hear a knock at the door. I wonder, *who could possibly be at the door?*

I open the door to investigate.

"Hello, I am Giovanna Berizzi," she said, "a pupil of Ugo Orlandi."

I see a slim young lady with long blonde hair.

"He gave me your address," she continued, "but not your telephone number, so I took a chance in coming to visit you."

We immediately start to chat and find that we have so many interesting things to talk about that our conversation extends over many hours, punctuated only by coffee and homemade hot cross buns.

Giovanna tells me that she is studying English at the University of Brescia and is spending six months in England as part of a special exchange with the University of York.

I tell her about my life: teaching the violin, playing the mandolin, passing my Master's degree, being mother to a seven-year-old boy who has just started life as a cathedral chorister.

I abandon all ideas of church, feeling somehow that this is an auspicious meeting: the start of a friendship that might lead me back to Italy and mandolin lessons.

―◦―

Giovanna has returned to Italy and sends me a letter thanking me for my hospitality and being anxious to repay the kindness in some way. (She and her fellow student stayed with me briefly before returning home.) I had asked for information about the National (Italian Mandolin) Conference, which I understand to be at Busto Arsizio. I have absolutely no idea where Busto Arsizio is, but I quickly discover that it is northwest of Milan. I have read about the conference in a magazine called *Plectrum*, a quarterly newsletter published by the Italian Mandolin Federation. The magazine mysteriously arrived by post. Giovanna explains in her letter that she had enquired about the conference and Ugo had said that the location changed every year. He couldn't tell me anything about it yet, but Giovanna would let me know where and when it was as soon as possible.

Giovanna also has news of a concert in Germany that she is taking part in. The concert is to be given by the *Orchestra di Mandolini e Chitarre 'Citta di Brescia'*, the City of Brescia Mandolin and Guitar Orchestra, of which she is a member. Sometimes, the orchestra is more simply known as *Orchestra a Plettro 'Citta di Brescia'*, The City of Brescia Plectrum Orchestra.

I first became acquainted with this orchestra when I was invited to a rehearsal as part of the mandolin course I attended in Brescia. In addition, Giovanna tells me that she will be attending a mandolin course at Salo, on Lake Garda. She says that it would be the same course as the one I attended at Brescia three years previously.

July and a postcard arrives from Giovanna. It was postmarked Heidelberg, Germany. It says that she is there with all the other members of the orchestra, but she has stopped to write my postcard and now she is lost!

September and Giovanna writes again, telling me her news about the mandolin course she attended in Salo. She tells me that it was most interesting and that she met a violinist from Ferrara who was studying mandolin on the course. Apparently, he and I met at the Brescia course. His name is Sergio Zigiotti and he asked Giovanna to say hello to me. I can't remember him clearly. There is still no news about the conference, although Giovanna reassures me that I would be welcome to stay with her and her parents at their home.

Halfway through October and a postcard showing an atmospheric photograph of Venice at sunset arrives. Giovanna, as promised, is writing with details of the conference, which she now attractively describes as a mandolin festival. It is to be in Venice on the 30th and 31st of October. Her mandolin orchestra is to play there on both days and she hopes to see me there. I am dismayed that after months of asking for information I have less than two weeks' notice to arrange the trip. Needless to say, it is impossible. I arrange to stay with Giovanna for a week in November instead. At least I can visit Ugo and the orchestra and have some contact with the mandolin world in Italy, even if I am unable to take advantage of the structured events, the concerts and discussions of the conference.

Here I am in Brescia, perhaps by mistake or by default, perhaps by design.

I spend two of five days visiting Ugo in his new house situated in a small village called Monticelli Brusati, which lies to the north-west of Brescia and is very close to Lake Iseo. The houses in Ugo's road are all modern and constructed mostly with basements, instead of second floors. There are shutters at all the windows with rows of terracotta pots filled with pelargoniums and herbs. All around are vineyards and one neighbour has filled his slightly extended garden full of vines, under which small dark brown chickens run freely.

Giovanna accompanies me on both of the visits. I take my newly acquired Embergher mandolin to show Ugo on the first visit. Luigi Embergher was responsible for evolving a concert mandolin which was, and still is, considered by many to be the Stradivarius of the mandolin world. I already have an instrument made by Embergher's pupil Pasquale Pecoraro, but my new Embergher is a superior instrument. However, Embergher died in 1943 and my instrument is dated 1957, which is a mystery. There is not the same tradition of fakes and forgery in the mandolin world as there has been in the violin world. The most likely explanation is that when Embergher's most favoured apprentice, Domenico Cerrone, inherited the instrument making business in 1938, the instrument labels continued to bear Embergher's name.

Ugo admires my new instrument and suggests that I have some adjustments made to the bridge to ensure the instrument is in perfect working order. I don't have anyone at home who I know would be willing to undertake the work. Most luthiers just don't have the experience of mandolins and are reticent to experiment with something unknown to them. Ugo has a solution. He sends me to Filippo Fasser, *liutaio*, luthier, who has a workshop in the historical centre of Brescia. Giovanna kindly takes the instrument to Filippo on Wednesday morning and I collect it on Thursday evening. It feels quite strange and wonderful to me. Here I am in a foreign country taking my instrument to be repaired and it is as if, for a brief moment, I am really living here, and yet I know that I live somewhere else.

My first visit to Ugo's house is also a memorable occasion on account of the *spaghetti alla carbonara,* which Ugo makes for lunch. He shows me, step by step, how to prepare the dish. First he fries some cubed bacon called *pancetta*. He then adds chopped garlic and a surprise ingredient, fresh sage from his garden. He takes about six of the sage leaves, tears them up and sprinkles them into the frying pan. Finally he adds the cooked spaghetti, beaten eggs and grated *parmigiano*, Parmesan cheese. It is delicious. We follow it with a salad of fresh green leaves from the garden and homemade salami, made by Ugo's father-in-law. Ugo's wife, Marina Ferrari – also an accomplished mandolinist and music teacher – is at home today and shares the meal with us.

After my second visit to his house, Ugo proposes a pizza lunch en route to the airport. I am very grateful for a lift all the way back to the airport, since I have noticed that even the small suitcase I have brought is a nuisance on trains and buses. It would be all right if I didn't have to contend with an awkward shaped mandolin case without a strap!

During the car journey, Ugo randomly asks: "Yes, but what are you going to do with your mandolin playing?"

I tell him about my plans for researching repertoire and giving concerts of the music I have discovered, but he doesn't mean that. I say that I don't really understand the question. I have a Master's degree in performance and that is really as far as I can take my playing in terms of studying. Yes, I know that I have done a lot of the practical work by myself – I am mostly self-taught – but I have achieved something very important and significant for the mandolin. I have taken the playing as far as I can academically. The only other thing I could do now would be to write a thesis for a PhD, but that would be purely academic.

Ugo has a different idea. He thinks I should join the diploma course at Padua in order to continue my studies. I am stunned. It is a ridiculous idea. Never, even in my wildest dreams, would it be possible. For a start, I live and work in England and the course is in Italy. I ask for details. He says I could visit once a month for a year or maybe two years. It would only be the mandolin lesson. I wouldn't have to study history, harmony etc., because I have already studied those for my violin diploma, which I had gained in England.

It was possible, he said. It would be easy – but I am not convinced that we were discussing reality. I am a mother with a small child, albeit at choir school, who I am responsible for. There are violin pupils, with their exams, to consider and my concerts to think about.

On my return home, I am filled with conflicting emotions. I like the idea of being able to study the mandolin further and in one way I find the idea of the structured course attractive. On the other hand, the idea of any more formalised study is daunting. The idea of more exams, especially practical exams, would be a challenge, which seems at this moment too difficult to contemplate. I have done such a lot of studying for the Master's degree and I am quite exhausted from it. I also thought that the Master's degree would be the end of formalised study. Even if my family agreed to support me in this crazy plan, I would still have the problem of funding the project.

I also notice on my return, apparently quite by chance, an advert in *The Times*. Under the section marked 'scholarships' is an advert placed by a Trust inviting applications for research in Venice and the territories once subject to it. The areas of interest included music and culture. Padua was at one time part of the

Venetian Republic. The Venetian composer, Antonio Vivaldi, had bestowed the mandolin repertoire with a number of important works, including the much admired solo mandolin concerto. Today, an important part of Italian culture is being preserved, renovated and developed, in the shape of the Italian school of mandolin playing. This cultural phenomenon is happening within the old Venetian Republic. Even the other important centre of mandolin renaissance and development, Brescia, had been part of the Republic during the fifteenth century. There are it seems numerous connections between the Italian school of mandolin playing and Venice. It also seems an excellent project to investigate the performance practice and cultural traditions, which are so alive in Padua, and to make them known in England. I obtain and complete an application form.

It is the beginning of the year and a brown envelope arrives containing a pale lavender envelope and a letter, both of which have been roughly torn into a total of about six pieces. The accompanying photo-copied letter from the Italian Post Office informs me casually that my letter has been damaged by their sorting machine. They send me their 'distinguished salutations'. My letter has been eaten by their machine and looks like, and is indeed, a puzzle. I place the pieces together, and with the odd word or letter missing due to the ragged edges, I am able to make out the contents. Giovanna says that Claudio Scimone (principal of the conservatoire at Padua and conductor of *I Solisti Veneti*) has sent a letter of reference on my behalf to the Trust. I only hope that the letter was in better condition than the one I have just received.

Somehow, despite other overlapping letters, Giovanna and I manage to arrange for me to make another trip during the spring. My plan is to fly to Verona and spend the first night in a hotel in Padua. I shall spend the following day at the *Conservatorio,* the conservatoire, and then travel by train to Brescia where I shall spend the rest of the week. At the last minute, I learn, by letter, that a one-day masterclass in which some German mandolinists are taking part is to take place at the *Conservatorio* on the day of my visit. Giovanna also requests that I bring for her a number of English novels. She needs them for her course at the university and they are more expensive to purchase in Italy than they are in England. I only have five books to buy, including a personal favourite of mine, Jane Austen's *Emma*, but it is amazing how such a small quantity of books can be so bulky and heavy to carry.

I stay the first night at the Hotel Corso in the *Corso del Popolo,* which is the main road leading from the station into the centre of Padua. After breakfast, I ask for directions to the *Conservatorio*. I had received conflicting information about its location. I have two addresses for the music college. A phone call to Ugo confirms that the correct address is in *Via Eremitani*. The other address is an annex. My map doesn't show *Via Eremitani,* but the hotel receptionist says that it is an easy walk of five to ten minutes. It is straight until I meet a junction where a road forks off to the left. The road to the left is *Via Eremitani*. It is obvious really because set back to the left at the beginning of the road is the *Chiesa degli Eremitani*, the Hermit's Church, and next to it is the *Nuovo Museo Civico*, the New Civic

Museum. I leave my suitcase, heavy with books, at the hotel reception so that I am unencumbered and I arrange to collect it as I return past the hotel on my way to the station.

In my music bag, I have some music – a concerto by Nicola Conforto. I am so pleased. The music has the appearance of printed music that you can buy from a music shop, although it is not possible to buy this music from a shop. I have made this edition of music myself by inputting information into a computer using a special programme for writing music. I have recently acquired a CD on which Ugo has recorded this among a number of other Italian mandolin concertos. Like me, Ugo had requested the microfilm from the *Bibliotheque Nationale* in Paris. He had written it out by hand, being frustrated by technology and finding the simplest methods best. I have a vision of making all the Baroque concertos, available at present only in manuscript, accessible to anybody who desires to play them. After discussing the intricacies of plectrum strokes, whether to use a down or an up stroke and so on, I present Ugo with a copy of my edition. He reciprocates, unexpectedly, by presenting me with a copy of *Cinque Sonate, Five Sonatas,* for mandolin by Domenico Scarlatti, published in Italy, with revision by himself. Inside the cover is a handwritten dedication:

> 'a Frances Taylor, la speranza mandolinistica inglese! Ugo Orlandi. Marzo '94.'

The writing is a little difficult to make out, especially the final letters of the phrase *'la speranza mandolinistica'*, so I am unsure of the exact significance. I don't know whether I am the English mandolin's hope or a hopeful English mandolinist! Nevertheless, my new music is the result of some interesting scholarship which had uncovered new evidence pointing to the conclusion that five Scarlatti sonatas, previously thought to be for keyboard, were probably meant for mandolin. I am absolutely delighted with the new repertoire.

The Germans take most of the day to materialise. Eventually, they arrive by car in the late afternoon. Giovanna has studied German as well as English, and is enlisted to translate their talk about the German school of mandolin playing. However, they seem to prefer talking in English, which leads somehow to me becoming involved in the clarification of a discussion on the differences between the German and Italian schools of playing. The delay in the day's proceedings means that suddenly I find myself as one of a group of about six people, trying to walk and run intermittently, as fast as possible, towards the station. I have to collect the heavy suitcase and am grateful when one of the boys in our group chivalrously offers to take it for me. He wheels the case along on its small plastic wheels at breakneck speed and I can see that it will never recover from the experience. The spare space in the suitcase, released by the books, is put to good use on the homeward journey. Giovanna's mother thoughtfully gives me a beautifully boxed, traditional Easter cake, called *colomba,* because, as its name suggests, it is in the shape of a dove.

—◦—

A family holiday to Umbria during April, in which we travel to Florence by train from London, fuels the idea that it might be possible to travel to Italy by train. The following month I receive a letter from the Trust telling me that regretfully they are unable to grant my request for funds to pursue research in Venice. They had so many excellent applications to consider, and the advisory board was faced with a difficult task in making its selections. I do understand their position and it is a polite letter wishing me well for the future. I am already making applications to a number of other charitable trusts. Nevertheless, it is disappointing and the future is uncertain.

᠃

Much confusion follows surrounding the bureaucracy to enter the course. I decide to proceed with my application for the course, despite the uncertainty, and I write to Giovanna asking what the procedure is. A hasty reply explains that I must urgently copy an attached sample letter, naturally written in Italian, filling in my personal details and send it immediately to the *Conservatorio*. Seemingly, I have missed filling in the correct form, which was due at the end of April. This letter is to ask for special permission to be accepted onto the course, even though I have not filled in the correct form, because of my special circumstances – these circumstances being that I was waiting to hear about funding for my travel expenses. The fact that they are not forthcoming is not addressed. The whole language and structure of the letter is legalistic and archaic, using phrases such as 'I the undersigned'.

᠃

I send a number of letters and faxes to Ugo since I understand from Giovanna's letter that he might still be able to obtain the form for admission to the *Conservatorio*. I receive a short letter from Giovanna saying that Ugo is surprised that I haven't had any communication from the *Conservatorio*. The brief note also tells me that my audition for admittance to the course is on the 13th and 14th of October. I then receive, finally, a letter from the *Conservatorio* stating that the *esame di ammisione*, the admission exam, is at eleven o'clock in the morning on Friday the 14th October. I have already booked my train ticket, but a phone call to Ugo confirms that Thursday the 13th is fine.

il primo anno

1

I am sitting on the train, which has stopped. We have just passed some grey roofs of houses, which were huddled together and built lower than the train track. Over the roofs, I had glimpsed at the sea in the distance. It is dove grey, flat and still. A few seagulls swoop and squeal near the train track. Their cries beckon me back to halcyon childhood holidays: the sea breeze through my hair, the taste of salt on my lips, the walk along the water's edge searching for beautiful shells, feeling the shock of the cold water as it lapped over my bare feet. For a moment, I am bathed in the memory of being carefree: breathing in fresh sea air, being joyful; just being. Suddenly the train jolts and we are moving back in the direction from which we had come. We make a slight detour, since we are now on a different track, and arrive at Folkestone Station.

Actually, I don't feel at all carefree. I think about the components of my journey. I am beginning to feel tense and I know that I will not be able to relax properly until I am on the train from Paris to Padua, because then I will have no more connections to worry about. The overnight train from France to Italy is the only long and continuous part of my journey, lasting twelve hours, which is exactly half of the entire twenty-four hour journey.

I pass through customs into the departure lounge ready for the next sea crossing. It is basic in design and reminds me of an airport lounge from a 1960's film. The coffee bar is a 1990's addition to the set and I treat myself to a cappuccino, knowing that tomorrow I shall have the authentic article. My next task is to avail myself of the ladies' toilets. I regard this as a key skill for successful journeys: always locate and use any available loo, since you never know where the next one is. Unfortunately, this one is made for extremely thin people and is not to be recommended for people carrying mandolin cases.

I sit down to wait and take advantage of the time to study the Paris underground system. I have a compact plasticised map of the city centre and the metro. It is small and easy to use, without attracting a lot of attention to myself. Nevertheless I am cautious of being in a strange city, with little knowledge of the language, and I have decided to memorise the route so that I minimise the appearance of looking lost or ill at ease. The French train I will catch from Boulogne will take just under three hours to arrive at *Paris Nord*. At about four-thirty, the beginning of the rush hour, I shall be embarking upon a trip across Paris, along with the native commuters. My preferred plan is to take the number five line, which is depicted orange, in the direction of *Place d'Italie*. I thought the destination would be easy for me to remember. I will count seven stations until *Bastille* where I will change. I must then travel on the light orange number one line, in the direction of *Chateau de Vincennes*, for one stop in order to arrive at *Gare de Lyon*.

The ferry is a catamaran with a huge interior, the size of a dance floor, filled with rows of seating. I manage to find a seat on the port side of the vessel. My aisle of seats has three seats across, a gangway, and another three seats across. Just this little strip of seating looks like a whole aeroplane. I am pleased to be near the large windows because I have a good view of whatever is happening outside without having to venture up onto the outside deck. I am sensitive to the cold and I have my modest, but at times awkward, luggage to carry. Travelling by myself feels a huge responsibility. I am conscious that I must keep my luggage with me at all times. At *all* times!

I settle down with a coffee and a sandwich for lunch, and I amuse myself by viewing the 'in-flight' movie, a tourist's guide to Boulogne. I am captivated by the images of the historical centre. It would be lovely to have sufficient time to stop and buy cheeses at the specialist cheese shop or to wander around the church with an Italianate cupola.

In France, there is much walking and many flights of stairs to negotiate between the ferry and the train. Some people contend with huge suitcases and I am happy to have my portable luggage. I tell myself that I am on French soil now and that I have completed the first stage of my journey by arriving in the first foreign country. I remind myself that we have switched languages and that I must give the appropriate response to the official at passport control. After a polite '*merci*', I am boarding the train for Paris. No more sea now, it will be *terra firma* all the way. I am a little tired but I am anxious to see everything from the train window. I don't want to miss any part of this experience.

I am struck by how similar the countryside is to the countryside at home: patchwork fields of green and brown, and copses of trees. It is, perhaps, not altogether surprising if, as we are told by geologists, England and France were united once as a single landmass. I fall asleep and I awake at Amiens. I notice a terrace of stone cottages high above the track. The windows are enticing the onlooker with painted wooden shutters. I especially admire the pale blue ones. It is a shame I'm not able to stop and explore. It is just after three o'clock and quite a lot of people board the train.

After the approach to Paris, in which I notice the sleek and famous *TGV* parked with other trains, I arrive at *Gare du Nord* and alight from the train. As I walk along the platform, I feel a sense of quickening. I realise that I must muster some energy and keep my wits about me. I feel the urgency, or perhaps fear, of being about to enter the urban jungle. I know that in my native urban jungle, London, I am familiar with all the clues, signals and messages, which help me to avoid danger – but here I am struggling just to scan the signs and symbols that will alert me to the metro. I think I know where I am going. I checked out the metro entrance in the spring when I travelled to Florence. I didn't travel on the underground then because we had lots of luggage and took a taxi between the overground stations. This is my first time on the metro. I find myself temporarily walking against the flow of commuters. I must have misread a sign and entered at the wrong entrance. I don't know. I'm confused. I retrace my steps and see the ticket office. I have rehearsed my lines from the phrase book and taken notice of its advice. I ask for a *carnet* of tickets. Now I have ten small rectangles of green cardboard and I am ready to use the first one in the automatic ticket machine. I watch the lady in front of me and copy the procedure. It is easy and I am now a commuter in Paris.

The labyrinthine passages through which I must venture at the Bastille seem shabby and dimly lit. I am jostled by the crowd, which is moving with me and I take care to protect the mandolin by holding the flat top of the case close to the front of my body. My body feels weary and my legs ache, even though I have spent most of the day sitting. This is a low point in the day. I hear in my mind all the complaints and lamentations of my friends who have to cope everyday with the underground at home. I decide that underground train travel certainly is the worst kind of travel in the world, and that I am probably on the worst underground system in the world. I have forgotten all the grim stations at home.

Just as I am being assaulted by this deluge of negativity, I step onto what must certainly be one of the most beautiful underground platforms in the world. I am stunned first by the shaft of natural light and then by the breathtaking views of the harbour with all its moored boats down below. To one side of the water's edge, a vibrant market is in progress. All this is visible because one side of the platform tunnel is exposed above ground and is covered by glass. I could wait forever for the train, so entertaining are the comings and goings down below. I am right over someone's houseboat. I have a privileged view of a little slice of Parisian life through this glass and it reminds me of watching exotic reptiles in the reptile house at the zoo. My thoughts are interrupted by a turquoise train, which might have emanated from the pages of a Tintin cartoon.

At *Gare du Lyon,* I head for a new looking development of subterranean shops and restaurants. I find the restaurant we had eaten in during the previous spring. It is an unpretentious establishment and I feel a sense of security knowing that I have visited it on an earlier occasion. I am also encouraged by knowing that they cook quite an acceptable French version of pizza. I am nourished by a pizza *forestiere*, which is topped by ham, mushrooms and an egg. I have a window seat and as I quietly sip my mineral water, I watch, from the safe haven of my table, anxious commuters hurrying along outside. I also have a salad and then a coffee. I take as long as I can over my meal. I read the menu three times, translating all the words I am able to, and I watch the progress of the other customers, listening carefully to the spoken language. I am comforted by the food and warmth of the restaurant. Eventually I am unable to waste any further time having a leisurely supper and I pay my bill, remembering to take advantage of the ladies' room before departing.

It is half past six and I have about an hour and a half before the departure of my train to Italy. I am at a loose end and find myself wandering aimlessly. I look in the windows of some of the shops. There is a wonderful chocolate shop. I feel as if I am on automatic pilot. The pleasure of window shopping eludes me. There seems nowhere suitable to sit down and rest so I am trying to occupy myself by looking at the shops. Normally I enjoy window shopping, but now my eyes seem glazed over. I have seen so many images flashing past me during the course of the day and it is probably only natural that I should feel tired. I long for a comfortable, inconspicuous chair where I can sit down and relax, and just be.

Near the platforms for international departures, there are benches to sit down on. These benches are made of metal and are reminiscent of park benches. The whole area is partially exposed to the elements and the night air is cold and sharp. I find a place to sit and from which I can see information about my train. It is still early evening and yet this station, like many others throughout the world, acts as a magnet to marginalised people. The homeless, the drunk, the mad and the sad, all intermingle with international travellers.

I am profoundly grateful when I enter the safety of the overnight train to Venice. I easily find my carriage and compartment. The compartment is divided into six couchettes, three on each side. Each berth is provided with a small pillow, a blanket and a plastic bag containing a clean pillow case and a sheet. My bed is at the top, which I had thought would give me even more security and privacy once I had made the journey up the ladder. I quickly take up my belongings and arrange them in a recessed shelf near my head. I then set to work making up my bed. It is neat and cosy and I look forward to collapsing on it, but I feel I cannot collapse just yet. It is so odd sharing one's bedroom, my compartment, with five complete strangers. The train moves out of the station and everyone mills around in the corridors looking out of the windows at the illuminated city melting away into darkness.

A lady in uniform passes through the corridor informing people that the buffet is ready to serve supper. The thought is tempting: a thin, moist steak accompanied by French fries and a glass of red wine. I wish for a moment that I hadn't eaten earlier, but I console myself with the thought that it was a better plan. I am now better organised. I don't, for example, have the hassle of taking all my belongings with me to the buffet car. I have, as it is, to take a small calculated risk by leaving my stowed away belongings whilst I visit the bathroom and clean my teeth. I feel uncomfortable about it, but I am exhausted and it is too complicated. I think, anyway, that taking my mandolin to the bathroom will only attract unnecessary attention to it. I also have enough trouble keeping my balance in the short walk between the compartment and the bathroom. The train seems to move about considerably more than I remembered from the spring rehearsal.

At last I am tucked up in bed and I try to relax and rest. I am not wearing night clothes. I wear instead the underneath layers of my day clothes: a long-sleeved cotton polo neck sweater and cotton leggings. They are chosen for comfort and their quality of being non-creasing. It is the most practical solution to the problem of travelling in this way.

I do not sleep well on the train. I am restless. At times, I become too hot. I remove the blanket a little but I leave the sheet in place. I have arranged it to be folded in half with the fold on the outward edge of the bunk. In this way, I feel I will be contained and less likely to fall out of my lofty bed. I hear the voice of the customs official at the Swiss border. I handed my passport to the carriage steward soon after boarding the train. Passengers are re-issued with their documents in the morning. This ensures that passengers are not disturbed from their sleep. I lie awake on the still train thinking that I have just arrived in Switzerland, the second foreign country of my journey. I also think about the Calace *Preludio* I have to play for my audition. I run the opening bars over in my head, imagining how my fingers feel to play it. This should send me to sleep but it doesn't. I remember how once I had found that listening to my own imagined playing of this piece had comforted me in hospital. When I was very ill, it soothed me and made me soporific. Now it only served to increase my anxiety because I worry that I haven't been able to practise on the journey. Then I worry that I have had insufficient sleep and I will be too tired to play properly.

I stir. I realise something is happening. The train has stopped and I must have finally fallen asleep. A deep loudspeaker voice announces 'Verona *Porta Nuova*'. I have arrived in Italy. I look at my watch. It is a quarter to seven. I snuggle under my blanket, feeling its warmth and comfort. Now I don't want to leave the place of my repose. It seems that all night I struggled to be in a place as relaxing as this and now that I have found it, I must abruptly abandon it. Sluggishly and somewhat resentfully, I make an effort to prepare myself for the day. I put on my boots and my jacket. I tidy the bed. When I have retrieved the ladder – there is only one per compartment – and descended by it, I run my fingers through my hair. I glance in the window at my tangled hairstyle and strategically place a hair band on my head. I feel fractionally more civilised. I join other people in the corridor to watch fields and farms flash by in the ever increasing daylight as we speed towards Padua.

My first priority at Padua station is to make for the station buffet in order to have breakfast. Lots of commuters are taking their coffee at the bar but I need to be a little more leisurely, so I sit at one of the small round tables. To my left, there are huge glass doors which look out onto platform one and afford me a generous view of the station's comings and goings. I order a cappuccino, a *brioche* and a glass of water. The *brioche* is warm and contains apricot jam. It is delicious. I am so happy to have arrived and to be sitting in Italy eating my breakfast.

Next, I find the ladies' toilets. The lady attendant indicates a particular door. I pass the first open door and see the continental 'hole in the tiled floor' model of toilet. I am pleased that my cubical contains a proper toilet. I am feeling a little soiled by this stage. I knew that this trip would be like a camping expedition, so I have come prepared with individually wrapped baby wipes for intimate and difficult cleaning. Outside, I go to the large sinks to wash my hands. I also need to clean my teeth and wash my face, but I feel self-conscious. I look at the attendant and engage her eyes. I ask her if it is okay for me to wash my face and teeth quickly. I explain that I have just arrived on the overnight train from Paris and that I have, in fact, been travelling for twenty-four hours from my original point of departure in London.

The attendant becomes animated and is most accommodating. She asks me about the purpose of my visit and as I smooth some moisture cream on my face I tell her that I am going to study mandolin at the *Conservatorio*. She seems very impressed and wishes me good luck. I happily leave some money in her little bowl. I feel I have had very good service.

I leave the station and make my way towards the historical centre. There are many other people walking purposefully with me in the same direction. Some are dressed smartly in suits and look as if they might be going to an office. Others wear trousers or jeans, casual jackets and fashionably coloured rucksacks, and are probably heading for the university. Founded in 1222, the university is one of the most distinguished seats of learning in Europe. The list of alumni includes such famous names as Petrarch, Dante and Galileo.

The crowd of people I am walking with find it difficult at times to make its way along the pavement. There are all types of obstacles: ladders leaning against windows being washed, people unloading boxes from cars into shops and cordoned off excavations of the pavement's surface. To the right is a main road full of chaotic traffic. Buses, cars and *Vespa* motorcycles all compete with each other to be first. People have to take care not to enter into this competition with the traffic by stepping inadvertently off the pavement. The crowd also has to stop occasionally at intersections to respect the traffic lights. On the corner of one intersection is the hotel where I stayed on my last visit. As I wait for the lights to change, my ears are assailed by a high-pitched siren. Within seconds, a police car screeches through the intersection with an officer leaning out of the window waving something that looks like a table-tennis bat.

At the other side of the road, the pavement widens out, making my progress much easier. To the left is the *Piovego* Canal, which runs beneath the pavement and the main road. I notice a barge tied to the bank of the canal. As I continue past the public gardens, I am pleased that this time I know my way to the *Conservatorio*. I look at my watch and realise that I am far too early. It is only nine o'clock. I decide to seek refuge in the *Chiesa degli Eremitani*.

The church is dark, cool and peaceful. It is almost empty of people. One lady kneels and prays. A couple, probably tourists, wander along the sides of the nave, looking intently at everything. I sit down in a pew, glad of the rest. For a short space of time, I am able to be myself. I can think, pray and reflect on my forthcoming day. Even if I had no religious conviction, the church would still provide a safe retreat to hide in and to be myself. There is no need to react to people around me or to the situation I find myself in, as is necessary out on the street. There is always the tension of having to be constantly mindful and aware on the street. Here, all I need to do is just sit and be. It is a wonderful release.

After a period of quiet, I am restored and I begin to feel intrigued by my surroundings. A great treasure of early

Renaissance art, the Church of the *Eremitani* was sadly damaged by an air raid in 1944. Its jewel, the *Ovetari* chapel frescoed by Andrea Mantegna in the mid-fifteenth century, was devastated. A mini exhibition tells the story of piecing together the salvaged fragments. I suddenly remember that I should be continuing on my way to the *Conservatorio*. The frescos are absorbing and I resolve to return another time in order to respond fully to them.

Two minutes later, I am at the door of the *Conservatorio*. The building is salmon pink in colour. To the right of the imposing entrance is a plaque, which reads: '*Conservatorio di Musica Cesare Pollini*'. The stone framework of the entrance, the height of about two tall men, is filled with dark panelled wood. At the top is a decorative grill and in the centre are two enormous doors, which are unlocked and left open. As I pass through the doors, there is a porter's window to my right and huge glass doors in front of me. The other side of the glass doors is the vestibule proper.

The entrance hall is palatial space with a marble floor and lighting suspended from on high. Noticeboards on the walls display information about forthcoming concerts, and the arrangements for various classes and examinations. After the notices, on the left-hand side, is a stairwell encasing a grand marble staircase with ornate wrought iron railings. Long benches covered in brown leather flank the walls and at the far end of the lobby are more oversized glass doors, mirroring the front doors and leading onto a courtyard filled with foliage and bicycles.

I place my mandolin case and bag down on one of the benches. Almost immediately, I am approached by a young man carrying a mandolin case. He is from Naples and is here today to sit his diploma exam. I tell him that I am from England and that I have just arrived today by train to take my admission exam. We chat as if we have known each other for years. I tell him that I had read about him in *Corriere della Sera*. In a short article, the newspaper had outlined the plight of those wishing to study the mandolin. It said that it was impossible to study the mandolin in Naples, the birth place of the mandolin (the Neapolitan mandolin, that is). As a result, one young man was having to make an unprecedented lengthy journey for his lesson. Every week, the young man commuted the round trip between Naples and Padua. This was surely the longest trip anyone has had to make for a mandolin lesson, the newspaper claimed. That is, until today. We both laugh. The idea of travelling between London and Padua seems at once both wonderful and ridiculous.

Other mandolinists are attracted to us. It is a strange experience being part of a group of people who are seriously studying the mandolin. Our common interest is a unifying force. I feel immediately at home and comfortable with these complete strangers. Two others, both young men, are taking their diploma exam today. A third is a young lady called Deborah who, like me, has also come to take her admission exam. They have all brought friends and companions, so we are quite a crowd. They chatter extensively and nervously. They ask each other what time their exam is, where Ugo is and what is happening next. No one knows where Ugo is, neither do they know what is happening next – but they are all certain, like me, that their exam is at the fast approaching eleven o'clock. At this moment, it becomes clear that we all have the same appointment.

A rival group begins to manifest. A ripple of awareness moves through our group. The rival group is a collection of

Maestros lead by Ugo. They are the examining panel and they make their way to one of the teaching rooms. At intervals we are invited in to listen to the recitals, which form the basis of the final diploma exams.

The recitals consist of three pieces: two with piano accompaniment and one unaccompanied. Each recital is about forty minutes in length and so each exam, taking into account a few other requirements such as the chat with the examiners, lasts about an hour. It will be teatime before the admission exams even begin. Deborah is concerned about catching the train home. She has to return to *Piemonte*, Piedmont, where she lives close to the French border. I assure her that my train will leave mid-evening, so I am happy for her to have her exam first. She is happy too and we go to the nearby *Caffé Eremitani* for lunch.

Deborah talks a great deal. Her Piedmontese accent, influenced by hard French sounds, and the quickness of her speech makes it almost impossible to understand – but she is so patient and kind, taking care to slow down, repeat and clarify whenever I ask her to, that I am drawn to her. Her companion is a lady of about her mother's age, a family friend, who has accompanied her on the long journey. I thought the lady was her mother, but her own mother is unable to make the journey today. As we eat our *panini*, rolls, and drink mineral water, I tell my new friend about my journey and my family. After a quick espresso, we return to the examinations.

The afternoon passes happily, listening to beautiful music. Some of the pieces I have never heard before. One of these is the concerto in A minor by Raffaele Calace. It is a real treat to listen to such a richly romantic work. I am transported by the most luscious sounds, the most exquisite nuances, to the

Neapolitan coastline. I feel the warmth of the sun on my face, I smell the scent of the lemon trees and I visualise the sapphire blue sea as I look over to the island of Ischia. Absolute paradise!

Later I am intrigued by another piece of music which is new to me: *La Fustemberg* by Antoine Riggieri. It is a theme, a simple tune, with a set of ten intricate variations on the theme. I am fascinated by the complex patterns and shapes of the music formed by string crossing. The plectrum dances backwards and forwards, often between two strings, with the left-hand fingers changing constantly to alter the pitch of the notes. Sometimes, the two strings are close together, next to each other. Other times, the strings are far apart with one or two strings between them, which the performer must take care not to touch. In my analysis of this music, I assume, as usual and for the sake of simplicity, that the mandolin has just four strings like the violin. In fact, it really has four pairs or courses of strings. Each pair of strings is tuned to the same pitch and when playing it is essential to think of each pair as one thick string.

At the end of the afternoon, the candidates are recalled individually to hear the amount of marks they gained and whether they have succeeded in passing the exam. I am a little shocked to learn that one of the candidates has failed and that there is no possibility of retaking the exam. Seven years of study is crowned by glorious success with the passing of the final exam and receiving the diploma certificate. Alternatively, seven years of study is negated by the failure to pass the final hurdle and the lack of a piece of paper. It seems a harsh system compared to England, where it is possible to resit such exams. I am touched by the devastation that the failed candidate feels. There is nothing appropriate to say.

I wait for Deborah to sit her exam. Now, it is my turn. It is half past five and I am totally exhausted. I am physically tired from travelling; I am mentally tired from listening to a foreign language all day; and I am aurally tired from listening to so much music. I am worried because I haven't found a moment's privacy to warm up or practise. I am anxious because of the diploma results. I begin to doubt myself, thinking, *If one who has lived and studied here can fail, then what chance do I have?* I try to ignore the great tension in my body and I begin to play. I give a performance of a Calace prelude. It is not bad, especially considering the circumstances, but it certainly isn't good. Ugo asks me why I chose something that is so difficult and complicated to play. I thought the piece was a good vehicle to exemplify various aspects of my technique. He advises me to study something simple, the solo sonatas of Francesco Lecce, and tells me to come back for a lesson next month.

At least I have passed the exam. I cheer myself up with the thought of an Italian supper. I return towards the station to find a *pizzeria* that I had noticed on my way to the *Conservatorio* this morning. It is in a parade of shops, which are near to the station. I decide that the most sensible plan is to relax eating a meal somewhere close to the station. Then I don't have to worry about the time, because it will only take a few minutes to walk to the station. The *pizzeria* is small, plain and simple. The pizzas are reasonably priced and their quality is excellent. I have a *pizza ai funghi,* a mushroom pizza, with a salad. I also have a quarter litre of local white wine, brought in a handmade pottery jug, and half a litre of mineral water.

I feel a little naughty ordering wine when I am eating alone. I justify myself by remembering that the significant word is 'eating' and not 'alone'. Alone is academic because I am amid other people eating. It is just that some people, like me, have a table all to themselves. Drinking wine with food is the culturally accepted norm in Italy. It compliments and enhances food, and is meant to be made use of in conjunction with food. It is not something to be consumed by itself for its own sake. I come from a culture in which drinking is traditionally something separate from food. For the majority of ordinary people, drinking is something which happens in the pub. Although it is often represented as a social activity, it is also often presented as something medicinal. I remember as a child that a person who had suffered a shock would always be offered a good stiff drink to steady the nerves.

I enjoy my wine and water, mixed, *mezzo e mezzo*, half and half, just as the Italians do. I had learnt from my many Italian holidays that I enjoy drinking wine much better this way. The pizza is also fantastic. It is such a pleasure to be eating an authentic pizza with a wafer-thin base and fresh, simple ingredients. Although I have had some good pizzas in London, they are never quite the same – despite all the claims – as those made in Italy. They are usually complicated with too many ingredients and often a tomato sauce, which is uncharacteristically spicy. In Italy, most pizzas have only one ingredient in addition to the bread base, tomato sauce and mozzarella cheese. If it is a pepperoni pizza, for example, it will only have pepperoni sausage added to the basic ingredients.

After a healthy bowl of *macedonia*, fruit salad, and an espresso, I return to the station. The overnight train to Paris doesn't come too soon for me. It has been a long day. A second long day. The station is cold and the waiting room hosts quite a lot of people with disturbing behaviour. I walk up and down the platform in order to keep warm and to avoid contact with unwelcome strangers. As soon as I am able, I board the train, hand in my passport, arrange my bed and settle down to sleep.

In Paris, I am not restored by my night's sleep. I feel pretty ghastly and I would love to have a bath. I am, however, delightfully distracted at the Bastille station by a young lady playing a harp. It is a large harp, the sort found in an orchestra. I am amazed at its presence amongst the throng of early morning commuters. The frame of the harp flashes gold and the celestial sounds of the strings echo all around. The buskers I have encountered have portable instruments and live in fear of being moved on. This one is ensconced in the centre of the platform. I know nothing about the French attitude to busking or of the likelihood that this one will be moved on or even prosecuted. I know only that the Parisian commuters seem respectful of this precious instrument and that perhaps they are even thankful for the inspirational music encouraging them on their way.

At *Gare du Nord,* I embrace the comforts of a civilised society by hiring a bathroom for a modest fee. The bathroom is just a small room containing a toilet and a hand basin, but it is perfect for my purpose. With a flannel, a bar of soap, hot water and privacy, I am able to carry out my ablutions in an old-fashioned but most satisfactory way. I am so grateful for this opportunity and I am so grateful for hot water.

Breakfast is good: fresh croissant and milky coffee. Soon, I am on a train heading for the English Channel. The return journey is slow and tedious. The channel crossing is uneventful. Kent is also tiring – all the more so, because, although we are not far from London, the train is particularly sluggish. I hit the

London rush hour and take the District Line from Victoria station to Mile End. I change there onto the Central Line, because I just have to walk across the station platform, which is easier with my luggage. I walk the five minutes' walk from the Central Line station to arrive home in the early evening. I have been for my first mandolin lesson and I feel in a state of collapse.

2

I have not been home a complete week when Ugo rings me to say that he has arrived in London for a series of concerts. We have a confusing conversation in which he tells me that he is staying very near to where I live. He would like me to meet him for lunch. It turns out that he is staying at the Forum Hotel in Kensington. It is nowhere near where I live, being on the diametrically opposite side of London. I explain that he is in the west of London and I am in the east. Yes, we are connected by tube, but it will take over an hour, maybe the best part of two hours, before I can reach him. He is undeterred, tells me his room number, and says that he looks forward to meeting me shortly.

I arrive at the hotel an hour and a half later. I speak with the receptionist and she rings through to Ugo's room, but there is no reply. I tell her that I will wait.

The reception area is massive. There are all sorts of coming and goings. I notice three clocks giving the various times around the world. I order coffee. I visit the ladies' room. On my return to the reception, Ugo materialises just as I had given up hope of seeing him.

He says that he became involved in talking with members of the orchestra and that he wasn't in his own room. He is here now and he has some paperwork to do with me. We order sandwiches for lunch and we sit down to look at the papers.

I have some forms to fill in. Forms are always tedious and Italian ones are especially so. I also have to give him some money for some taxes that have to be paid. I don't really understand these taxes. There are three different sums to be paid. One is a yearly tax for students attending a course. Another is, I think, because I am joining the course. The final one is because I have been late in sorting out the paperwork for entering the course. It is a sort of fine, I suppose.

The three sums, 26,000 lire, 53,200 lire, and 11,700 lire, make a total of 90,900 lire. I felt quite alarmed. It sounds so much and it is unexpected – at the best of times, I have always found numbers so confusing.

In reality, the bill is not so bad. It is approximately 100,000 lire, which is about forty pounds. It is just that it is an extra sum to find for my, as yet, not funded course of study.

There is another very important task I am told that I have to undertake before I return to Italy. I have to take all my certificates to the Italian Consulate in order to obtain a *Certificato di Equipollenza*, a certificate of equivalence. It is at this point that things begin to take a complicated turn.

I am told that my Master's degree and my Violin Diploma are not sufficient to convince the Italian authorities that I am proficient in theory, harmony, history of music, keyboard skills and so on. I am a little aghast but I try not to show it. The authorities require my grade certificates for piano and theory, dating back to my childhood. They also want to see the syllabuses for my diploma and degree courses, in order to understand that I have already covered all the other aspects of the mandolin diploma course. This is because Ugo is trying to arrange it for me to visit only for the mandolin lesson.

One significant problem in all this is that the authorities require proof of an exam they call *Licenza di Teoria e Solfeggio*. *Licenza* means certificate or diploma, so it is an examination that includes both theory and *solfeggio*. I feel fine about the theory because I know, whatever the standard, I have covered everything. The *solfeggio* is another matter. *Solfeggio* is a system of identifying sound names with the pitch of written notes. It is a foolproof method of being able to sing from sight. It is a fundamental skill, which is useful and some would say essential to any musician, instrumentalists and singers alike.

I have been exposed to *solfeggio* but I haven't used this system exclusively. The issue is that *solfeggio* is a method of ear training that helps the musician to perform more efficiently. He or she learns a vocabulary of rhythms and pitches separately from the instrument. When the performer uses the instrument, he or she can concentrate more fully on the technique of the instrument since the rhythms and pitches are second nature. It is an excellent idea.

However, training the ear, or aural work as it is often called, is organised differently in England. The same work, recognising pitches and rhythms, is divided into a range of listening activities. These activities, singing back a tune or clapping a rhythm in the early stages, become progressively more difficult as studies continue. They are examined at each stage with the practical examinations. So, for example, someone who has the Grade Eight Violin exam has studied aural work to a high level. The aural work is an integral part of the instrumental exam and not given a separate certificate.

How I am to overcome this difficulty is beyond me at present. I feel overwhelmed. I am told that I must get all my certificates translated into Italian before I take them to the consulate and that I should act in a convincing manner. Ugo must have noticed my lack of confidence. I go home in a complete daze.

―◌―

It is almost 6.30 pm and I am sitting in the Italian Institute in Belgrave Square. I am here to listen to a concert given by an Italian orchestra. The programme is to include a mandolin concerto by Giovanni Battista Pergolesi, with Ugo as the soloist. I have not seen Ugo since yesterday lunchtime.

Outside it is twilight and I look at the silhouettes of the autumnal trees. The windows are bare but harmoniously framed by painted wooden shutters. The large expanse of room with its stucco ceiling is decorated in minimalist white. It is on the first floor at the front of the building looking out onto the square. I love the atmosphere of this room and I imagine it full of people dancing.

This is to be an intimate concert. Half the room is arranged with rows of chairs for the audience and the other half contains a group of chairs forming an arc, from which music stands periodically mushroom.

The orchestra members take their places. The men wear the traditional uniform of formal evening suits with tailed jackets. The ladies wear long black clothes of their own choice. They follow the same dress code as female orchestral players in England, but I am struck by how stunningly different and glamorous they look. Some of them wear trousers instead of long skirts. The trousers are beautifully cut garments in soft draping fabrics, which move elegantly with the wearer. I also admire the abundance of exquisite lace and see-through material used so seductively in the blouses that accompany the trousers. One of the violinists has sleeves like mantillas. I see several outfits that I would love to wear and I consider the problem of trying to find shops that sell suitable clothing for concerts.

Ugo appears and begins to introduce the concert.

It is quite an extensive talk, given entirely in Italian. I listen to the sound of the words as if they themselves were notes of music. Sometimes, the words are fast and bubbling with intensity. Other times, they are enunciated slowly with elegiac precision. It is difficult for me to understand the intricate detail of the speech. I am distracted by the beautiful sounds of the words and often forget to connect their meanings. Also, the odd word, usually a conjugation of a verb, throws me and I miss the nuance of meaning. Overall, I have a general impression of the sense of what has been said, but I fear I may have missed some important detail.

The programme consists of unknown works written by Neapolitan Baroque composers. Two of the works are in four movements following a contrasting pattern –slow, fast, slow, fast. Two other works follow a tertiary plan – fast, slow, and fast. Our attention is drawn to the slow movements, in which seventeenth and eighteenth century Neapolitan composers were influenced by the close proximity of the sea. In these slow and reflective movements, we will experience a gentle, hypnotic, lilting rhythm, reminding us of the sea lapping against the boats.

The theme of the sea might be a wildly romantic notion, but is nonetheless a clever connection with the title of the orchestra, *I Musici dell'Aquarium*, The Musicians of the Aquarium. The use of the English word aquarium is correct, if perhaps a little ironic, since so many English ensembles choose to Italianise their names in order to add romantic charm. This ensemble is an association for culture and education, which is connected to an International Marine Biological Laboratory. It is a puzzling collaboration.

The first work is a concerto for oboe and orchestra by Francesco Mancini. This is followed by a violin concerto by a composer I have never heard of called Angelo Ragazzi.

Next is the moment I have been waiting for: the mandolin concerto. First, there is a bit of retuning. The orchestra is a small chamber orchestra consisting of six violins, two violas, one cello, a doublebass and a harpsichord. Ugo sits down on a chair that has been placed in front of the orchestra and to the left of the conductor. They start to play, all the instruments co-operating in filling the room with vibrant energy. The room is alive with the resonance of sequential rhythms and the rhetorical banter between the soloist and the group of instruments. The middle movement is my favourite. Entitled *Largo*, it is music of languishing lyricism, packed full of emotional intensity. It is hard to understand how such tenderness is possible from a plucked metal string. And it seems to me remarkable that Baroque music is at times so romantic and sentimental. I have a strange sensation. It is as if I have discovered this truth for the very first time.

The concert concludes with another work by Pergolesi, a concertino for strings, and three songs sung by a soprano and accompanied by the orchestra.

After the concert, when Ugo has changed back into smart casual clothes, my husband and I take him to an Italian restaurant for dinner. I have booked a table at *Orso*, which is situated in Covent Garden, very near to the Royal Opera House. We find a parking place reasonably close by and walk the short distance to the restaurant. As we pass the Drury Lane Theatre Royal, I am startled by a quick movement and a noise. The strap on Ugo's mandolin case has snapped at one end and the bowl of the instrument, still contained within the padded case, briefly makes contact with the pavement. I am worried that the instrument is damaged, but Ugo is relaxed and thinks it is fine without inspecting inside the case.

Orso is neither a traditional *trattoria* nor one of the new pizza/pasta establishments currently opening up everywhere. Instead, it offers a menu that is changed daily and which includes the best fresh ingredients available, together with the exotic elements of Italian cuisine. The menu might include delicacies such as fried mozzarella cheese with anchovies and capers, or grilled swordfish with roasted peppers and ravioli made with wild mushrooms. The meal is always initiated with bread served with aromatic olive oil flavoured with herbs. The food, intrinsically attractive, is enhanced by being presented on beautifully hand-painted, rustic crockery.

The restaurant has a contemporary, uncluttered appearance and the ambience transmits a feeling of energy provided by the clientele of artistic and media personalities. Both the location and the food is perfect for an after concert celebration.

When we have eaten, we embark upon a sightseeing tour of London at night. This entails a short detour east, in the car, to Tower Bridge. We weave backwards and forwards across the Thames in a westerly direction. Our intention is to return Ugo to his hotel, but first we must point out all the illuminated bridges and buildings of importance: The Royal Festival Hall, The Houses of Parliament and Big Ben, and so on. It is late, but I am happy and proud to be pointing out the significant sights.

The phone rings at breakfast time. It is Ugo wanting to do some music shopping and requiring my assistance. I have a mandolin pupil arriving shortly, so we arrange to meet at my house. My pupil arrives and the lesson progresses. Towards the end, Ugo arrives and I leave him in the sitting room looking through my record collection. I return to my pupil in the music room and complete the lesson.

My pupil departs and I make some coffee. Ugo and I sit in the morning room adjoining the kitchen of my Victorian house. He is interested in my use of pale yellow for the walls and my partiality for shades of green in my crockery. My design brings the warmth of Italian sunshine into the eating area. The room I had inherited was a dismal depressing grey that reminded me of London drizzle. Now I am collecting hand-painted Italian plates, bowls and mugs, in various shades of blue, green and yellow.

"Ah! Green the colour of *speranza*, hope," Ugo sighs. He continues: "In Italy, grey is a good colour for a kitchen."

I learn a number of useful things from Ugo that are unconnected to music. I am experiencing problems with a glut of homegrown tomatoes – more precisely, allotment-grown tomatoes. Pounds of them are stacked in boxes on the floor. We grow them to make sauces for pasta, but this year we have more than I can manage. I don't have time, with my forthcoming trips to Italy and mandolin practice, to bottle them.

Ugo tells me that tomatoes can be frozen easily without any preparation. Just place them in plastic bags and put them in the freezer. When you want to use them, they are hard like golf balls. Place them in boiling water, as you would do normally, to remove the skins. The skins come away easily and the flesh begins to defrost. The tomatoes can be chopped up and used in the normal way. The heat from cooking quickly completes the defrosting process.

This is a useful tip about freezing tomatoes. I have never read about this idea in any of my many Italian cookery books. Ugo also says that it is possible to freeze *castagne*, chestnuts, in the same way. When the nuts are removed from the freezer, it is important to pierce the shell and then you can proceed to roast them on an open fire in the usual way. They take a bit longer because they defrost first and then cook. But this method of storage is excellent because it prevents the nuts drying out.

We travel on the tube to Oxford Circus. We talk most of the time about the mandolin. At our destination, we head directly for Schott's in Great Marlborough Street. I find nothing of interest today but Ugo sees a sale of old music placed in some cardboard boxes. He thumbs through and finds a number of interesting pieces that might be useful for mandolin. Suddenly, the shop is filled with chattering foreigners. It is the Neapolitan orchestra. Ugo talks with his friends and I find myself translating and helping the players with their enquiries.

It is Sunday evening in the Duke's Hall at the Royal Academy of Music. It is the venue for the second London concert of *I Musici dell'Aquarium*.

I have been busy ringing up all the other professional mandolinists to tell them about the concert. I notice that some of them are here. I see my friend Sue and we greet each other with a kiss. I promise to introduce her to Ugo after the concert.

This evening, I am with my family and we are complete with my ten-year-old son. It has been an onerous day. This morning I attended my church and this afternoon I heard my son sing at St. Paul's Cathedral. Now, I am about to listen to an evening of music. My usual routine on Sundays is to attend my own church in the morning and the cathedral in the afternoon. On special feast days, I might give my own church a miss and attend the cathedral twice. Today is different because half-term holiday began after Evensong and my son who boards at school is anxious to get home. He is very tired and we have had to stay in town for tea and to while away a couple of hours before the concert. There wasn't time to go home and come back again.

The programme is identical to the other evening except for one detail, the inclusion of an extra mandolin concerto: the *Conforto*. I have a particular interest in this concerto as it is the first one I have made an edition of, using my new computer programme, and I took it show Ugo earlier this year in the spring. Although I have a recording of Ugo playing this work, I am enraptured to hear a live performance.

At the end of the concert, I introduce Sue to Ugo, but I have an exhausted little boy tugging at my hand and I have to depart quickly.

This morning, my task is to take my certificates to the Italian Consulate for ratification. Ugo has returned to Italy but I have the company of my son, as it is his half-term holiday.

At the offices of the Italian Consul, I have to wait before I am able to present my documents. All my certificates have accompanying pieces of paper with Italian translations of the wording. I began these translations but quickly found myself out of my depth. An Italian friend of mine helped me enormously by correcting them and typing them out on her word processor, so I am sure that they are accurate.

The administrator that I see does not agree with some of the wording, a nuance, or a difference in cultural meaning. She starts to type out a document on headed paper, which will explain my qualifications for the Italian authorities. She looks suspiciously at each certificate in turn. I feel nervous, a little stressed. My son is sitting on a chair and I sense he is restless. I have warned him not to speak unless he is spoken to. He is the sort of child who is always asking questions and striking up conversations with the people we meet – but he is also at the age where in his innocence he may contradict me, and undermine my position. I feel the delicate tension of this moment. So much hangs on the *Certificato di Equipollenza*. Without it, I might not be able to proceed with my mandolin studies.

I am pleased to have the *Certificato di Equipollenza* in my possession, although I am surprised that all my certificates, even my degree, have been stamped and signed on the back as being authentic. I feel confused. I don't know whether to be pleased or dismayed. I feel my certificates have been violated in some way, but perhaps in years to come, it will be the only evidence of a remarkable story. It is only the advent of the European Community that makes my impending cultural exchange possible. If I had to pay tuition fees as well as travelling expenses, then the whole project would be out of the question.

3

My second lesson is taking me on another adventure. This time, I am going all the way to Venice where I will spend a night in a hotel and the first part of my trip will be on the new Eurostar train. I am really excited at the prospect of going directly from London to Paris, via the channel tunnel, in three hours.

My husband is accompanying me on this trip. He is anxious to try out the new train. He also wants to see where I am going for my lessons and it is generally a good excuse for a few days away from it all.

The plan for this short break seems attractive to me because we will have a day free to relax in Venice. After a good night's sleep in a hotel bed, we will take the short train ride back to Padua where I shall attend the mandolin class. At the conclusion of the day, we will return to Paris on the overnight train in the usual way.

The Eurostar is an absolute dream. The journey time, from city centre to city centre, is cut by about four hours. The concept of being linked to Europe by land and the feeling of Italy being more accessible is thrilling. I also have this feeling of being present in an important moment in history. I am one of the first passengers to try out this new method of transport – the first train to travel beneath the sea. I wonder whether the first tube travellers to make the journey beneath the Thames viewed their experience in the same way. Were some of those passengers also nervous of travelling in a tunnel under the water?

A communal sigh of relief is audible when the train arrives in France after thirty-five minutes of darkness. It really hasn't been very long. It was just like travelling on the underground, without all the interruptions of the stops.

The whole journey, especially in France, is so quick that it is difficult to enjoy looking out of the window. Fortunately, I have brought with me a magazine to indulge in. The internal design of the carriage gives me the impression of being on an aeroplane. Reading and having a drink seem more appropriate than looking out of the window.

In Paris, we retrace my journey of the previous month. I feel a little easier travelling across Paris on the metro this time, and the wait for the overnight train to Venice is tolerable since I have some company.

The journey to Venice passes without incident. I wake as before at Verona, which means that the last part of the journey is a little longer. It is about forty minutes after Padua, and just before nine o'clock, when we arrive at *Venezia Santa Lucia*.

Our first priority is to check our luggage into the left-luggage office. I feel liberated with nothing but a small handbag to carry as we walk out of the station and down the big steps that lead to the Grand Canal.

The second priority is breakfast. We turn into a street to the left of the station and find a bar. We order *brioche* and cappuccino, and stand with the locals eating our breakfast. We could be in deepest Italy, except that we are only a few minutes from an international railway station. There are no foreigners, other than ourselves, and we are hoping to be undetected. My husband has dark hair and is Mediterranean in appearance. I speak sufficient Italian to get by. We are passable Italians, as we nibble at our *brioche*. I take care to hold the white paper serviette around the pastry. It is a delicate business. I don't want to get my fingers sticky with the apricot jam and I don't want to be smothered in crumbs. There are other women dressed in elegant trouser suits who are managing the same operation with great aplomb. I think I am doing well. No one seems to have noticed that we are tourists yet.

We walk out into the chill November air. I have postcards from previous trips of Venice enshrouded in mist and I have always wanted to visit it in the dead of winter. November is not quite winter, but it is certainly the approach.

Our plan is to walk towards St. Mark's Square through the streets and myriad alleyways. We begin to make our nostalgic pilgrimage to the basilica, pointing out to each other the places we remember from our earlier holidays. It is difficult to explain the allure of Venice. I have visited it on three other occasions, but I am always ready to return and hungry to experience it again.

Some people say that its enchantment is a result of it being a city on water. They quote the fact that it is a city whose transport system relies entirely on boats. The buses and cars all have to stop in the *Piazzale Roma* at the entrance of the city where it is joined to the mainland by a bridge. The same bridge carries trains to the terminal nearby. Aircraft land at the airport, which is just across the lagoon, on the mainland. It is a peaceful city, people say, without the stress of modern transportation.

The Venice that I am visiting is charged, as if with electricity. At certain times, when shops are open for business, it is particularly energetic and lively. It always seems to hum and throb. Its pulse, its vibrations, its movement is constant. Even when it appears quiet, it is never still. There is always water lapping against the stones or bricks somewhere. I listen to the rise and fall of the engine noise of the *vaporetti*. I hear these water-buses knocking against the landing-stages as they unload their passengers and refill with new ones. I am reminded of a time when I stayed in an inexpensive hotel near the station that backed onto the Grand Canal. All through the night, I was woken each hour by the thud and resultant vibrations of the *Accelerato* water-bus as it stopped and started near my window.

Walking through the *calli*, or alleys, is like being in a maze. High up between the buildings of the narrow streets and alleys are strips of blue sky. Down here, I find it impossible to have any sense of direction. I am distracted at frequent intervals: a window, a balcony, some pots with late flowering plants, a cat. I see a linen shop and stop to admire some embroidered pillowcases and duvet covers. I never imagined that I could be so domestically inclined. I am rushed on. My husband is always confident of the route and always pressing ahead relentlessly. I am always ready to linger and to waste a little time.

We walk over tiny bridges. We see a barge laden exquisitely with fruit and vegetables: shining aubergines, large green and red peppers, swollen bulbs of fennel and salad leaves. The boat is moored on one side of the canal and is being used as a market stall. A group of ladies, with their shopping bags, wait to be served.

Just a little way further is a modern shop window with handmade wooden toys arranged on glass shelving. I am looking for something to take home for my son. My eyes trace over the various patterns of wood grain. I compare them with the patterns I have seen on the bowls of mandolins. I don't see the gift I am looking for, but I am fascinated by the stark contrast of the old and the new: an ultra-modern shop fitting within a cluster of ancient buildings.

Periodically we cross a *campo*, the Venetian equivalent of the *piazza*. These wide, open spaces are a welcome relief with their greater light. I let my eyes focus on some distant detail: the Baroque façade of a church or the shape of a campanile.

In the *Calle dello Spezier,* I hear the music of Vivaldi, a violin concerto. We are a long way from Vivaldi's church. I follow the sound of the music and it takes me across a pretty courtyard, decorated with potted plants. I feel as if I am entering someone's private house. At the other side of the courtyard is a shop window, in which is displayed a lute and books of music. The lute is placed on its front so that the round bowl is visible. I survey the ribs carefully, noticing the contrasting flaming in the alternating strips of wood. It is extremely attractive.

I remember a former visit when I tried to study the paintings by Pietro Longhi that are housed in the *Ca' Rezzonico*, the last home of Robert Browning. In a painting called '*La Polenta*', the lute like instrument was viewed from the back. Another picture I wanted to see had been moved, I was told, to the *Galleria Querini-Stampalia*. When I tried to locate it, nobody knew of its whereabouts. I am anxious to collect iconographic evidence of all lute type instruments, as they contribute in some way to the evolution of the mandolin. It is, at times, a frustrating investigation.

I am dragged away from my thoughts to the *Pasticceria Marchini*, one of the many confectioners of the city. I can smell the sweet sugary fragrance before we see the array of pastries. The Austrian influence in Venetian history is reflected in the wonderful *Sachertorte*s and various types of strudel. I am tempted to buy some nougat, but I resist and press on.

A shop that specialises in marbled paper catches my eyes. I love the designs. The paper is handmade and very expensive. I steal a few moments evaluating the different patterns and colour combinations. I prefer the blues and green to the reds and oranges. I decide to experiment with marbling when I return home. I would like to use the designs as cover paper for my editions of music. My son's class did some beautiful work when they tried marbling at school. I resolve to seek his teacher's advice on the matter.

We enter the *Piazza San Marco*. Even though I have seen it several times before, and despite the nuisance of the pigeons, I am struck by its vastness and by the glory of the decorated basilica. The gold and jewel-like colours of the paintings on the façade of the building glitter in the sun. Slowly we walk across the asymmetrical 'square' towards the Campanile, savouring the experience. Turning right, we walk past the Doge's Palace in the direction of the water. Turning left, we walk a little way along the *Riva degli Schiavoni*, until we find a café with outdoor tables. We sit down and order our morning coffee.

The water changes endlessly. Sunlight falls on the undulating surface, making it iridescent: slate grey, turquoise, opaque, limpid, sparkling.

I stare at the crooked sticks growing from the water, protecting the parked gondolas that bob up and down ceaselessly.

My gaze extends to the ambiguous horizon and then focuses on the church of *Maria della Salute*, across the water. I have a silk screen print of this church at home. My picture is predominantly turquoise: a symbol of hope and gratitude, it was built to honour the deliverance of the city from the plague.

Apart from a short gap during which we consume delicious pizzas, the rest of the day is spent walking around: exploring, admiring and reminiscing. At about five o'clock, I start to worry that I haven't done any practice. My legs are tired and I want to go to our hotel. We take the *vaporetto* to the station and collect our luggage. We take another *vaporetto* along the Grand Canal towards our stop at the *Accademia*. The water-bus is crowded with people returning home from work. A tired baby is crying and being comforted by its mother. Through the glass door at the front of the boat, I see the famous Canaletto scenes of Venice drenched in the pink light of the setting sun. Probably this scene has been observed and described thousands of times, but I am left with a sense of privilege at having seen it first-hand.

In the hotel, I have a shower and change. It is bliss to be clean and to be able to relax in the privacy of our room. I begin to practise. My husband is restless and departs for another short walk. I think he should rest but he wants to make the most of every minute. I say nothing. It is no use trying to dissuade him. It only makes matters worse.

My need to practise is urgent and my mind is quickly focused on the notes. I have prepared the first three sonatas by Lecce, out of a book of eighteen. Each sonata is just a single movement. My teacher has written out the notes by hand, copying them from the original manuscript. My book is a photocopy of his work, bound together with a red spiral binding and plastic covers. I imagine how the book would look with notes printed by the computer and handmade marble paper beneath the plastic covers.

I sit on the edge of the bed with my music propped up by pillows and I begin to play. The music is reasonably clear in comparison to some handwritten examples I have seen. I play the first phrase a couple of times. It contains four G major chords. I love the quality of their sound, but one of the chords is a little tricky because it is short – only a semiquaver in length (or really quick for the uninitiated). I try it a few times until I am satisfied and then I move on.

I am soothed by the patterns that follow. Arpeggios and chords in various inversions, the notes played separately and repetitively. They create a harmony, an order, a peace, a stillness within me. At the same time, the relentless semiquavers imbue me with an energy; intensified by a dominant seventh here or lightened by the decoration of a trill there. At the cadence points, there is always just a skeleton of notes to suggest the punctuation. Such simplicity. Such beauty.

An hour has disappeared as if it were a few seconds, and I am content.

My husband returns. He takes a shower whilst I watch the Italian news on television. I love watching Italian television because there is no need to be interactive. I can relax knowing that I am soaking up the language at my own pace. If there is something I don't understand, it doesn't matter because I don't need to respond.

I am hungry and ready for my dinner. I have in my mind several good restaurants where we have eaten before, but my husband has a better plan. In his search for perfection and the avoidance of other tourists, he thinks we should take the *vaporetto* to the *Giudecca*, where we are sure to find a quiet restaurant used only by the locals.

The *Giudecca* is certainly quiet and seems largely unlit. We stumble along in the dark looking for the restaurant of our dreams. We see shops closing and one or two bars, but no eating places. We decide to return to the other side of the canal and head for the two restaurants I thought of earlier. The first is near the barge that doubles as a greengrocer's. I remember having a memorable meal of spaghetti with *seppie*, but when we arrive, there is a notice that says it is closed for a wedding party. We walk on into *Campo S. Margherita* where we have already been once today and where my second choice of eating establishment is. Here, we are also disappointed. It is closed this evening, and on this same night every week. I feel disheartened.

Our search for a restaurant continues. I am cold, tired and hungry. We have, it seems, walked miles today. I just want some hot, delicious food and my bed. Eventually, on the well-beaten track towards St. Mark's Square, we find a restaurant that is open. It looks as if it welcomes tourists and I am suspicious of its quality. Nevertheless, we enjoy a simple meal: grilled vegetables drizzled with extra virgin olive oil, a slice of pan-fried veal, salad, wine and water.

I sleep soundly, but when I wake, I realise yesterday has taken its toll. I have a migraine beginning and my stomach feels unsettled.

On the way to the station, we stop for breakfast at the same bar as yesterday. I have nothing except a few sips of water. The sweet smell of the shop makes my stomach heave and I go outside to wait.

The short train journey doesn't improve matters. On my walk from the station to the *Conservatorio,* I resolve to be stoical.

When I arrive at the *Conservatorio,* the classes are already in progress. I knock on the door.

"*Avanti.*"

I open the double doors and enter. The class is busy. There are lots of people waiting for their lesson. The day is run rather like what is termed a masterclass in England. Everybody attends. One person at a time receives a lesson whilst the others observe, making comments if they are invited to do so.

After a short while, my husband is restless again. Attending a lesson is not like a concert. There are lots of stops and starts, and discussion in between. The discussion is technical and difficult to follow in Italian. He departs for a walk.

I try to concentrate on the discussion. When it is my turn, I make my excuses, saying that I feel a little fragile. The Maestro jokes that it is probably Venice with the constant movement of water that has caused my nausea. I find it difficult to think of the correct form of address as we talk. I notice that the other students address him formally with *Lei,* but I have always used the informal *tu.* This is because we met as colleagues from different countries. Now it dawns upon me that I am his pupil and must afford him the appropriate respect when we are in the teaching context. It is confusing.

My playing goes well and I am happy. I am advised to use fourth fingers for descending passages. (This is a subtle difference between violin playing and mandolin playing only for those interested in the technicalities – otherwise, skip the rest of the paragraph. The mandolin is plucked and an open string will continue to resonate, if not stopped by a finger. By using the fourth finger instead of the open string, when followed by a note a tone below, it is possible to avoid a discordant clash. On the violin, this doesn't occur because the bow is responsible for making the string sound, and when the bow is on the next string, playing the next note, the previous note has ceased.)

I am also sent to buy a new scale book. I follow the directions to the music shop, *Musica Musica*, which is just around the corner from the *Conservatorio*. The new scale book, by Luigi Schinina, is really intended for violinists and as I am familiar with other violin scale books, I don't anticipate too much difference between what I have been used to and the new book.

I manage a little light lunch with my husband in the middle of the day. At the end of the day, I check possible dates with the Maestro for the following month. Then, I begin my journey home.

When I awake on the train approaching Paris, I am still not feeling well. This does not bode well for the day, since we have arranged to have some free time in Paris before catching the Eurostar home.

We embark upon a tour of the *Louvre*. It is too big to see everything, so we decide to concentrate on the Italian paintings. It becomes increasingly difficult for me to focus on the paintings. I am unsteady, and I have a great desire to sit down and close my eyes. I am battling constantly with myself, trying not to become absorbed by the raging pain in my head and behind my left eye.

At the pyramid shopping centre, there are stylish, modern shops and wonderful places to eat – but I am not able to enjoy any of this. Here I am in Paris, with the fragrant smell of crêpes and other cooking. Normally, I would find the atmosphere delicious and irresistible. Instead, everything is too noisy and the pungent aromas of Parisian cuisine seem to be making me feel sick. I collapse on a bench. My body is racked by pain. How can a migraine be so debilitating? I cannot concentrate on any thought. It seems that my consciousness, my very soul, is ignited with the searing fire of pain. I feel embarrassed and angry with myself. My man is mad with me. I am absolutely exhausted and my journey, on this occasion, has been spoiled.

4

This morning, I have arrived in Padua again for another mandolin lesson. On this trip I have reverted to the old-fashioned train and sea crossing by catamaran. The Eurostar is too expensive this month.

I walk along with the other commuters through the subway beneath the platforms of Padua station. I am feeling confident that I am establishing a pattern in my journeys. I know where to go and what to expect. I have my breakfast at the station, visit the ladies' room and walk to the *Conservatorio*.

I begin to recognise the faces of those who work at the *Conservatorio*. The porters: a young man with dark hair and glasses and a gentleman of mature years wearing a casual shirt and a grandfatherly cardigan. Often they sit behind a wooden table near the entrance, reading the newspaper.

I am in good time this morning, but after a while I begin to feel uneasy because I haven't seen anybody else I recognise from the mandolin course. I pluck up the courage to speak with one of the porters. I ask the elderly gentleman if Maestro Orlandi has arrived and, if so, has the room changed since there is no one in the usual room. I use the word *classe* for classroom but I suddenly remember *aula*, which seems to work better. He tells me that Maestro Orlandi has not yet arrived.

After a further period of time, I begin to feel quite anxious and I speak again with the porter. He makes a phone call to the secretary on the first floor but the answer is the same. The Maestro has not yet arrived. No one has seen him or knows of his whereabouts.

I decide I should phone Ugo's house in case this throws some light on my problem. I find some change and wait by the telephone at the bottom of the stairwell. A girl is speaking effusively on the telephone. When she has finished, I take my turn and pick up the receiver. Suddenly I notice some large dangling earrings next to the receiver, and I run up the stairs after the girl to return the earrings. She is grateful but I am a little flustered that I can't remember the word for earrings.

I try to phone Ugo but the telephone does not work. I imagine that I have done something wrong. I check the number. I have dialled correctly, using the complete code, since it is another city. All I can hear is what I think is the unobtainable signal. All the phone signals sound slightly different here. The phone has eaten up all my money and is now out of order. I can't believe it!

Just as I wonder what to do, I turn around and a lady approaches. She tells me that there has been a telephone message from Maestro Orlandi, saying that he is unable to attend the *Conservatorio* because his child is sick, and that I should telephone him at home. I am extremely thankful for this communication, but at the same time dismayed at the thought of missing my mandolin lesson.

Unexpectedly, I see a face that I recognise from the mandolin course. It is Gianluigi, from Naples, here for some history and harmony lessons. I explain, as best I am able to, all my troubles. By now, I feel panic-stricken at the thought of all the time and money that would be wasted if I didn't succeed in having my lesson. The stress causes some short-circuiting in my thinking process. The Italian language becomes more difficult than usual. I am conscious of missing out words, using the wrong words, and failing to make the correct agreements to word endings. Words are inadequate. It all seems too awful.

Gianluigi calmly removes something from his pocket and places it in my hand. It is a phone card. He tells me that there are telephones equipped for phone cards just a short distance away. He points through the arcade opposite the entrance of the *Conservatorio* and to the left.

I find the telephones and manage to get through to Ugo. He wants me to go to his house in Brescia for my lesson. This means returning to Brescia, which is almost two hours away. I had already passed through Brescia whilst sleeping on the train early this morning. Another complication is that I also have to get to Ugo's house, which is on the outskirts of Brescia. It sounds impossible to me, but Ugo says it is possible and that I should ring him when I get to Brescia.

At the *Conservatorio,* I explain to Gianluigi what has happened. I return his phone card and thank him for his kindness and help. I am deeply touched by his warmth and generosity. He says it is nothing. *È niente*. I disagree. For me, it was quite a lot. His manner is casual, almost self-effacing. I thank him once again for rescuing me and I depart for the station.

At Brescia, I phone Ugo and he says that Giovanna will collect me from the station. My spirits lift. This is the silver lining to the cloud. I hadn't expected to see my friend Giovanna on this or on any of my trips at present. She is working hard studying for her degree.

As we drive out into the countryside, Giovanna and I chat continuously, catching up on all our news. We talk in English, which is a great relief to me. She leaves me at Ugo's house and we resolve to see each other later at the rehearsal of the Mandolin and Guitar orchestra. I have checked the train details and found out that I can join the overnight train to Paris at Brescia. I just need to be at the station at about ten o'clock.

I am now able to begin my mandolin lesson. This and the promise of playing again with the mandolin orchestra has redeemed what, only a few hours ago, seemed a disastrous day.

We start with scales: G major with a new fingering. I have to play it twice and follow immediately with the arpeggio, which is also repeated. It is like an exercise playing the scales and arpeggios in this manner. I am told not to worry about mistakes. It is fluency and the right-hand movement that are important. Do not stop for mistakes, just keep going. One note after another with unbending fixation.

How different this is to my study of the violin. The scales have the same fingering, the same patterns, but the issue for the violin is completely different. Every note on the violin must be made from scratch. The violinist has no markings on the fingerboard to guide the fingers. The violinist must choose the exact spot to place a finger in order to make the pitch of the note. This is before all other musical considerations: the rhythm, dynamics, articulation.

A violinist sometimes feels lost trying to find the notes. It takes hours of practice to learn the feel of where the notes are. Hours of practice with Sevcik exercises, learning the geography of the fingerboard. Violinists are envious of pianists who have their notes already made for them. They are sometimes envious of other string instrumentalists who have frets for their fingers to fall between.

Consequently, I spent hours practising my violin scales slowly, checking each note for intonation, and making slight adjustments. Now I feel as if I must race on carelessly and sometimes the frets get in the way of my fingers.

The lesson continues with more soothing sonatas by Lecce. There is a lovely passage in the fourth sonata that conveys the illusion of alternating sevenths and sixths. In reality, all the notes are played separately, rapidly and repeatedly. The effect is one of a harmonic progression. The two chords continuously follow each other: one is discordant and full of tension, and the other is harmonious and relaxed.

The arrangement of the notes in this passage is a little awkward for the plectrum. The direction of the plectrum must change each time one changes string. At speed, this is the equivalent of a tongue-twister for the mandolinist. My teacher suggests an alternative arrangement of strokes. Now the strokes are down, up on each string. The arrangement works perfectly and I play the passage with ease. The harmony has its potency restored, and is reminiscent of the music of Vivaldi.

I also start work on the preludes and cadenzas of Munier. A name little known outside mandolinistic circles, Carlo Munier was one of the most important figures in mandolin playing in the second half of the nineteenth century. Born in 1859 in Naples, he moved to Florence when he was twenty-two years old and remained there for the rest of his life. He enjoyed a distinguished career as a performer and teacher, one of his most famous pupils being Queen Margherita of Italy.

The interpretation of the preludes and cadenzas is extremely interesting to me. We have to discuss where it is appropriate to increase or decrease the speed of the notes in order to generate excitement. This music should reflect its improvisatory nature, even though the notes are written out. A sense of impetuosity must be cultivated so as to enhance the virtuosic content. It is a fascinating discussion.

I eat supper with Ugo's family. We talk about Christmas. Ugo's children, like all Brescian children, had presents last week on the Feast of Santa Lucia. Traditionally, presents are given to children in this part of Italy on December 8th instead of Christmas day. I am quite surprised by this.

I tell them that when I arrive in London tomorrow evening, I have to go directly to the Barbican Centre, where my son is singing with his choir in Britten's Ceremony of Carols. It seems so strange. Here am I eating supper with an Italian family in the Italian countryside. Tomorrow, I shall be in London listening to my son singing in one of the world's most prestigious concert venues. Tonight, I will rehearse with the Brescia Mandolin Orchestra. Tomorrow, I will have breakfast in Paris.

At the orchestra, I am deliriously happy just to be part of the sound. I don't worry if I can't manage all the notes because it is just so thrilling to be part of a plucked string ensemble. The deep throb of vibrations when we strike chords together is exhilarating. It is as if not only the strings and the instruments are vibrating, but we and everything else in the room vibrates in sympathy.

Giovanna drives me back to the station. Before I depart, she gives me a Christmas present. It is a small, round wooden box. On the lid is an array of mountain flowers in pink, red, yellow and blue on a green background. She explains that it has been hand-painted in the traditional Austrian manner by a friend of hers. The box contains traditional nougat sweets. This unexpected kindness completes a perfect day. I clutch my Italian Christmas present and begin my journey home.

5

The New Year starts with a number of complications. I have quite a bit of professional work to undertake: three performances of *Otello* with the Royal Opera and a solo recital of mandolin music with piano accompaniment.

I also have rehearsals for these engagements. The opera is less of a problem. There is just one rehearsal I must attend at Covent Garden and two performances in January. The third performance is at the beginning of February. The recital, on the other hand, requires hours of rehearsal time spent with my pianist. The performance is also at the beginning of February, just a few days after the last *Otello*.

I want to do and will enjoy all of this work, but it is the nature of concert work to be unpredictable. It either comes all at once like this or not at all. The freelance musician is either stressed by too much to do or is bored waiting for the next opportunity.

My real problem is not only trying to fit in a few days away in Italy for my lesson, but also trying to manage all the conflicting requirements. In particular, I have been addressing the issue of changing my hand position. The seed for this change began at Brescia over four years ago. Now beginning on the mandolin course, I have to face up to this challenge once and for all.

One friend wisely said that one must take what is helpful from the experience and disregard what is not useful. This is certainly true at one level, but I have embarked upon a course of study based on certain technical principals. I have to embrace those principals with trust. I have a choice: either I trust my teacher and change my technique, believing that I will then progress to the finer details of style and interpretation, or I walk away. It is not possible to deal with style and interpretation, the actual music, the artistic process, without first having an appropriate technique.

The real difficulty for me at present is that I need some space to concentrate on changing a habit: the habit of holding my right wrist in an arched manner. Instead, I must learn to keep it straight and in contact with the instrument. Intellectually this posture makes sense, but emotionally it is difficult to come to terms with since any habit is hard to change.

At the same time, I have to perform music professionally. I am absorbed, even obsessed, with thinking about the hand position whilst I am practising. But I realise that I mustn't think about it whilst I am performing or else everything will go wrong. I cannot get out of my professional obligations. I just somehow have to get through this period. Some days are brighter than other days, and I feel that I am making progress and that my hand position is evolving. On other days, I feel the strain and impossibility of what I am trying to achieve, and my mood becomes one of despair.

This month, the old-fashioned train is not operating. I don't yet know if this is a permanent change of plan. The Eurostar, however, has a new timetable and is affordable this month.

My trips are beginning to attract a lot of attention from

everyone that knows me: my family, friends, colleagues and so on. Everyone is interested in the fact that I am making these trips with such regularity. They are interested in the eccentricity of travelling by train. I explain my motives time and time again. Cheap airfares require an overnight stop on Saturday. I need the cheapest available fare, but I also need to be at home on Saturdays when my son has his lunch leave from the choir school and also so that I can attend Evensong on Saturday afternoon, so that I can support him by hearing him sing

Some people look at me blankly. They don't understand my passion for the mandolin and its music. They don't understand my desire to improve my skill and the fact that I am prepared to travel across Europe to do it. Even less they understand about cathedrals, the English choral tradition and what it is like to be a chorister parent. Other people are utterly amazed by the madness of my undertaking, but like the glamour, romance and, perhaps, the novelty factor. Fortunately, I also have a nucleus of supportive and understanding friends who value the importance of what I am doing. They know it is unique, special and worth doing.

On the train to Paris, I sit next to a lovely French lady who tells me that she lives in London during the week where her husband works. At the weekends, she travels home to Paris to be with her daughter who is still at school. I tell her about my study of the mandolin in Italy. Perhaps, there are other people like me, who have or who are growing roots in two cultures, and who commute between them.

In Paris, there is an incident in the waiting room at the station whilst I am waiting for the overnight train. Last month, I was pleased to discover the waiting room since it is supervised. This month, I head directly for the waiting room after having eaten, knowing that it will be safe and warm, only to find that it is without a station official.

I sit down and read. Suddenly, a man begins a great commotion. He shouts and his behaviour is threatening and violent, and probably all the more so to me because I don't understand his language. I try not to notice the disturbance, feeling that this is the best course of action. After a while, the man leaves. Everyone starts to chatter with relief.

A man next to me begins to engage me in conversation. All at once, I am involved in a complex discussion and it dawns on me that there is little difference between this man and the one who has just left. How could I have got caught up in this conversation? He says that he had worked at the opera in Verona, but further questioning reveals he sold soft drinks and ice cream. He has a friend in London. The friend works in a restaurant. He wants to visit me in London. I smell danger. The conversation has gone too far. I tell him it will not be possible. He asks me why? I say, truthfully, because I have a jealous husband. With this final remark, I declare that I have to leave and I depart with amazing confidence. When I feel it is safe, I glance over my shoulder to check I am not being followed. He said that he was staying in Paris, so he will not be travelling on my train. I feel safe when I board the Venice train.

My sense of security is quickly shattered. When I arrive at

my compartment, there is a discussion going on between an elderly lady and the carriage steward. I have a top couchette again and I briskly arrange my belongings and make up my bed. At first, I am pleased that it is not too crowded. There is another man in our compartment, but that is all. We are half full. There are sheets and pillows on the other beds, so I imagine that there will be other passengers later.

The steward goes away and then returns. More discussion ensues. Finally, the debate is resolved and the lady is moved to another compartment. Apparently, there had been some misunderstanding about her booking. Being elderly, she required a bottom bed and she had been allocated a middle bed. It is not clear to me why she cannot have the bottom bed in our compartment. There is no reservation ticket on the door for the bottom bed.

Abruptly, I realise that I am about to spend the night travelling alone with a man who is a complete stranger. I make polite conversation with him in an attempt to disguise my internal agitation. He is Italian, so language is not a problem. He has a shoe factory in France and is returning to Padua on business. He seems nice enough, but then criminals can be deceptively nice. This man is probably honest and honourable, but how am I to know?

I weigh up the pros and cons of whether to speak to the steward about this situation. I don't want to make a scene. He told the elderly lady very firmly that reservations for couchettes couldn't be changed. He will probably think I am being silly. Perhaps I am.

I am reticent to become embroiled in conflict with the steward. Instead I face the fear, imagined or otherwise, of unwanted attention or personal attack. I console myself that I am less vulnerable high up on my top bed. He is on the other side on the bottom bed. There is a notice above the door warning passengers to lock the door in order to avoid being prey to robbers, but I am disinclined to lock the door. I don't want to be locked in with a complete stranger.

The night is uneventful, except that my sleep is disturbed by anxious thoughts. I feel responsible for putting myself at risk and yet I didn't knowingly choose to travel alone with a stranger. It is unwise to say the least, but it is one of the disadvantages of travelling unaccompanied during the winter months. I am just thankful that it is morning and I am safe.

⁓

At my lesson, the scales lull me after my difficult night. The ones in sixths, octaves and broken thirds are especially calming. I manage them quite well. They were also my favourites whilst studying the violin.

⁓

My journey home is easier. There are more people in my carriage. My apprehension disappears. I relax and fall asleep.

⁓

In Paris, I awake with a migraine. This is so often the pattern. The attack begins not during a period of stress or tension, but afterwards in the calm that follows.

I ache to be at home in my bed. I am so uncomfortable in the seats of the new Eurostar lounge at *Gare du Nord*. They are not designed for ill people. I wish that I lived in Italy so that I didn't have this extensive journey to do. I begin to wonder about the wisdom of what I am doing. I am making enormous sacrifices for my art and at present I am not convinced that I have the strength to continue.

6

I receive a postcard from Delhi. It says: '*Quando ci vediamo?*' 'When shall we see each other?'

It is Ugo. He is in India touring with *I Solisti Veneti*.

I do not know the answer to his question. I have successfully completed all my professional engagements, but now there are other complications. Ugo doesn't return to Italy until halfway through February. At the end of the month, my son has his half-term holiday and I must, of course, be at home for that.

It is at this point that I become aware of a huge difference between the English and Italian scholastic year. The Italians do not have the same arrangement of holidays that we do. At Christmas and Easter, we have long holidays of two or three weeks. My son's holidays are always delayed by a week because he has to sing in services up until Christmas Day and Easter Day respectively. In Italy, there is only a short holiday of a few days for both these Christian festivals. In addition, the concept of a week's half-term holiday three times a year just doesn't exist. Naturally, being a Mediterranean country, Italy enjoys a long summer holiday of at least three months, whereas in England we have only six weeks. Our overall holiday time is probably about the same, it is just distributed differently.

I suppose I had read about this somewhere in my study of

Italian culture. At my Italian evening classes, we often receive articles to read about Italian life. Somehow these facts hadn't registered with me and it is only now as I am trying to practically live part of my life in Italy that they are doing so.

I am unable to book a train ticket in the few days I have available this month. It is unfortunate but cannot be helped. I don't want to miss a month because a month is quite a long enough gap as it is. All the other students have lessons weekly. If I lived in Italy, I could have lessons weekly. But I don't live in Italy, and I have just discovered that the course finishes for the summer on June 1st. This means I will only be able to squeeze in another three, possibly four, visits. The course starts on November 1st and finishes on June 1st. The entire academic year for the mandolin course is only seven months. I am shocked that the course appears to be so short. It is going to be quite a challenge to fit in the requisite lessons. Our courses begin in September or October and complete in mid-July. It would be lovely if I could spend some nights in Italy in order to take more time over this study, instead of being in continual transit.

7

It is March and I have accepted an invitation from Giovanna to stay with her at Brescia for a few days.

I fly from Heathrow to Venice. I take a bus to Mestre station and then catch the train to Brescia. Giovanna collects me by car from Brescia station.

It is absolutely wonderful to be part of an Italian family again. Giovanna's parents always make me feel so welcome and Giovanna's mother cooks wonderful food. The pace is so different. There is the siesta hour, or hours, which I adore. I was astonished at first when Giovanna's mother told me to rest after lunch. I thought that I had perhaps misunderstood her instructions. It is so relaxing to have a little rest. It suits my personality perfectly, but at home I usually feel guilty if I take a rest. In Italy, it is just an accepted part of the culture and it is a great comfort having permission to take a nap in the afternoon.

Giovanna and I talk a great deal; we always have so much to discuss about music and life. We also play duets together in the evenings after dinner. We are so happy to be reunited again. We work on our music and when we feel we are ready, we ask her parents to come and listen. This evening, Giovanna's brother calls in. He lives locally with his wife. We have three people in the audience for our concert and they are all totally delighted. Even Giovanna's black cat, Caligola, seems to enjoy the music.

―❀

At the *Conservatorio,* I have to take an exam. I have to play some short pieces and answer some questions in order to confirm which year I am in on the course. I have prepared a sonata by Lecce and two preludes and a cadenza by Munier.

During the lesson, Ugo tells me that Gianluigi is taking the same exam and has prepared the same Lecce sonata as I have. He asks me to look at another sonata that I have studied. He thinks it would be better if we don't play the same music.

As I play through the music, my teacher gives precise instructions, reminding me where to take a breath between notes and where to ensure they are linked, where to slow down the pulse and where to fasten it up, in order to create the greatest possible dramatic effect. It is a curious business playing a plucked instrument. We use the fingers independently all the time, so that the act of lifting a finger off the string stops the vibrations. Sometimes, it is even necessary to place the fingers over the strings – not in any particular place – just to deaden the sound of a chord. Using the fingers independently, continuously, is strange for me. On the violin, I was trained to leave fingers down wherever possible to help intonation. In a violin scale, we leave fingers down in case we return quickly to them. It prevents wasted energy finding the exact spot to place the finger down again.

I need to practise. I need to remember everything my teacher has told me and I need to rehearse the music, making the necessary adjustments. It is like reciting a piece of poetry. One must set the right pace, breathe in the correct place, emphasise important words. There are no practice rooms available. My teacher tells me to bring my mandolin and music. I follow him out of the room into the entrance hall, out of the glass door into the courtyard, up some steps and in through a door. We are in a corridor behind the concert hall of the *Conservatorio*. Beyond, in the annex, there are other steps and corridors, and other rooms all in use. Along the wall to the left runs a bench, probably intended for instrument cases during concerts.

"You can sit here and practise for a while," my teacher tells me. And I do.

―⁂―

I am nervous waiting outside the room for my exam. On the wall is a large portrait of Cesare Pollini, after who the *Conservatorio* is named. Underneath are chairs and sofas, nineteenth century in style, upholstered in wine coloured velvet. I don't know whether they are authentic or reproduction, but they add a sense of richness to the ambience. An administrator sits behind a big, dark wooden desk. Behind her a pool of golden light falls on the floor from a standard lamp. The room has a high ceiling and dark panelled door at one end, through which I must pass to my examination. It is all rather imposing and adds to my sense of unease.

Doubts flicker through my mind. It is a nuisance I am not playing the Lecce I prepared. It was in a comfortable key, G major. I can hardly comprehend that I am about to take an exam in which I will play something I have only spent a couple of hours preparing. On the other hand, I find this Italian quality of spontaneity so attractive.

Gianluigi emerges from the examination room. His face relaxes into a smile of relief.

When I am invited to enter the room, I am startled to see that there are five professors, including my own teacher. They look formal and serious.

My teacher introduces me, explaining that I am English and commuting from London for my studies. This breaks the ice a little and I settle down to play the pieces. As soon as I start to play, I think about the music and forget my nerves.

The music is followed by questions from the professors. They want to know what else I have studied. They ask me about musical history. They ask me about my piano playing. They have the photocopies and translations of all my certificates before them. They want to know what I covered in my study of harmony. They confer between themselves and study the prospectus for the violin diploma course I followed. I feel like a criminal being cross-questioned. *Why don't they understand that I successfully coach pupils to pass exams in violin, theory and aural training? I couldn't do this without passing my own exams. Are my certificates invalid, meaningless?*

My teacher is very happy. The exam went well. I satisfied the examiners and passed the exam with *otto voti*, eight marks. It doesn't sound much, eight marks. Apparently, it is eight marks out of ten and it is very good. I convert my marks to eighty per cent, since it makes more sense to me.

I am quite pleased with myself. My teacher is delighted that I am such a quick learner, that I was able to assimilate the new information about the pieces in a short time. Then, he explains that my exam has confirmed my position in the fourth year. My feeling of jubilation is checked by the sudden realisation that if I am in the fourth year of a seven-year course, I have another three years of study after the end of this year. My project of studying mandolin in Italy was only to be a year or two at the most. Suddenly, I am embarked upon an extensive mission.

I voice my doubts about continuing with the incessant travelling by train. To continue for another three years after this academic year seems an unbearable undertaking, despite the charms and pleasures that Italy has to offer. I never have time to savour them. It would be different if I had somewhere to stay.

However, my teacher has a plan.

―○―

In the afternoon, there is a knock at the door.

"*Avanti.*"

A pre-Raphaelite apparition enters the room. I have seen this apparition once before, at distance, but I have never met her. She is tall, thin and beautiful. She is wearing a suit in pale aquamarine that enhances her long copper hair, which falls in ringlets about her shoulders and down her back.

"This is Maria Cleofe Miotti," says my teacher, introducing her to me.

Maria Cleofe was on tour with Ugo in India. She is a former pupil of his and she was performing in the double mandolin concerto by Vivaldi. She would like to study English and would be happy for me to stay with her when I visit Italy for my mandolin lesson.

We chat together. She lives in Bologna. I am not sure about the journey by air, but I will make some enquiries. She writes her telephone number down in the back of my diary. She also writes down the name 'Ette'. All her family and friends call her Ette and in future I should do the same. I promise to ring her soon after my return to England.

8

April arrives quickly and Bologna beckons.

I have never visited this city before so I am excited at the prospect and a little apprehensive about the unknown, a different journey and staying with someone new.

Like last time, I am going on Wednesday and returning on Sunday, so as to stay a Saturday night and qualify for the cheapest ticket price. I haven't exactly come to terms with being absent for Saturdays, but I think this is a compromise that I am going to have to accept and that will hopefully get easier as my son gets older.

My flight is between Gatwick and Verona, the latter being the nearest location to my destination that I could find. In fact, Verona is nowhere near Bologna. It is considerably north of my final destination and a train journey is necessary to reach it.

On the Central Line, I meet a friend who I haven't seen for some time. We catch up with our news and I explain that the mandolin case is not because I'm going to a rehearsal in town, but because I'm going to Italy for a mandolin lesson. I tell her about the train journeys, the new development of finding somewhere to stay, and the flight I am taking to Verona.

"I don't know how it is going to turn out exactly," I tell her, "but I am learning to take one month at a time. It is going to be a challenge trying to find the next cheapest flight each time I return home and I don't know where the money is coming from, but I have found sufficient funds up till now. I'm still looking at various bursaries. I will just have to see what happens."

At Mile End I change to the District Line, which takes me to Blackfriars station. Here, I catch a train that takes me directly to Gatwick airport. As the train departs across Blackfriars Bridge, I stare at the symbols of London, my English heritage, my life. I look intently at the huge dome of St. Paul's; I think of my son and wonder where he is and what he is doing. I feel love, pride and sadness all at once. I say a prayer for him. I gaze at the magnificence of our favourite bridge, Tower Bridge. I think how strange it is that music brings us so close together and yet today pulls us apart. I consider the pain of love, how we have to let each other be ourselves and live our own lives. I am bound to be back safely in a few days and yet undertaking this journey, and all my journeys, seems to intensify my emotions.

At Verona, I catch a bus to the station. I have just missed the train to Bologna. It is late afternoon and quite warm. I phone Ette and tell her the time of the train I am catching and she says that she will meet me at the station. I have a little time to waste, so I find a table at one of the station's bars and I order a *toast* and cappuccino. The *toast* is really a toasted sandwich with a filling of ham and cheese. I sit quietly savouring my snack and watching the world go by.

The train to Bologna hurtles across the plains of Emilia-Romagna. The landscape is so flat in comparison to the train route between Milan and Venice. I look at the distant farmhouses, each with their row of protective trees. The late afternoon sun envelops the fields in amber light. The train is warm. I am sitting on the left, but those on the right have drawn every available piece of curtain to protect themselves. There are a number of windows open in my open-plan carriage and the ensuing breeze is humid. I feel quite mellow and sleepy.

―♊

As I step down from the train, I see a familiar face. Ette has somehow chosen the correct spot on a long busy platform to meet me. She smiles at me and greets me like a long-lost friend. In these first minutes of our meeting, I have such a sense of welcome and being cared for.

We drive to her flat in her white Ford Fiesta. The slow chaos of city traffic gives way to the speed and order of the *tangenziale*, the by-pass. We appear to be heading into the country on a motorway, but my friend tells me that we are still in Bologna, just moving towards the *periferia* – the outskirts. All around, I can see farmland and rustic dwellings scattered here and there. In the distance, I notice the cupola of an important landmark: the Sanctuary of the *Madonna di San Luca*. To the right are the tennis courts where her husband, Marco, plays tennis. To the left, there is a new shopping mall and a huge sporting stadium that sometimes acts as a venue for pop concerts.

Abruptly, we leave the motorway. We wind our way through a country lane. On the right, there is a house with neatly tended grapevines and chickens running between them. A dog barks as we drive past. I notice trees covered in pink and white blossom. The white trees are *pesca*, peach, and the pink ones are *ciliegia*, cherry. Ette explains that she is passionate about cherries and that her parents grow copious quantities of them on their farm. I ask about the farm. Her parents are almost self-sufficient, but their main source of income is from the growing of grapes for wine production. I am absolutely enchanted by this connection with country life.

At the end of the country lane is a T-junction with a main road. Opposite is a row of shops and a bus stop. We turn right, then almost immediately left. Behind the shops is a new housing development: blocks of flats coloured in shades of apricot and cream. We have reached our destination.

The flat is on the first floor and reached by a lift, although there are stairs for emergencies. It faces the elements, with a red tiled pathway connecting the entrances of all the dwellings on this level. I look over the iron balustrade, down at the communal gardens below, and then return my gaze to the flat. The hidden windows are secure with closed brown shutters. Ette struggles with the keys for the heavy wooden door. She turns them many times, it seems, and finally the door is released and falls open.

Inside it is dark at first and we have to put on the hall light whilst the shutters are opened to let in the daylight.

It is a simple and stylish flat. Painted white throughout, it is furnished with a blend of ultra-modern and dark antique-looking furniture. In the living area, there is a contemporary sofa in creamy, off-white colour fabric. This is contrasted with a dark wooden table and a sideboard. The walls are also embellished with the same juxtaposition of old and new. On one wall, there are framed prints that are about one hundred years old. On another wall, there are soft, dreamy sketches of reclining nude ladies, drawn by a friend of the family who resides in Vicenza.

Ette gives me a guided tour. It is a bit unusual, she tells me, in that the flat is on two levels. The entrance area gives way to the L-shaped living space. Immediately on the right of the front door is a door leading into the kitchen. Opposite the kitchen, on the left of the front door, is a small second bathroom. There are two more doors on the right, after the kitchen. The first leads to the cupboard under the stairs, which is useful storage space for shoes and coats. I will find spare *carta igenica*, toilet paper, if I need any. The second door leads to the stairs.

At the top of the stairs is the main bathroom and three bedrooms, one of which is laid out as a study.

In the room that is to be mine, Ette thoughtfully shows me how to operate the shutters for the windows. On this floor, all the shutters are adjusted with internal chords. The chord is pulled downwards in order to raise the shutter and is pulled towards you in order to lower it. I had found these difficult to operate in the past but the mystery is now dispelled. It is just a matter of knowing the technique of how to do it. Now, it is effortless and no longer a struggle. It is even possible to adjust the shutter so that there are little gaps between the metal slats, enabling a glimmer of light to permeate the room in the morning. I prefer not to sleep in the absolute dark so favoured by Italians and I like to know when morning has arrived.

Ette is at pains to make sure I understand that I should relax and feel at home. She tells me that I may take a shower, watch television, read, whatever I like. There is a little time before her husband arrives home and she has preparations to attend to in the kitchen. She asks me whether I like turkey and asparagus and I assure her that I do. She leaves me alone to unpack.

There isn't a great deal to unpack but I am glad of these few minutes alone. My bed is of the metal fold-up variety, which is used for occasional visitors. It is simple but clean, comfortable and perfectly adequate. A woollen crocheted blanket, made up of different coloured squares, covers the bed. I haven't seen a blanket such as this since my childhood. My grandmother made one that I had on my bed, but it was knitted, not crocheted. I admire the stitches, mostly trebles. They are similar to the treble pattern of the black jacket I am making. The jacket is really a crochet cardigan that I am making in black for my concerts. The idea was inspired by the preponderance of lace I have seen at Italian concerts and the difficulty I have in getting suitable clothes for my own concerts.

I look around the room. It is light and airy. There are white muslin curtains at the window. On one side, there are fitted wardrobes with plain white doors. In a recess between two pairs of double doors is an old-fashioned wardrobe in dark wood. It has a mirror on the door and is not dissimilar to one I have at home. This wardrobe is really the linen cupboard. Inside are shelves packed with towels, sheets and pillowcases. Ette introduced me to the linen cupboard in case I had need of extra towels or an extra cover for the bed. I peep inside at the neatly folded linen. I love the traditional pillowcases and smooth linen towels with their edges, handcrafted in crochet or embroidery. Some of them even have boarders delicately decorated with holes made by drawing the threads of the fabric away.

I close the door of the cupboard gently and go downstairs, to investigate the progress of the preparations for dinner.

At dinner, I meet Ette's husband, Marco, who is an engineer. Engineering is the most esteemed of professions in Italy. Both Giovanna's father and brother are also engineers, and I am proud to say that my father is a retired engineer. In Italy, he would be well-regarded.

We eat our meal in the small kitchen. Behind me, there is a portable television on the counter, which informs us with the news programme, the *telegornale*, and entertains us with the *publicità*, or adverts. The turkey is wafer-thin slices of breast, pan-fried with a creamy asparagus sauce. The sauce is delicious and we all mop up the residue with bits of bread.

I sleep well, despite the heat. I drink freshly squeezed orange juice and tea without milk for breakfast. I also consume a good quantity of biscuits since there is nothing else. The biscuits are excellent but I am not sure they will sustain me until lunchtime. I don't eat a traditional cooked English breakfast at home, except on special occasions, but I do like to eat cereal with fresh milk. I can see that the lack of cereal and fresh milk is going to take some getting used to.

The plan is that Ette will accompany me to the lesson today, taking me by car to the station and showing me the route. She has also realised that I have brought the wrong clothes with me; they are too warm for this weather. She shows me a selection of T-shirts and asks me to select one. I choose a beautiful turquoise blue. This, with my leggings and navy blue blazer, make a passable outfit. We hardly know each other yet, so I am a little embarrassed to borrow the T-shirt, but I am also touched by her kindness.

Before we depart, Ette cleans the floors throughout the flat, easily and quickly, by passing a kind of broom, with its head covered in a duster, over the surfaces. Her husband suffers from an allergy to dust and pollen. She likes to keep the floors clean by attending to them regularly. The floors are tiled and easy to clean in this manner. My house is full of fitted carpets and the most rigorous vacuuming has little effect on dust levels. Even steam cleaning and shampooing are only temporarily effective. I am most interested in these easy-to-clean floors.

The trip to Padua goes smoothly. I am keen to notice every detail of the passing countryside. Mists enshroud the flat fields. Later, they will disappear as the scorching heat of the sun pervades the atmosphere. I fancy that the fields look flooded. We pass over a huge suspension bridge above a wide and energetic river I take to be the Po. I ask Ette if the flooded fields are where the rice is grown, but she is not sure. I buy Italian brown rice at home and I am interested to know where it is grown. Ette, like me, is new to this region. She has only lived in Bologna since her marriage in the autumn. Marco's family live in Bologna, but Ette's family is from Breganze, north of Vicenza.

The train journey takes just over an hour and a quarter. We are taking the faster EuroCity train for which we have had to pay the *supplemento*, an extra charge. The EuroCity is an international express train and our train is going to Vienna via Venice. Once again, I notice the feeling of being connected to other European countries in a way I have not been used to in England.

The lesson also goes well. I must begin to prepare a sonata in D major by Emanuelle Barbella for the lower diploma that I shall have to take in the autumn. Apparently, there is a recording of the Barbella played by Fabio Menditto. I scribble the details in my notebook for later investigation.

Another issue raised in the lesson was the business of summer mandolin courses. The Maestro thinks it would be helpful for me to attend the plectrum course in Spain. It is to be held in Logroño in Rioja and he is to be one of the course tutors. A number of other students are planning to go. I don't know what to say about this unexpected proposal. I start to say something but no sound emerges. I clear my throat and manage to croak that I will think about it. Privately, I can't help thinking that I have enough on my hands just coming to Italy without entertaining a new project of a trip to Spain.

Friday morning is taken up with a trip into central Bologna. We leave the car parked just outside the historic centre and take a bus from *Via Saragozza* the rest of the way. From the bus stop onwards, I am aware of the perpetual *portici*, arcades, which line the streets everywhere. Seemingly, they were built in the twelfth century to house thousands of university students. Originally, they were built over the streets on to existing buildings. Over the centuries, the Bolognese, mindful of the protection they offer from the elements, continued to add further *portici*. I have read that Bologna has more *portici* than any other city in the world – more than 35 km to be precise.

When we alight from the bus, I am taken on a fleeting tour of some of the principal sights. We walk across *Piazza Maggiore*, scattering the pigeons as we go. The sides are flanked by overgrown medieval *palazzi*, but the largest building is the *Basilica di San Petronio* – a symbol of municipal prestige. Everywhere I see the characteristic red bricks of Bologna, instead of the marble and ornate plaster decorations that are used so extensively in other parts of Italy to indicate wealth and importance. I try to drink in every detail, but we do not linger as long as we might since we have a pressing task to undertake. We are shopping for English books – that is to say, books for learning English.

In a nearby street, we find a bookshop and descend into the basement to find language books. We look through the various books and Ette seems to like the two that I advise her as suitable. We purchase them and return to the dazzling sunshine and smart shop windows, filled with designer labels and the sartorial elegance of luxury bags, shoes and suits.

In a gastronomic shop, we select some cheese for lunch. Both cheeses are local and one is smoked.

We catch the bus and return to *Via Saragozza*. Ette wants to show me the church of *San Luca* set on a hill and reached by a long uphill walk through yet more *portici*. We cheat and go most of the way by car. The views from outside the Sanctuary of the *Madonna* of *San Luca* are stunning. The south of the city is skirted by luscious green hills planted with grapevines. Looking back at the city centre, I see the patchwork of terracotta roofs pierced at intervals by the campaniles of various churches.

On the way home, we stop to visit the *mama di Marco*, Marco's mother and Ette's mother-in-law. The street is quiet and full of lush gardens surrounding low blocks of flats, with about three floors. The gardens are protected with fences of metal railings. Ette presses a button by the side of the gate. Some incomprehensible speech comes from the metal grill at the side. Ette replies and we hear a buzz and a click. The gate swings open and our attention is drawn above our heads to the balcony, where a smiling lady is waving and calling.

'*Ciao*,' the lady says, with obvious pleasure at seeing us.

Ette explains that she is Marco's mother. Inside, we are formally introduced.

Marco's mother is cheerful and chatty. She has prepared some pasta for Ette to take home, but first we sit down to have a little chat. She asks me about my journey and what we have been doing this morning. We tell her about our visit to the church of *San Luca*. She asks whether we walked up the hill under the *portici* and we say that we drove there in the car. Marco's mother says it is a beautiful walk and especially useful as a kind of penitential pilgrimage. For a moment, her expression is wistful. I ask her about the cloth and pattern, pinned and half-cut on the table. Suddenly, she is animated again. She works part-time as a tailor. An unfinished jacket adorns a dressmaker's dummy behind me. The sun streams in through the balcony door and illuminates the pale wooden floor. I tell her that my mother is a gifted dressmaker and we have lots to talk about.

As we prepare to leave, Marco's mother darts into her tiny kitchen and retrieves foil containers from the freezer. The containers are filled with homemade lasagne. She places them in a plastic carrier bag and we take our leave.

The cheese we have purchased for lunch is served fried. I had imagined that we would eat it just as it was. Accompanied by salad, it is surprisingly good, but too rich and filling for either of us to finish the last mouthful. We thankfully retire to our respective bedrooms for an afternoon rest.

The evening is partly taken up with Ette's evening class in *difesa personale*, self-defence. I accompany her to the *palestra*, the sports-centre. I am really pleased at this opportunity because I have always wanted to attend a self-defence course. Although I am only allowed to observe, I am sure I shall learn something from the experience.

Saturday brings a problem that needs to be resolved. My flight leaves Verona just before eight o'clock on Sunday morning. It is very early and after I booked it, I realised I would have some difficulty getting from Bologna to the airport. I tried to book a hotel room, just for the Saturday night in Verona, but I was unable to find a place because it was the week of the Agricultural Trade Fair.

There is a train that travels through the night, but it is uncertain, despite enquiries, whether the bus connecting the station and airport will be operating early in the morning.

Ette is unhappy about this journey and feels the only solution is for me to go with her to her parents' farm, and to stay there for the Saturday night. She will drive me to the airport in the morning and then continue on home to Bologna. I am anxious not to cause her or her family any inconvenience, but she is sure that this is the best plan.

―o―

North of Vicenza, and after several hours of dull motorway driving, we are approaching Breganze. As we enter the village, we look up into the hills ahead and see at their summit a life-size cross. Ette tells me that when we reach the cross, we will have reached her parent's farm.

We negotiate steep gradients and tricky bends in the narrow leafy lanes of the hills. The car struggles and strains to take us higher and higher. We drive through a concealed entrance and find ourselves in a farmyard. Behind us as we drive in, on one side of the yard, is an ancient farmhouse. We park on the right side of the yard. On the other side is a row of barns used for housing animals and storage. As we get out of the car and stretch the stiffness from our bodies, I can see just how high up we are. In the foreground, the land falls away in a series of gentle pleats. We are facing south and I notice how incredibly flat the land is in the distance. It seems to stretch for miles and disappears into a lavender haze, which makes the meeting point of sky and land indistinguishable.

Ette runs across to the barn to greet the dogs. There are five dogs, each with their respective kennel under the shelter of an open section of the barn. All the dogs bark excitedly, vying for attention. Ette talks to each one in turn, patting and fondling their ears. Her chatter is high-pitched with feverish rhythms. I cannot understand this Italian dog talk. They are extremely appreciative of her attention and affection. She obviously adores them and misses them terribly. The one with long ears and long, wavy copper hair wags his tail the most. He is her special one: the one that belonged to her when she lived at home. I remember seeing a beautiful photo of them posing together at the flat.

It is about five o'clock and my friend is fortunately in the habit of stopping for a cup of tea at this time in the afternoon. We go inside and find a saucepan to boil some water in. The kitchen is furnished with old-fashioned kitchen cupboards. Ette searches through one of the cupboards for the tea and some biscuits. In the middle of the room is a kitchen table. At one side, the chairs are lined up against the wall, as if in a doctor's waiting room. We draw two chairs to the table and sit down to drink our tea without milk, and to eat our biscuits. I find myself mirroring my friend, dipping each biscuit into the light brown liquid before placing it in my mouth.

After our refreshment, we go outside and meet Ette's mother, Pina, coming into the yard. She had been busy at the other house. I am a little confused by this, but they take me by the arm to show me. We go back to the road from which we had entered. We cross it. As we do, Ette stops and points out a large pink house further along the lane. "That is a monastery," she tells me. "Just a few monks live there." There is a beautiful chapel in which special prayers were said for the marriage of Marco and Ette. They attended the chapel with their close family and friends the night before their wedding. Their official wedding was a civil ceremony the following day.

On the other side of the road, we continue down a dusty track and past a vegetable plot, until we are in front of a magnificent new building. This is the other house. Ette explains that her parents are building a new farmhouse. It is painted white and has brown wooden shutters. At one end there is a covered tiled area with three tall arches, each edged with red brick. This area is for entertaining and was used for her wedding banquet. At the back, there is a locked room which I am shown into. At one end is a built-in brick chimney fitted with spits for barbecuing food. Outside Ette points out the decorations made from corn, which are still in place from the wedding celebrations. She also tells me about the electric blinds that come down between each arch, to provide further protection from the sun.

Through another door, which is carefully unlocked, we go into the *cantina*, cellar, where all the future wine production will take place. Ette proudly shows me all the equipment. There is even an office.

Upstairs, we pass a lemon tree growing in a large terracotta pot. I view the fruit with disbelief and then delight. We climb a small staircase to enter another door. Here is a palatial room with a good acoustic, plain white-washed walls, a red tiled floor and a fireplace at one end. We open a pair of shutters to let the light in. Out of the window, a steeply inclined hill is planted with vines. I am shown an adjoining bathroom that is stylishly up-to-the minute in design and pristinely clean.

The other end of the building is unfinished. We walk around rooms lined with concrete and look out of the rectangle holes left for windows. Ette and her mother discuss where different things should be. The plan is to make rooms that can be hired out to self-catering tourists. It is a new market developing in Italy called 'agritourism'. It simply means that the accommodation is on a working farm. As they chatter, the words drift over my head. I have an urge to pinch myself to see if it is true. But it is true. I really am standing in this Italian pastoral paradise.

We return to the old house. Pina goes inside and Ette takes me for a walk around the fields. These fields are so different from the fields at home, where everywhere is planted with cereal or used for grazing animals. Here the fields are mostly planted with vines, so the vegetation is higher and you have to walk between it. It is like a maze. I feel a sense of innocence with each moment as I notice some new tree or plant: a fig tree, an apricot tree, a cherry tree. I am constantly delighted at each discovery.

I try to analyse the fascination I have with these plants. The vines, olive trees and fig trees are biblical plants. Perhaps it is a sense of history and a sense of connection with another time and another place. All those New Testament stories with references to these plants are suddenly brought to life and given new meaning.

I stand for a moment and breathe in the damp, woody smells. The air is so good. I can hear a disorientated cockerel crowing. I gaze out at the sublime panorama and I am filled with pure joy.

In the kitchen, there is a constant stream of visitors coming and going: family, friends and neighbours bringing things, collecting things or just dropping by for a little chat. They are all introduced to me and I am introduced to them. It is like one continuous party, entertaining and enjoyable, but Ette assures me this is quite normal for her parents. They are always having visitors. I notice the laughter, interest and concern, warmth and affection that is exchanged between them all, and in which I have also become included.

A wonderful aroma fills the room. It is only a simple tomato sauce, which Pina is cooking, and yet it smells divine. It is made from an onion softened in olive oil, to which homemade *passato* is added. The *passato* is just mashed tomatoes, which have been preserved in jars. I do not know whether it is the simple, fresh ingredients or the country air which makes the cooking smell so good. Probably, it is a combination of all of these elements.

The table is quickly laid with everyone helping, and we all sit down to eat. There are six of us around the table. In addition to Ette, Pina and myself, there is Franca, Ette's sister, Firmino, Ette's father, and Gino, who is a farmhand.

We begin with spaghetti and the tomato sauce. The Parmesan cheese is passed around, as is bread, and Gino pours red wine into our glasses. It is delicious. Next, there is a choice of local cheese, homemade salami or a slice of home-reared steak. I choose the steak and accompany it with salad leaves dressed in olive oil and a sprinkling of salt. The salad is undressed and we all add our own seasoning to our own taste. Somehow I seem to have become ravenous and I accept a second helping of the steak, which nobody else seems to want. It is pan-fried, thin and melts in the mouth.

I have been trying to follow the conversation whilst I have been absorbed in enjoying my food, but it has been hard to follow. I thought that the difficulty might have been because I was getting tired or because I was concentrating on the food. Now I discover that the men have been talking in *dialetto*, dialect. Ette warned me that her father talked mostly in Veneto dialect, but I had forgotten all about it. Suddenly, as they turn their attention towards me, I find I am having a comprehensive discussion about the European community and current farming practices in Italy. I feel elated at being able to communicate with them about their life and work. They too seem delighted. Firmino invites me to return with my family for a holiday. It is a very generous offer and I am delighted by it, but I think it is unlikely that we will be able to take it up. This summer, I am probably going to Spain.

Early Sunday morning, when it is still dark, Ette knocks on my bedroom door to wake me up. In the kitchen, Pina prepares me coffee. She hands me the sugar and offers me biscuits, which I accept. We whisper quietly so as not to wake the others.

The car journey is mostly silent except for the English-speaking radio station, broadcast from the American Forces base. The sun rises and the mountains look dramatic. I feel confused: I am anxious to get home but also want to stay.

At Verona airport, Ette stops the car momentarily whilst I get out. I thank her for everything and tell her I will ring her soon with news of my next visit. I will try to get a flight directly to Bologna. We kiss each other on both cheeks. This has certainly been a memorable mandolin lesson.

9

It is the first week of May and I am returning to Bologna directly. I have managed to purchase a cheap ticket on a chartered flight from Gatwick airport.

The flight is a bit cramped and the service brusque. I find myself sitting near an exit and I am not particularly happy that they have to take my mandolin away to store it under a stranger's seat. The Italian lady next to me is even less happy about them taking away her precious box containing a china tea set.

At Bologna airport, Ette is extremely pleased with my travel arrangements since the airport is only ten minutes away from her home. I am also pleased that, despite the minor discomforts of the flight, I am just minutes from Ette's flat only two hours after leaving English soil. In addition, my ticket has cost me half the price of the train fare.

The mandolin lesson is the source of more confusion this month. I am alarmed to learn that there is no lesson at Padua. At the same time, I am delighted to hear that Ette is taking part in a concert with *I Solisti Veneti*. She and Ugo are to be soloists in the Vivaldi double mandolin concerto, and I am to accompany her to the rehearsal and performance. If my understanding is correct, I am to have my lesson between the rehearsal and the concert.

I have to say that I do feel a little bit anxious about all this. It is quite a big responsibility booking air flights when I can barely afford the cost. Naturally, I check the dates are convenient with everybody in Italy before I confirm a reservation. However, it is disconcerting when the plans change after I have made the reservation. Economy tickets cannot be changed once they are booked. From this point of view, the whole operation of commuting to a foreign country for music lessons is a risky business.

The concert is in a place called Sabbioneta in Lombardy. I had never heard of it. We travel north-west by car, taking the motorway from Bologna towards Milan. At Parma, we turn right and progress northwards towards Mantua. Just after we cross the River Po, we turn left onto a local road, which takes us the short distance to Sabbioneta.

Our arrival in the town of Sabbioneta comes after a hot and tiring journey. It is mid-afternoon and nothing much is open. We find a bar and we each buy a cone of ice cream. The streets are dark and narrow, offering shelter from the desiccating sun. We stand in the shade, greedily eating our melting and messy ice-cream cones.

We walk a short way to find the venue for the rehearsal and concert, the *Teatro Olimpico*. It is locked and there is no one around. We walk around the surrounding streets trying to amuse ourselves. The streets are lined with buildings from the late Renaissance. There is a wealth of history to explore here, but we are preoccupied with the rehearsal and the fact that no one has arrived and the theatre is closed. We are unable to concentrate on the details of our surroundings. We just absorb the atmosphere, ancient and full of shadows.

We meet a couple of people from the orchestra. They say that the theatre is now open, so we collect our belongings from the car and go to investigate. The theatre is refreshingly cool inside. Built in 1588, it has a simple wooden stage and an auditorium constructed of tiered wooden steps in a horseshoe shape. These wooden steps or benches are the seating for the audience. I am taken aback by the age and simplicity of the design. High up at the back of the theatre is a little balcony with classical statues of ancient Olympians. Apparently the building is modelled on Palladio's theatre at Vicenza, which I haven't yet seen.

Eventually Ugo arrives and so do the rest of the orchestra. It transpires that the coach bringing most of the orchestra has been held up in motorway congestion caused by a car accident.

Quickly, the orchestra assembles itself on the stage and starts to rehearse. Up until now, the journey, the waiting and the heat have all conspired to make me feel lethargic with the tedium of the day – but with the first vibrations of sound emanating from the players, and resonating around the *teatro*, I am awakened and energised. Claudio Scimone, the conductor, puts the orchestra through its paces and it is a fascinating process to watch. One of the works in the programme is, most inappropriately for this heat, the *Winter Concerto* from Vivalidi's *Four Seasons*. Scimone's slim body moves lithely, sometimes with vigour to establish the characteristic pulsating rhythms and at other times with softness to coax the most delicate *pianissimo*. At the moment when all the violins play tremolo, to imitate teeth chattering with cold, I see the conductor pretending to shiver with cold. This exuberance may seem over the top to some people, but it gives me great pleasure to see musicians enjoying their music and the sense of drama seems to enhance the performance.

Before the rehearsal is quite complete, I notice with some amusement that two ladies have already begun to wash the tiled floor at the front of the auditorium. How lovely it is that with the simplicity of a mop and water, the dust is banished.

There isn't much time before the concert is due to begin and there isn't much space in the communal changing rooms. Thus, I find myself backstage, in the wings of the *Teatro Olimpico*, Sabbioneta, having my mandolin lesson. We improvise, using a table as a music stand, and there are no chairs so we have to stand up to play.

We study the Barbella sonata for the impending exam.

My teacher is anxious to show me the character of each movement, as well as to clarify technical details. Often, the two are imperceptibly entwined. In the opening *Largo,* he demonstrates how to play various chords. The plectrum must be as light as possible. It must glide gently over the strings in order to allow the strings to vibrate as much as possible. In this way, the instrument is given the optimum chance to make the most beautiful sound. If the plectrum is held with tension and the strings are hit harshly, the sound is strangled because the strings aren't allowed to vibrate freely.

I watch my teacher playing effortlessly, as if the plectrum were a feather stroking silken strings. I find it difficult to relax and feel the same sense of abandon. I try too hard to imitate what I have been shown and I struggle with the plastic plectrum and the metal strings.

Surprisingly, the *Fugato* goes well. The rhythms of this third movement are straightforward and I understand the concept of a fugue with its conversational style. I am able to forget the plectrum and just enjoy the music.

The *Andantino* is marked '*alla Francese*', which, according to my teacher, implies inequality of notes. This means that the movement has to be played in the French style – that is, the style favoured in France during the Baroque era. It means that pairs of even notes are executed with the first note of each pair longer and the second note shorter. This tradition of playing notes unequally is well known in less formal traditions such as folk and jazz music. However, I will have to make quite an effort to remember to play the music differently from how it is notated. I also make a mental note to look up the subject of inequality in one of my books on performance practice when I return home.

I mention that I have managed to make some arrangements for the Spanish plectrum course. This news is met with approval. I have booked a villa in Rioja for my family. It is in a quiet hamlet, some distance from Longroño, roughly about three quarters of an hour's drive. It is difficult to be sure because some of the roads are in the depth of untamed countryside.

Our playing and our discussion are interrupted from time to time with people brushing past or asking a question. Now the auditorium is filling up and my teacher takes me to find a place to sit. We walk right through the auditorium and out the back into the foyer, through a small door and up some tiny twisting stairs. I find myself amongst half a dozen special guests sitting on the small balcony, high up at the rear of the auditorium. It gives me a wonderful view and a good sound.

The concert is brilliant: the music is exquisitely beautiful and well-received by the audience. Afterwards, there is a buffet supper backstage, consisting of bread, salami, *prosciutto*, cheese, slices of pizza, wine and water.

On the way home, as we drive along the motorway at midnight, we see flashing lights searching the night sky. Ette says it is a discotheque.

10

It is the final day of May and I am returning for my June lesson. It seems strange to think that I was in Italy at the beginning of the month and now I am here for the end of the month. As I missed February I am anxious to take the opportunity to fit in another lesson, despite the fact that the course officially closes for the summer holiday at the start of June.

When I meet Ette, she tells me that my lesson has been rearranged for Saturday. She also wonders if I would mind if we visited her parents' farm this weekend. It is the harvest of the cherries that allures her to return home. Naturally, I am delighted by the prospect of revisiting the farm.

On Saturday, I take the train from Bologna to Padua and attend the *Conservatorio* for my lesson. Everything is progressing well with my playing and I feel content. When the lesson is finished, I return to the station, as arranged, to meet Marco and Ette who are coming by car from Bologna. Together, we continue on to Breganze.

At the farm, we are told that Ette's parents are in the fields. Ette and I go to look for them. We are met with an extraordinary sight. A white figure resembling a beekeeper is high up in the tree. On closer inspection, it turns out to be Ette's mum dressed in men's overalls. The tree trembles as Pina divests it of its fruit. On the ground, Gino holds a ladder and a basket. Pina descends from the tree and inspects the harvest, which is divided between a number of baskets. We all help to carry the baskets back to the house, tramping between the leafy vines.

In the kitchen, Ette and I sit at the table sorting out the cherries. We spread newspaper on the table and tip the contents of the baskets onto the surface. Then, we begin to divide them into three categories: the best and most perfect cherries, the slightly bruised cherries, and the bad and mouldy cherries. The three different piles of fruit slowly rise up and are then dispersed into cardboard boxes, which Pina has found. Each cherry is dark red, like the colour of wine. The best specimens have skins that gleam as if they have been polished. Ette continually samples cherries as she sorts through them. She encourages me to do the same, but I am reticent. A little pile of stones is growing at the corner edge of the table near her elbow. We are both so happy, laughing and chattering as we sort through the mound of fruit. So many of the cherries are complete with stalks and many of these are joined in pairs or threes. Suddenly we are little girls again, bedecking our ears with the most beautiful jewels that nature has to offer. We giggle as we show off our dangling earrings to each other and then settle again to the meditative work of sorting. It is a simple, soothing pleasure.

The evening is taken up with a special supper put on for the friends of Ette's parents. Apparently, the weather isn't that good. It seems fine to me. The consequence is that it has been decided that eating will take place indoors in the new house. Long tables have been laid out with white tablecloths in the room with the built-in barbecue. Gino is in charge of building the fire and brings twigs and other suitable wood to the hearth. Pina explains that there isn't room for the wives as the meal is inside, so only the men will be attending. Ette's sister is going out for the evening with her friends. Thus there are only three ladies, Ette, her mum and myself, amongst a male-dominated gathering.

There are lots of jobs to be done, so I busy myself with carrying and fetching things. There are big bowls of pasta salad to be eaten before the roast meat and big bowls of salad leaves to follow. There is also a collection of desserts, covered over with clothes to protect them from flies. I help to set the tables with cutlery, glasses and serviettes. I feel really pleased to be included as part of the team. When everything is organised, Ette and I go back to the old house to use the bathroom and to change for dinner.

On our return, the party has already started. In the courtyard, guests are chatting and drinking glasses of wine. Gino is cutting up homemade salami. He carefully removes the outer skins of the sausage slices and places them on pieces of toasted bread, which have been rubbed with garlic and drizzled with olive oil. He offers me one and I accept. It is delicious.

The air is warm and sweetly fragrant with the smell of wood smoke and roasting meat. I notice the progress of the lemons on the little tree by the steps. A bird is singing blissfully and for a few moments I am still, alone with my own thoughts. I feel so tremendously lucky just to be here, overlooking hills draped in vines. I reflect upon the people I would love to share this view with.

Abruptly my introspection is shattered, as I become the

centre of attention. Everyone it seems is introduced to me. Some want to practise their English. Others are interested in my reasons for visiting Italy, my music and my thoughts on Italian life and culture. Others still want to know about England and English life. I become involved in lots of different conversations. Each one is fascinating and thoroughly enjoyable. I am so busy talking that I could easily forget to eat. However, I love good food too and somehow I manage to juggle the two activities of which Italians are so passionate: eating and talking.

The roast pigeon is very good and much better than I had expected. I was cautious in accepting the meat because I have only tried pigeon once before and that was in a pie cooked by Giovanna's mother. In the pie, it had been combined with a variety of other ingredients and it is difficult to recall exactly, or to separate in my memory, the flavour. This time, though, the meat is excellent. Simply roasted with olive oil and rosemary over a wood fire, the gamy flavours emerge. It is beautifully moist with a tasty, crunchy texture on the outside.

There is also a choice of roast farm-reared pork, which I had declined, not being a great fan of pork. Ette prefers the pork and brings over a morsel, which she insists I try. My prejudice melts away. It is also excellent.

As the meal drifts towards its conclusion, the dessert is served – a choice between fresh fruit salad and *tiramisù*. Unexpectedly, it is accompanied by music as chatter on the other side of the room dissolves into singing. The singing is high spirited but it certainly isn't drunken singing. Rather it is cultured; operatic arias and traditional songs sung in dialect.

Pina serves coffee and a bottle of *grappa* is passed along the tables for those who like a shot of it in their coffee. Three tenor voices soar above the others in competition with each other. First, they try to outdo each other by singing the loudest and longest note. After this power struggle, they give way to a more refined approach by seeing who can ornament the end of the phrase with the greatest art. They trill and twiddle with notes to their own – and to our – amusement. Then, one of the tenors decides he wants to sing a song especially for me. I have to go and stand by him whilst he performs a love song with exaggerated operatic gestures. I feel a mixture of being slightly embarrassed and, at the same time, being greatly honoured by this serenade.

The singing is quite remarkable. These are ordinary folk doing ordinary jobs and yet they are singing the music of their heritage, the music that underpins western art music and is often thought to be the music of the privileged. The singing is an expression of pure joy and a celebration of life. Tonight it is the men of Breganze who are privileged, to know this joy and to be engaged in this celebration.

At about midnight, I return to the old house accompanied by Ette and Marco, who holds a small torch. I am tired but happy. It is pitch black and we huddle together following the tiny pool of torchlight. As we stumble along the dusty track, we notice lights twinkling in the distance and we comment upon the sound of the men, still singing and laughing, which fades away behind us.

After Sunday lunch, I help Ette and her mum with the final bit of clearing up after the previous evening's meal. Ette and I sweep the tiled floor of the room where we had eaten and of the courtyard outside. Pina washes with a mop after we have swept. I look out over the hills and catch myself thinking that *this is fun, even therapeutic*. I don't understand my thought process. I absolutely hate the chores at home.

I follow Ette and her mum to the *orto*, the vegetable garden. We pick green salad leaves. Ette shows me which ones are best. Normally, I don't like doing this kind of job. I worry about the insects and getting dirty. Now I am not thinking about those things, I am just noticing the lacy edge of the leaves. I don't know this plant and I ask what it is called. *Rucola,* I am told. I am none the wiser, it is completely new to me. It is strange but I am like a small child, wanting to know everything about their world. Ette tells me that it is very good as a salad leaf and we are taking a quantity back to Bologna with us, so we will be able to try it. She also promises to show me a very good recipe, which uses *rucola* with pasta.

We pack the car with our overnight bags, the mandolin and the food, cherries, *rucola*, farm-reared steak and homemade salami.

In Bologna, Ette shows me the recipe for *rucola* with pasta. Whilst the pasta is cooking, a tub of *mascarpone* cheese, another new ingredient to me, is heated together with a little butter in a saucepan. When the two ingredients are melted and nicely amalgamated, the *rucola* is added and allowed to wilt just like spinach. This only takes a minute. Finally, the cooked pasta is folded into the mixture and is served with a sprinkling of Parmesan cheese. It is a superb dish, simple and nourishing. It would make a good light supper just on its own. I add lots of freshly ground black pepper to my bowl of pasta and I think I would add the cheese to the saucepan at the final stage of preparation, just before serving.

Ette and I discuss plans for the summer. My idea to go to Spain for the plectrum course has come to nothing as a result of a letter I received just before coming to Italy. The letter explained that, unfortunately, no one else had booked our 'off the tourist trail' villa and the owners had decided to withdraw it from the brochure. We could have a full refund of our deposit or choose another villa, but neither option helps with the course. The brochure doesn't feature other villas near to Longroño.

I discover from a phone conversation with Giovanna that there is to be a mandolin course in Brescia, the week before the Spanish course. This would be far more convenient. Ette suggests that I take up her parents' offer to bring my family to stay on the farm, whilst I attend the mandolin course in Brescia. It seems an excellent plan.

11

I have returned to the farm with my family. Both my husband and my son are delighted with the location, although for different reasons. My husband dreams of a life of self-sufficiency in the country, whilst my son is liberated in a way he has not yet experienced – by being free to wander outside the house by himself. In our London suburb, children are not encouraged to play outside in the street or to go with their friends to the park. We are constantly fed information, which makes parents believe, rightly or wrongly, that our streets are unsafe. Here, though, it feels secure and comfortable.

We are staying in the room in the new house, which is at the top of the steps by the lemon tree. Two of the lemons have been harvested and are now in our room. Pina has thoughtfully placed them with a knife on a small plate, along with tea-making things, in case we want to make a cup of tea in the privacy of our own room.

I decide to have a little practice whilst my family have gone off to explore our new environment. I put the mandolin case on the bed and open it up. There is just one shutter partially open and I need a little more light, so I open up another shutter. As I open the shutter, the sun pours in, immediately lighting up the previously darkened room as if I had switched a light on.

It is late afternoon and I begin to play the Conforto mandolin concerto, which I am preparing for the exam I am taking in the autumn.

"Da-da-da-da, dum dum, dum dum. Da-da-da-da, dum dum, dum dum."

I sing the opening bars and play at the same time. I try to be conscious of the pulse to make sure my timing is secure, but I am troubled at first by the opening semiquavers. On my copy of the music, the words 'right hand *molto rilassato*' have been written. *Molto rilassato* meaning very relaxed. Also written, in capital letters, is the word 'LIGHT'. This word and the other words are instructions written by the Maestro. The right hand is required to be light and relaxed, so that the music is fluid and delicate. Somehow, the semiquavers at the beginning seem too fast. I seem to play them awkwardly and I feel that sensation when you trip over something and then recover your balance, and feel for a few seconds out of control.

After a few more attempts, I recover sufficiently to satisfy myself and the music continues to dance along happily. My notes blend and merge alternately with the murmur of a cicada and the sound of a gentle breeze rustling the vine leaves. In a performance of the concerto, a small ensemble of string instruments would accompany the mandolin: a few violins, a cello and perhaps a harpsichord. In an exam, for practical reasons, the piano would provide a prosaic accompaniment. Here, the sounds of nature conspire together to make an improvised and poetic accompaniment.

I play for some time. When I stop, the sun is lower but still potent. Outside, its heat seeps into everything: the soil, the plants, the stones, and even people. Inside, it is cool. I love the simplicity of my surroundings. The bare white walls are conducive to study, giving the room an atmosphere of a studio. It is plain and without distraction. An echo enhances the sound of my mandolin. I am undisturbed, solitary in my sanctuary. It feels as if a few minutes have elapsed, but when I look at my watch I realise that the minutes are hours. Bliss.

After lunch on Saturday, Pina thinks we should explore the environs. She suggests that we go to Marostica to look at the *scacchi*. She keeps talking about the *scacchi* (pronounced scakki) and tries to explain their significance, but I am none the wiser. I really don't know what she is talking about and I have left my pocket dictionary over at the new house. She also thinks we could take in Bassano del Grappa. She arranges for us to take a family friend as a guide, a doctor from Milan who is also staying for a few days at the farm.

The doctor, a heart surgeon, is elderly, gentle in manner and speaks some English.

Refreshed from a post-lunch nap, we drive towards Marostica. It is about four o'clock in the afternoon and everywhere there are signs of life sleepily stirring. A shutter opens, out of a door an old man shuffles, and young people congregate on motorcycles. It seems so strange venturing out at this time of day. In England, the shops would soon be shutting, instead of opening up for the second half of the day's trading.

The sun is still blinding and blistering hot. My husband is driving, I am sitting in the back with my son, and the doctor is sitting in the front passenger seat. Unexpectedly there is some confusion about the turning to take and, simultaneously, the crazy antics of a car overtaking us on a bend. Somehow, in the confusion, my husband accidentally knocks his sunglasses off. From where I am sitting, it is difficult to understand exactly what happened. I only know that the glasses have fallen off and as they are retrieved from the floor, it becomes apparent that they are broken. My husband is extremely agitated because the sun is so bright and it is difficult to concentrate on an unknown road.

When we park outside the city walls of Marostica, our first task is to find a new pair of sunglasses. A pair of sunglasses, as well as being a fashion statement, is an essential item in Italy. The sun is so much stronger than in England and it is also consistent, giving a predictable summer. Despite changes in the weather pattern, caused in recent years by the greenhouse effect, we still suffer capricious weather during the summer months at home.

Almost immediately, we find a shop that sells cameras, binoculars and sunglasses. As we walk inside, I feel a sense of trepidation, knowing that my husband finds shopping for personal things stressful, and I fear that we might be heading for a family crisis. A middle-aged man behind the glass counter is deep in conversation with a customer interested in a camera. A lady, possibly the shopkeeper's wife, comes to our rescue. I tell her that my husband needs a new pair of sunglasses. She shows us to another counter at the other end of the shop. We show her the broken pair and she takes out about six pairs of metal frame glasses, which are similar in design. My husband tries on the different pairs. He looks at himself in a mirror that stands on the counter. He rejects one or two pairs. The lady attentively wipes and cleans the lenses of the glasses to be tried and, when necessary, makes adjustments to the glasses with a small screwdriver. The whole process is intensely fascinating.

Eventually, it seems that my spouse has tried on just about every pair of spectacles in the shop. In reality, we have probably only looked at about twenty pairs. My opinion is sought yet again, but there is still a flicker of indecision in the purchaser's mind. It is between two pairs of glasses. Both are fine, but I have expressed my preference. I am astonished at the assistant's patience. She is not at all bothered. The doctor also has an opinion. He feels that one pair is supremely better than the other pair. They are more elegant and more refined for a man. It is done. My husband produces a plastic card and unflinchingly pays the designer frame price for what is undoubtedly the best pair of sunglasses he has ever owned.

Outside the shop, looking every inch an Italian behind the new shades, my husband informs me that he was sold this pair of glasses. I don't quite comprehend his meaning for a moment. I wonder is he dissatisfied? Then he clarifies his position and explains that the assistant took an inordinate amount of care and time to make sure that he bought the correct pair, the most suitable pair. I had to agree with him. We had had wonderful service and the shopping was a pleasurable experience.

In the *piazza* of Marostica, everything becomes clear to me. *Scacchi* is chess. Marostica is a fairytale medieval town with two castles, one high up on a hill and the other one lower in the *piazza*. It is also a town obsessed by the game of chess. The *piazza* is marked out in huge grey and white squares, which host a biennial re-enactment of a human chess game, played in 1454. The game was a pacifist version of a dual to win the hand of Linora Parisio. Her father refused to let the suitors fight the traditional dual for humanitarian reasons. He wanted neither of the men to die or to become enemies, so he decided that the two rivals should play a game of chess. He also devised a perfect compromise: the winner would have the hand of Linora and the loser would take her younger sister, Oldrada, as a consolation prize.

The re-enactment uses period costumes, the knights being mounted on horses, and is carried out with announcements in Venetian dialect since Marostica was under Venetian rule during the fifteenth century. Everywhere I see posters of the spectacle and I pick up a leaflet about it. The pictures depict the pageant in the foreground of the lower castle, which was the home of Linora. It looks a magnificent pageant and I wish I could attend. The programme boasts 500 people in costume, twenty horses, fireworks, and period music. Apparently Linora was secretly in love with one of the suitors and the leaflet explains that she sent a secret message to the people of Marostica saying that if her choice of suitor was successful, then the lower castle would be illuminated by white light. This was so that everyone could participate in her joy. I find the sentence construction in the leaflet awkward at this point. The Italian uses the subjective tense and the English translation is not clear. It suggests that the castle might be lit up if the correct suitor wins. I am anxious to know if Linora married the man she loved and was happy in her life. The next game will take place in September of next year, just over twelve months away. I can't wait that long!

We decide to adjourn to a bar at the side of the *piazza* for a quick drink. I have an apricot juice and I carry on reading my engrossing leaflet. This game of chess has captured my imagination. I read that the 1994 re-enactment used the moves of a famous game played in 1858 at the Paris Opera, during a performance of the *Barber of Seville*. I am slightly disappointed that the Marostica game doesn't use the original moves. Perhaps it is not recorded. This hiccup of authenticity doesn't throw me for long. I have in my mind a picture of a box like those at Covent Garden, with two gentlemen playing chess whilst the performance of the opera is in progress. I suppose the game is silent and wouldn't disturb other members of the audience. I also think how theatrical the game of chess looks in the picture before me. It could easily be an extravagant opera set.

I finish my apricot juice and walk outside to join the others. Under an arcade are small, pavement-size squares arranged as chessboards. Fathers and sons play chess with huge plastic chess pieces. So much is this game the preoccupation of Marostica that the town even has communal chess pieces. We watch for a while before moving on.

Bassano del Grappa is well described in my guidebook as charming, picturesque and trendy. Laying in the foothills of the Alps, the town takes part of its name from Mount Grappa which is situated to the north. It also gives its name to a burning liqueur distilled locally and much favoured by Italians in their coffee.

The doctor takes us first to view Bassano's most important landmark. We follow him through tiny twisting streets, up and down steps, until we come to a unique covered wooden bridge that majestically reaches across the Brenta River to connect the two sides of the town. It is called *Ponte degli Alpini* and was amazingly built for the first time in 1599 according to the design of Palladio. It has subsequently been rebuilt several times, always to the same design. This bridge seems to be a meeting place as well as a tourist attraction. We linger for a while, walking the length of the bridge and studying the movement of the water flowing beneath.

In the centre of the town, it is difficult to walk across the *Piazza Garibaldi* because it is being resurfaced and we have to weave our way between metal rods and plastic orange ribbon. My shoes become quite dusty with the sand being used to set the stones. I stop in a little pocket of space to look up at the square, medieval tower, *Torre di Ezzelino*. I can't stand still for long because it is very busy with people and I am afraid of losing the others. I move with a throng of people, keeping my eye on the others ahead. The doctor leads us into a quieter side street. He takes us into a gastronomic food shop and begins to do his shopping. He buys fresh pasta, *tortellini*, filled with ricotta cheese and spinach. The assistant delicately places the floured pasta on a cardboard tray and wraps them carefully in paper and ribbon. She warns the doctor to keep the parcel the right way up, to avoid damage to the pasta. The doctor also selects various salad items: olives, roasted peppers and artichokes preserved in olive oil. He is going to make a present of the food to Pina.

―✧―

Just before Sunday lunch, I find my son outside with Marco, who, along with Ette, has now arrived. My son is looking perplexed and is showing Marco a clean white handkerchief that he has just taken from his pocket. He looks up at me for help. I ask Marco what he has said so that I can help my son. Marco has kindly resurrected some schoolboy English and repeats the phrase slowly.

"You have angry?" he says.

It sounds like 'you have angry' to me. English pronunciation is sometimes difficult for Italians. I take a moment to think. I can see how it might sound like 'hanky', but I am sure this is not what Marco means. Marco is looking just as puzzled as my son and is frustrated by our incomprehension. My son doesn't look cross, so I don't think he is angry or that I have arrived at the tail-end of a dispute.

Someone has called out that lunch is now ready and various people are moving towards the house. In a change of tack, Marco tells me that lunch is ready.

"Yes," I say, "I'd heard. I was just coming."

Then, I have a moment of perception. Marco has asked my son if he was hungry, if he was ready for lunch. Probably he was trying to communicate that lunch was ready. The word that sounded like 'angry' was really 'hungry'. It is difficult for Italians to pronounce since it is necessary to aspirate the letter 'h', which is not used in the Italian alphabet.

I also realise that Marco had used the auxiliary verb 'to have', just as one does in Italian. He had translated the first part of the phrase literally from the Italian. In English, we use the auxiliary verb 'to be' with the word hungry. In Italian you *have* hunger and in English you *are* hungry. With these subtleties of language analysed and neatly sorted in my mind, we go in for lunch. The hanky story is repeated quite a few times and causes a fair amount of mirth. I think it is lovely that Marco makes such an effort to communicate, especially with my son, and I am encouraged that I am not the only one struggling with language.

Lunch has migrated from the kitchen to an adjoining room with a long table. There are at least a dozen people, a mixture of family and friends, seated around the table. The centrepiece of the meal is roast pheasant. I am once again suspicious, just as I had been about the pigeon on my last visit. Pheasant isn't something I remember eating before. It has connotations of the English aristocracy. My prejudice has this meat defined as exclusive to the rich and unpleasant because it is traditionally hung in England. The idea of meat that is purposely left to decay in order to increase its flavour seems extremely unpleasant to me.

Pina warns me to be careful of the lead shot. Firmino and his friends, assisted by the dogs, hunted for the birds. I pick at my meat, examining carefully for the lead shot. I place a small piece gingerly in my mouth. It is absolutely delicious. Pina tells me that they don't hang the meat. It is freshly frozen after the birds have been plucked. My prejudice melts away as I greedily clear my plate.

At the end of the meal, I help Pina to make coffee. As she places the coffee beans in a little grinding machine attached to the wall, I learn an important lesson for a busy mother. Pina explains emphatically her philosophy about coffee. There are three rules:

"*Forte, caldo è seduto.*" Strong, hot and seated.

These maxims are repeated several times. Obediently I sit down and drink my strong and hot coffee, savouring its richness and savouring the moment.

On Monday morning, my new pattern of commuting begins, travelling from Vicenza to Brescia by train for the mandolin course. I have to rise early, at about six o'clock. Pina prepares me a breakfast of coffee, yoghurt and biscuits. We talk in whispers, just as we had done on my first visit when I was bound for Verona airport, as everyone else in the house is still fast asleep. I have left my son sleeping in our quarters. My husband is also up in order to drive me to the station and Firmino is already out with his helpers in the fields.

Usually, I am allergic to getting up early. I love the cosy comfort of my bed too much. I want to take time over my waking. I like it to be a gentle experience. It is strange that my passion for the mandolin has the power to motivate me to inflict such harsh discipline on myself. I hear the alarm and half-sleeping switch it off, jump out of bed and stumble across the room towards my previously laid out clothes. I clean my teeth, wash my face, put some moisturiser on, comb my hair with my fingers and pick up the mandolin case and music bag as I leave the room. In ten minutes, I am ready. Five more minutes for breakfast and I am ready to drive to the station.

It takes about forty minutes to get to the station and my train journey takes about an hour and ten minutes. I have to buy a ticket with a *supplemento*, because it is a fast train, and I remember to place it in an orange machine so that my ticket is validated with the place, date and time.

I am surprised that there are so many other people up at this time of the morning, considering August is traditionally holiday time in Italy. Many people migrate to the sea or the mountains to take advantage of the comparatively cooler air during the stifling heat of the summer months. I am standing near two elderly nuns, one of whom is saying goodbye to a younger lady – perhaps a relative or friend. It occurs to me that a lot of people are probably visiting friends or family, rather than travelling to work. I begin to notice the overnight bags and other luggage of people near me.

A lady asks me if this is the correct platform for the train to Milan. I say that it is. She asks me what time it arrives and if it is on time. I tell her the answers. They require only simple, basic vocabulary. All the information is, in any case, displayed on the platform. Even so, she is very pleased with my information and I am pleased to be mistaken for a native commuter. I am happy that I didn't have to confess that I too am a visitor.

On the train, I find a seat and place my mandolin and music case in the overhead luggage rack. There are six seats in my compartment, three on each side. One of the nuns is sitting near the window. I open up my book and start to read. Presently, the glass door is slid open and we are disturbed from our private thoughts by the ticket inspector.

"*Buon giorno*," she says.

She is very young, slim and has long black hair. I can't help being struck by how attractive she is in her uniform, with its well-cut trousers and jacket. I show her my ticket. She clips it and hands it back to me.

She takes the nun's ticket, looks at it closely and then scowls. She tells the nun it has not been validated. The nun looks genuinely puzzled. She tells the nun that the ticket has to be placed in the orange machine before making the journey. The machine prints the place, date and time on the ticket. The nun says she wasn't aware that this was necessary. The inspector says that this is a legal requirement and that the law has been in place for over a year. The nun says that she hasn't been on a train for twenty years. The inspector is unwilling to make a concession. She writes out a ticket and the nun hands her the fine.

Only months earlier, on my way to Bologna, I had seen another similar incident involving a party of four American tourists. On that occasion, the surly inspector gently rebuked the tourists, wrote the place, date and time in biro on their respective tickets, and omitted to take any fines.

Smartly and purposefully, I walk down the *Via delle Battaglie*. It is a street that if ever visited by tourists is probably only done so by mistake. Visitors might well pass the end of the street, viewing the *Torre della Pallata*, but it is unlikely that they would have cause to venture down it. Although on the edge of the historic centre, it feels like uncharted territory. I glance up at the windows of the flats, which hide behind the ancient edifices of the street. I look intently for signs of life. An open shutter, a line of suspended washing, a straggling geranium plant. At street level, I notice a butcher slicing veal for a Brescian housewife. Framed by another open door, a lady works at her sewing machine. I strain to overhear snippets of conversation between neighbours. The street is narrow and the pavement is sometimes non-existent. Occasionally it is necessary for me to impress my back against a flaking wall when a motorcyclist – or worse still, a small Fiat car – makes its progress along the road.

I am both magnetised to and made uneasy by this neighbourhood. I hope that my quickness of step and the cursory nature of my glances will enhance my discretion. I wish to observe every detail carefully and yet at the same time I wish to appear casual and remain unnoticed. It is a delicate balance. I wish to be respectful so that I don't give offence by giving anybody or anything too much attention. Also, I don't want to attract unwanted attention to myself. However, I am curious about the people here and their way of life. I don't wish to be or appear to be voyeuristic. On the contrary, my deepest desire is to take part in the life being lived here. Silently, I affirm to myself that I *am* partaking in life here. For a moment I had forgotten and now I remind myself. I am attending the mandolin course at the end of the street. I am a musician attending a summer music school. I have a role, not as a visitor but as a musician, and, more specifically, as a student of the Italian school of mandolin playing.

When I arrive at the mandolin course, it is about half past nine. It has taken about half an hour of brisk walking from the station and I am gently perspiring, as well as feeling a little out of breath. I remember that when I attended my first mandolin course, it was possible to enter the building from *Via delle Battiglie*. Now a wall has been erected to prevent access and it is necessary to approach from a neighbouring road, which runs parallel to it. The walk around the block adds extra time to my journey.

As usual, the morning begins with technique. There is no opportunity for a slow start with crotchets and quavers today: the Maestro means business. We start straightaway with semiquavers on the open G-string. This is to provide the foundation for an even tremolo. However, I feel unsettled and very uneven. The whole room is rumbling with the low noise. Semiquavers are quick notes, which are grouped in fours. Each four is measured by a beat of the pulse. Somehow I feel the pulse is being quickened, or am I slowing down?

We are all playing the semiquavers together but the notes of the Maestro are slick and controlled, and yet also relaxed. He sits in his T-shirt and shorts inspecting each one of our right hands in turn. I notice he is wearing leather deck shoes without socks. I have never seen him wearing such informal attire. Abruptly, I am out of synchronisation with everyone and I have to focus very hard to find my way back. The semiquavers continue.

"Da-da-da-da, da-da-da-da, da-da-da-da, da-da-da-da..."

The semiquavers are incessant, unrelenting. They seem to go on forever. I wish they would stop. Every now and then my arm shudders with an involuntary spasm. I'd much rather have an idea of when we are going to stop. Twenty bars for instance. Then, I would have an aim. Twenty groups of four beats, each beat consisting of four semiquavers. Instead, I feel insecure with the concept of semiquavers to infinity.

Without warning, we stop. It is not like a ballet lesson or an aerobics class where the teacher might say 'and stop' to indicate what is required. We have to know instinctively by giving careful attention to the Maestro and perceiving unspoken messages, clues and signals. These skills of observation and communication are essential elements in music-making.

The Maestro makes each one of us undertake the exercise individually so that we can all examine the right-hand technique. Each of us is placed under scrutiny. When it is my turn, I feel as if I am under a microscope being analysed by experts. It is uncomfortable. The attention causes an increase of tension in my body. It seems hard to hold the plectrum in a relaxed manner. I squeeze the wafer-thin plastic hard without realising that I am doing so. The plectrum suffocates the strings and extinguishes the life of their sound.

The Maestro talks at great length about the tremolo. I study carefully his demonstration. His wrist swings backwards and forwards, or rather upwards and downwards, in continuous motion. The evenness and continuity of the movement looks mechanical, as if a hinge that opens and closes attaches his wrist. At the same time the wrist appears loose, enabling the whole hand to move with flexibility and independence from the forearm. I am part of a semicircle of students sitting only a few feet away from the Maestro. I can see everything clearly and yet I sense an invisible veil between the Maestro and myself. I contemplate the phenomenon of the tremolo, waiting for clues and insights. It all seems so transparent and yet I know my perception is clouded because my attempts do not please the Maestro. He is so gifted and it all seems simple to him. I feel that he is exasperated with me.

I am comforted by the fact that my friend Giovanna is sitting next to me. She has returned from the mountains where her family are making their summer retreat to their country house. Her family is staying on in the mountains and she will return to them at the end of the week after the course.

As the tremolo lecture continues, I observe how beautifully and appropriately dressed Giovanna is. She is wearing blue jeans, a sleeveless white blouse and moccasin type leather shoes. In fact, I notice that everyone except the Maestro is wearing jeans, shirts and similar shoes. My shoes are Italian and leather and quite stylish, but different. Mine are flat, fairly pointed and made of a basket weave. I quite like my shoes, although I also very much like this moccasin variety. I am happy that bare feet covered in leather shoes, as opposed to sandals, are obviously the most suitable footwear in this season. My T-shirt is also bearable, although less elegant than I would wish, but my leggings are totally unsuitable. They are just not practical. They are tight and clingy and too hot. I need the air to circulate. Clothes have been at the bottom of my priority list, not because I have little interest in them, but because I have had more urgent needs such as finding sufficient money to cover my travelling costs. In this moment, I feel aware of the group dynamic. I feel different and on the outside. I want to be the same and on the inside. I want to look the same. And I also have a pragmatic yearning to cope with the torrid heat.

My attention returns to the technical discussion but my mind is restless. I try to evaluate what it is exactly that I am doing wrong. The Maestro says that I have a good hand position now, but I do not use the plectrum lightly enough. I inhibit the plectrum from gliding over the strings. The Maestro is answering a question put by one of the young men on the course. The words just wash over me without registering their precise significance. I feel tired, hungry and thirsty. I am greatly relieved when the Maestro glances at his watch and announces a pause. I assume that this must be the coffee break.

We all put our mandolins away in their cases and wander outside into the bright sunlight. We amble as a group through the small garden next to the music centre and out into the narrow streets. We are all chatting in pairs and threes. I am asked the usual questions. Where am I staying? When did I arrive? At which airport? When do I return?

A discussion ensues about the bar we should go to for coffee. Each one we try is closed because the owners are taking their holidays. In fact, everywhere is closed. Ugo remembers a place a few streets away. We arrive and see that it is a temporary sort of affair. The bar is like a caravan, which could be moved from site to site. Chairs and tables flank it, all protected from the sun by umbrellas. Close by, at the front, is a pavement and busy traffic.

We take charge of two tables, rearranging the chairs to include everyone in a large ring. I wait for the others to order first. I am not clear what is on offer. Everyone appears to order watermelon and I do the same. It is delicious and refreshing. I remember that one of the first words I ever learnt in Italian was *cocomero*, watermelon. At last it had become a useful bit of vocabulary.

After a bit Giovanna decides to order a cappuccino as well and I quickly follow her example. Despite the heat, I have secretly longed for milky coffee all morning. We pour copious spoonfuls of white sugar into our beverages, lazily stir them and sip them slowly. This wonderful moment of relaxation is brought to a close as the Maestro settles his bill and signals a return to work.

We resume our studies by playing chamber music. We play lots of Baroque trio sonatas. They are not really works for three instruments. The term trio indicates not the number of instruments required, but the fact that originally it was written as three lines of music. A trio sonata usually comprises of two treble lines for two melodic instruments, such as mandolins, and a single bass line. The bass line would then be 'realised', a technical term for amplifying a simple line of single notes by adding other harmonising notes. Normally, the harpsichord or lute would provide these extra notes or chords. However, often a cello would strengthen the bass line by playing the single line of notes as well. Hence, trios sometimes consist of four instruments instead of three.

We play trios by Barbella. I play the second part with Giovanna and two of the boys play the first part. The Maestro plays the bass part on the mandola, adding in extra chords from time to time. The music seems completely new, like playing at sight, yet I know that I have seen some of this music previously in a different edition. This edition is a facsimile of the original edition and the notes seem wobbly and strange to my eyes. I find it quite a challenge to read, but enormous fun to be contributing to the sound we are making. One movement in triple time is particularly fast and leaves me breathless and confused.

Inside the cover of the music is a quotation about the composer. It reads:

> *'He seems to know music well, and to have a good deal of fancy in his compositions, with a tincture of not disagreeable madness.'*

It is written by Dr Charles Burney, the celebrated English music historian, who travelled extensively throughout Europe over 200 years ago. He wrote about his experiences meeting musicians and hearing them play formally in concerts and informally in private homes. During his time in Naples, Burney met Emanuele Barbella and they became friends.

Being trained first as a violinist, I like the idea that Barbella was a violinist as well as a composer. I also think the 'not disagreeable madness' is a beautifully accurate description of the music. There are certainly some surprising moments!

Time evaporates. It is four o'clock and the hours have passed quickly without my being aware of time. Music-making, as opposed to studying technique, is an experience of such intense pleasure that I am totally absorbed by it. I love the onomatopoeic nature of certain Italian words such as *divertimento*, which sounds like a diversion. *Divertimento* can mean fun and entertainment, but it can also mean pleasure and enjoyment. Being diverted, as I have been, is synonymous with pleasure and enjoyment.

On the way back to the station, I notice some of the shops are open and some of them have sales on. I see a pair of navy blue trousers, a mixture of wool and viscose, which I try on and with great abandon proceed to purchase.

I also realise I haven't eaten any lunch or had enough to drink. The mandolin course is casually constructed and run in a relaxed manner. Music courses I have attended in England provide written timetables with the times of meals and breaks, as well as the sessions to be followed. In addition to meals, there is normally a morning break for coffee and an afternoon break for tea. I stop at the station for a toasted sandwich and a bottle of mineral water.

—⁕—

It is Tuesday and there is an unanticipated interruption to the mandolin course. It is August 15th, a national holiday.

Ette has phoned Ugo on my behalf and established that the course will take place despite the holiday. However, she manages to obtain permission for me to have the day off so that I can be with my family and friends. I am filled with mixed emotions. I don't want to upset the Maestro by missing an important part of the course and appearing uncommitted. On the other hand, I don't want to give offence to my friend and her family. My internal dilemma is settled by remembering that travelling to Brescia by train is not a practical option since the service will be considerably restricted.

The plan for today is a trip up into the mountains. We pack a picnic and set out in one car. Marco drives and Ette sits with him in the front. My family and I sit in the back.

We are heading towards Asiago in the foothills of the Dolomites. I sit back and try to relax by taking in the panoramic views as they change with our ascent. This is made difficult by the fact that the road is a long series of suicidal hairpin bends with sheer drops beneath my window. Apart from dealing with my own fear, the discomforting pressure on my ears and the nauseous feeling in my stomach, I am conscious of anxiety from my family. My husband and son are bickering in undertones. My son is uncomfortable with his physical space. He feels squashed by both of his parents and is making a bid to get more room. My husband feels totally out of control because he is not driving and this is a hazardous road. In addition, he is the most fussed family member on account of the fact that we are unrestrained by seatbelts in the back of the car. Rear seatbelts are not yet obligatory in Italy and although there is a legal requirement to wear front seatbelts, it is a requirement that is frequently ignored by the indigenous population.

I do understand and have great sympathy with my husband's concerns about the seatbelts, but I am powerless to do anything about it. I am overwhelmingly embarrassed by my husband's agitation and decide not to translate our discussion literally for my friends.

I am glad when our perilous journey comes to an end at Asiago. An agreeable mountain resort with beautiful walks, Asiago attracts tourists in both summer and in winter. Many of the shops are open and we wander along the high street. In the *Farmacia*, the chemist's shop, I obtain a tube of cream to deal with mosquito bites. Italian mosquitoes seem to prefer English blood and managing the irritating bites is a high priority on a day when family tensions are running high. In another shop, we look at goods handcrafted locally in wood. My son is placated by a miniature squirrel, which he purchases for his collection of tiny souvenirs.

We drive a little further into the countryside looking for a picnic spot. I notice signs for the surrounding cemeteries where the British dead lie following the Battle of Asiago in 1918. A feeling of sadness envelops me but I say nothing. Soon we pass through woodland where lots of families have set up their picnics. Many of them are barbecuing food. Whole families of three generations sit on camping chairs, chatting around the fires.

Without warning, our car is besieged first by sleet, then violent rain and finally by hailstones. All the cars looking for picnic spots become a traffic jam as flash floods block the road. People are scattered as the picnic parties try to take cover and rescue their food.

After a while, Ette is unconvinced that there is any point in staying. My husband, who loves walking in the Brecon Beacons and other wild places, feels that the bad weather will pass. But it is useless to argue. Italians feel that good weather is essential to outdoor pursuits. We return to the farm the way that we came.

At the farm, we sit around the kitchen table in a subdued manner. I eat my salami and bread in silence. In my head, there is mandolin music.

I return home to the farm after another day of making music. I am so happy to be spending my time playing, talking, thinking and breathing mandolin music in Italy. My family is also happy with their day. My son likes having the farm as a base where he can relax with his own toys and possessions. He has voiced his discontent with his parent's overdosing on cultural visits and sightseeing. He doesn't want to be always driving off here or there, to see some boring house or church. This all came to a head on a previous self-catering holiday in Umbria. My son didn't just want to sleep in his Italian house. He wanted to live there. And I can understand how he feels.

My husband is also enjoying his idyllic existence. He has participated in the lifting of potatoes, he has watched Pina making *passata* and he has sampled a recipe I am unable to find in any cookery book: a risotto made with hops. Undoubtedly, this is a recipe passed down the generations in rural communities by an oral tradition. I am sorry to have missed this experience.

On occasions, my spouse disappears entirely and I locate him in the *cantina* with the other men, knowingly discussing and sampling wine. He emerges from the shadows of the damp, dark cellar, deep in conversation, or so it seems, with Firmino and the farmhands. I am not sure exactly how they communicate since my husband's Italian is limited and Firmino and his assistants usually speak in dialect. I discern a great deal of sign language and facial expressions. Small amounts of ruby red liquid are poured into tumblers after being siphoned from the tall, shabby tanks. This is perhaps the last *vendemmia* to be processed in the old *cantina*. If everything goes according to plan, the next harvest of grapes will be fermented in the new *cantina* under the new house.

The evening meal is eaten outside in the farmyard. We sit around a large table beneath the canopy of a grapevine. The foliage of the vine is trained over a pergola. Small maturing grapes hang in bunches from the ceiling like Chinese lanterns.

Here and there lighter green, smaller leaves give way to delicate tendrils that curl like springs.

The meal extends beyond the nourishment of physical needs. As we share the experiences of our individual days, our spirits are also nurtured and encouraged. Much of our discussion is tinged with humour and the sharing of food and minds takes on a sense of celebration. As far as my family is concerned, it is a winning formula for a happy holiday. All three of us spend the day doing things we enjoy and then in the evening, we come together to recount our pleasures over a glass of wine and some wonderful food. We are all content.

At the end of each meal, the number of people around the table is always greater than at the beginning of the meal. This is due the steady stream of people popping in to say hello. These visitors are always made welcome and offered a glass of wine or some dessert or a coffee. At the end of the meal, two bottles are passed around. One contains *grappa* and the other contains *prugna*. I avoid the *grappa*, which is far too strong for my liking, but I am intrigued by the *prugna*, which I have not encountered before. A local speciality, *prugna* is made from plums and has the taste and aroma of marzipan that is reminiscent of apricot brandy. I try a thimbleful of the liqueur in my espresso. I am won over immediately by this heavenly addition to my coffee.

One evening, as we sit sipping our coffee, my son enquires about the direction of Venice. The farm is cloaked in a darkness that is only found in the countryside. The only lights are the stars, which seem to sparkle with exceptional brightness. Pina points to the corner of the yard that is the entrance and the exit of the farm. My son checks his watch. It is ten o'clock. To the incomprehension of those around the table, he walks over to the corner of the yard which has been pointed out and stands shining his pocket torch in the direction of the distant twinkling lights. He has an agreement with his Italian godmother, who lives in England but is visiting her family near Venice. As various circumstances make it impossible for them to see each other in Italy, they arranged to think of each other at this time on this day. It is a very special moment.

As we sit chatting late at night, I am sometimes aware of the smell of animal dung wafting on a current of warm air. At times it is overpowering and yet there are overtones that are rich and sweet. I think of how the bad odour of waste and decay is recycled into the soil and nourishes the new life of grapes, peaches, apricots, figs and cherries. Even in the tasting of the wine we are drinking, I detect the smell of the soil, fragrant with warm damp grass and the haziest suggestion of manure, which is translated, not unpleasantly, into one of the many strands of its flavour. The smell of the land and the taste of its produce are imperceptibly entwined.

When eventually I retire to bed, the cicadas make music that soothes me to sleep. Their nocturnal song is rapid and perpetual. Sometimes it fades into the background, buzzing like the sound of an old-fashioned radio searching between the stations, or hissing like the white noise of an old seventy-eight record being played. Sometimes I hear only the tremolo exercise, played on an open string.

I have begun searching for new clothes that will make me look more normal here and are suitable for the climate and environment I find myself in. For example, I have noticed that women on the trains tend to wear shorter raincoats, not only, I suspect, because they are stylish, but also because they are more practical. Over the past year, I had realised that my long trenchcoat style raincoat had been a great handicap. The trains in Italy are much higher and it is necessary to climb widely spaced steps to gain access into the train. This is quite awkward with luggage, especially a mandolin case, when the hem of one's coat is getting constantly caught between the steps.

On Saturday evening, I return home to the farm feeling irritated. My family disappears and I sit down at the kitchen table to tell Pina my problems.

"We began the day with a visit to the historic centre at Vicenza," I tell her. "The *Teatro Olypico* with its illusion of perspective was incredible and I am really pleased that I had the opportunity to see it. But," I continue, "I was disappointed that when I returned to the exquisite blouse shop near the *Piazza dei Signori*, I found it shuttered up with a notice that said the shop was closed for its annual holidays."

I had found this shop, specialising in blouses of exceptional quality, one evening when we made a short stop on the way back from the station. I feel cross with myself for not entering the shop then when it was open. I had seen beautiful blouses ornately decorated with embroidered collars and pockets, or drawn thread work giving the impression of tiny holes along the edges of collars and cuffs. I suppose some examples would be better described as ladies' shirts, with their clean, simple cut and concealed buttons.

"Then," I resume, "we returned to Marostica and, in the lower castle, I saw the exhibition of the costumes used for the human chess game. They were fantastic! We were too late for lunch and found all the restaurants busy so we grabbed a sandwich. Our day culminated in a final trip to Bassano del Grappa. There I managed to purchase a bottle of *prugna*, but that was all. I was hoping to do some clothes shopping, but we arrived in the afternoon before the shops opened. By that time, my husband was restless to be in the countryside of the mountains or somewhere far away from the shops. My son was fed up with sightseeing and wanted to be at home on the farm. My family day out ended in misunderstandings and failed expectations."

Strangely, my family now seemed happy, as if nothing had happened, but I was still frustrated at not being able to undertake my shopping expedition.

Pina listens quietly. I mention that on the way back I had even seen some clothes I liked the look of in a shop window in Breganze, but I was unable to stop. Pina tells me that her husband isn't that keen on clothes shopping either. I am surprised because I thought Italian men were more interested in shopping than English men are. Pina gets up from her chair and tells me that she will be back in a couple of minutes. She returns having replaced her apron with a jacket and tells me that we are going shopping.

We drive, in Pina's car, down the hill from the farm into the town. After parking near the church, we walk to the shop window that I had seen. It is a tiny window, skirted by a thin strip of pavement with a steep gradient. It is on account of the road being so steep at this point, and the pathway being so narrow, that we slowly passed by earlier and I was close enough to be able to catch a glimpse of the window's contents. There are only two items visible behind the glass. One of them is the pale blue jumper that had caught my eye previously. It is a simple tunic shape with a jewel collar and side vents.

Inside, Pina talks to the two ladies in the shop. She seems to know them quite well. I try on a number of garments and I find myself feeling calmer. Pina advises me that the cotton pale blue jumper suits me well. I knew it would do. She also suggests I try a pure wool polo neck jumper in light pink. She thinks it is a good classical piece for the wardrobe I am building. I try it on in the fitting room and I listen to the ladies chatting on the other side of the curtain. It is such a good feeling, being looked after. I need no persuasion. I take the blue and pink jumpers. Both of them are in the sale so I have two bargains. It seems extraordinary that I am able to buy clothes that are so stunningly elegant and of the highest quality in such a small country shop. Pina and I go to a bar a few doors away and celebrate my successful shopping and my redeemed day with glasses of peach juice.

―❀―

The hired car is parked in the designated space at Marco Polo airport. As we unpack the luggage from the boot, I am alarmed to see one or two giant ants crawling over one of the bags. In a plastic carrier bag, there are some emergency food supplies: a bottle of mineral water, a half-eaten packet of biscuits and three figs. We pause for a few minutes to replenish ourselves. We each take a swig of water from the plastic bottle and I begin to carefully peel the figs, which Firmino had picked from the tree this morning. Instinctively, I throw the middle one to the ground as I realise that it is alive with giant ants. I shudder in the heat of the midday sun. The remaining two figs, however, are perfect. Their pink flesh is warm, fragrant and sweet. As I enjoy these most succulent of fruits, I look intently out towards the hazy Venetian lagoon and I take stock. The first year is over.

il secondo anno

1

The second year commences with the lower diploma exam. I have arranged to spend a whole week in Bologna, Sunday to Sunday. My plan is to commute between Bologna and Padua. I have to attend rehearsals with the piano for the exam, undertake the exam and in my spare time attend sessions of a mandolin course that is running at the same time. All of this takes place on the first four days of the week. However, when I attend the *Conservatorio* on the first day, the Maestro advises me that it would be prudent to remain in Padua for a couple of nights. On my way back to the station in the evening, I make a reservation at my usual hotel for the following two nights.

Ette is happy with my arrangement to stay in Padua for a couple of nights. She thinks it is sensible. To my delight, I find that Deborah is also sitting an exam and is staying at the same hotel as I am. I am pleased to have her company during these tense few days.

The rehearsal with the pianist goes well. At least it goes well once I remember to count in Italian.

"*Uno, due, tre,*" we count together since I have to begin the Barbella sonata on the fourth beat. It is really difficult to rehearse in a foreign language. I especially find it hard to translate the numbers. It is so instinctive to think in English numbers, but I have to give an indication of speed and communicate this to the accompanist who doesn't speak English. For a split second I am edgy and the thought flickers through my mind that she must think I am stupid. I file the thought away under the heading 'stupid': that is, 'stupid thought'. Almost immediately we become settled, communicating in the same language: music.

The pianist is a lady professor at the college. I discover that she has a son about the same age as my own son and this gives us a link. In the same moment I realise that she is about the same age as I am and I am becoming increasingly conscious that I am considerably older than the average student is. At the beginning of my study, I just didn't consider my age. I suppose, in my mind, I just thought that I was young. Now a number of people have asked me about my age and I feel embarrassed to admit that I am in my late thirties. Most people think I am much younger, because I look about ten years younger than I really am. When I was a teenager and I looked plain and studious, I was disgruntled that all my friends looked so mature and beautiful. Now it is quite an advantage to look younger than one's chronological years. It is just that I have the sensation of harbouring a guilty secret: I am approaching my fortieth birthday. In music, it is not only desirable, it is almost obligatory to be brilliant, talented and young, very young. When musicians are mature, they have usually made their mark in their chosen field. Consequently, I love stories about late starters. Edward Elgar, for instance, didn't make his mark on the world until he was the wrong side of forty.

Another hitch occurs in the rehearsal. This time it is with the name of the notes. We use the first seven letters of the alphabet but Italians use *solfeggio* names. The problem is that the *solfeggio*, or Tonic Sol-fa, I had experienced used the system of the moveable *doh*. In other words, whichever key you are in, the first note of the scale is always *doh*, the second *ray*, the third *me*, and so on. In Italy, however, the system used is that of a fixed *doh*, starting with C as *doh*. Therefore, C is always *doh*, D is always *ray*, and E is always *me*, and so on. A further complication is that the Italian spellings are slightly different. Thus C, D, E, F, G, A, B are represented by *do, re, mi, fa, sol, la* and *si*.

So when the pianist casually refers to one of my chords as "*la, mi, la*," I struggle, thinking at first that it is B, F, B, which makes no sense. I stare blankly, feeling again momentarily stupid. Then I make the connection that it is simply A, E, A, which makes perfect sense. I just don't have the fluency to think of these notes in the Italian language. If I think of their pitch names, I think of their English names.

A wave of panic threatens to engulf me when the Maestro offers me a bit of paper with the notes of the strings for other types of mandolins. The *Milanese* mandolin has six strings, for example, and in the viva voce part of the exam I may have to quote the notes of these strings using their Italian names. I decide upon a mnemonic. The strings are from the lowest to the highest, G B E A D G. Simply, it is the word 'BEAD' with a G on either side. Also, read backwards, it is the same as the Neapolitan mandolin strings preceded by G B for Giovanni Battista (Gervasio), Baroque mandolinist, or simpler still, Great Britain. There are a number of possibilities. Having remembered the sequence, I would then need to translate them into their Italian equivalents. At one level this is all quite straightforward, but under exam conditions such basic tasks of recall become almost impossible.

I reach a new zenith of pre-exam stress when I am introduced to Fabio Menditto, a former pupil of the Maestro, who has arrived to help adjudicate the exams. Fabio recently became Professor of Mandolin at Aquila, near Rome. He is the soloist on my CD of the Barbella sonata, the same sonata I have prepared for the exam. I worry about how he will view my interpretation. I feel agitated and nervous.

Outside the main entrance of the *Conservatorio,* I come face to face with Fabio. He lights up a cigarette and he asks me about myself. I tell him about my recitals and teaching in London, and about my commuting to Italy to learn about the Italian school of mandolin playing. He is fascinated. He confesses that he doesn't like to travel extensively. We are briefly interrupted by a red scooter, which we have to move out of the way for. Fabio slowly inhales more smoke from his cigarette. For a moment he is thoughtful, then he asks another question: "*É tu, sei al suo agio in Italia?*"

He is asking me if I am at my ease in Italy. I tell him how interested I am in the way of life: the culture, the cuisine and even the way of dressing. The warmth of the bright October sunshine is on my face. The street we are standing in is narrow with a few tables and some chairs belonging to the Bar Pollini behind us. A plant in a square terracotta pot catches my eye. The ambience is one of an outdoor culture, exotic and a world away from the grey skies of London. I glance at the passing Paduan women wearing impeccably tailored suits. My navy blue blazer jacket is a classic piece and blends in well. In an unguarded moment, my conversation seems to be flowing. I feel quite animated and I confide that I do feel at my ease. I do feel comfortable here.

Deborah and I arrange to eat together during the evening prior to the day of the exams. Deborah says she knows of a restaurant where we can eat good food cheaply. I'm not entirely sure what to make of this statement, but we meet at seven o'clock and walk from our hotel back towards the *Conservatorio* and the historic centre. The restaurant is only five minutes away from the *Conservatorio* but I had been unaware of its existence.

Nothing could have prepared me for the experience of the Brek Restaurant. To begin with, it is a self-service restaurant and this concept alone conjures up the image of canteen dinners at a college or a workplace. The idea of self-service means mediocre meals, kept warm for long periods of time, and, as a result, long past their best. It means massed produced menus with little attention to detail, quality or choice. It means stodgy dinners, unhealthy cuisine and fast meals. It represents everything that is an anathema to the Italian ideal of cuisine, and it represents everything that the Brek Restaurant is not!

I look around, slightly disorientated at first. I appear to be in a market where each of the stalls has canopies in green. Each market stall is in fact a counter for a different part of the meal. I take a tray and follow Deborah, watching the procedure carefully. We go to the pasta counter, which is set up like a field kitchen, with a number of gas rings and huge frying pans. The menu is changed on a daily basis and is chalked up on a board at the entrance and individually at each counter. We choose a sauce with *zucchini*, courgettes, and *farfalle*, pasta butterflies. The food is partially prepared. The pasta is reheated, perhaps completely cooked, in boiling water. The cook pours some olive oil into the skillet and fries some *pancetta* cubes. When they take on a nice golden colour, and they do quickly because the oil is hot, sliced courgettes are added. Finally, a dash of *passata* is added and the pasta is stirred into the mixture. The cook serves up to about six people at a time. Each plate has a lid to keep it warm. Parmesan cheese is added at the time of serving, but there is more available at the tables. The cook already has some more *pancetta* cooking for the next batch as we are served with our food.

Next we go to the salad counter with huge bowls of leafy salads, containing amongst other things *radicchio*, as well as bowls of single items such as tomatoes, grated carrot and fennel. The salad can be seasoned and dressed at the counter, but if you forget, it doesn't matter because all the tables are well supplied with olive oil and other condiments.

As we move onto the dessert counter, we pass the second course counter and smell steaks and slices of veal being seared and cooked as required. The patisserie counter is like a treasure chest with its beautiful fruit tarts, each studded with exquisite jewels: kiwi pieces as emeralds, strawberries as rubies, dark grapes as garnets and so on. I modestly help myself to a portion of fresh fruit salad.

Before paying, I survey the drinks: bottles and half bottles of wine, red and white, and the cheapest local wines available are on tap, decanted into the appropriate size carafe. Mineral water, *naturale* or *gassata*, still or sparkling, in big and small bottles, is also available. Additionally, there is a limited supply of soft drinks. The emphasis, however, is clearly on wine and water. I opt for the water.

As I wait briefly in the queue for the till, I notice that there is a wonderful selection of fresh bread and rolls, but I decline to choose anything further. I have quite a feast on my tray and I am pacing myself in preparation for tomorrow's exam.

Deborah and I meet up with Fabio and Gianluigi, who is also taking the lower diploma exam. We all sit together, eating and talking. When the meal is over and the conversation is not, we decide to have some coffee. The group consensus is that we should go to another establishment for our coffee, which would entail a *piccola passeggiata*, a little walk, enabling the conversation to continue.

Our *piccola passeggiata* turns into a *gran passeggiata* as we walk through the streets of Padua, talking about music and the world of the mandolin. We walk across the *Piazza delle Erbe*, around the *Palazzo della Ragione* and across the *Piazza della Frutta*. We walk under the porticos and past shuttered shops. We wind through tiny streets and sometimes Deborah and I stop to look at a stylish jumper or some other interesting garment that catches our eye in a window that isn't shuttered. We are almost back to our hotel when we stop at a bar for our coffee. Then, having gulped down our sweet espressos, we continue the walk since the conversation has not yet concluded.

The night air is mild and I feel as if we are experiencing the remnants of a departing summer. At last we pause in the *Piazza Cavour* and we sit on some steps. Fabio and I are absorbed in a deep and fervent dialogue about our chosen instrument. I feel heady from the atmosphere: the food, the gentle climate, and the ambience of the surrounding architecture, added to an exchange of views with people who share my passion for the mandolin. My body is pulsating with energy. I feel as if I could stay up all night discussing the intricacies of mandolin music and its performance. I have nearly forgotten the exam. There is just a flicker of it at the edge of my consciousness.

Eventually and reluctantly, we all return to our respective accommodation.

I am called into the exam room. As I walk in, I flash a glance at the formidable examining panel behind the long table on my left. I try to pretend to myself that they are not there. I sit on my chair, adjust the music stand and check my tuning. I signal a glance and a nod to the accompanist and we begin.

Everything goes as rehearsed: the Conforto concerto, the Barbella sonata and the unaccompanied prelude and cadenza by Munier. From time to time, I have the strange sensation of hearing beautiful music, but I somehow feel disconnected from it. It is almost as if I am not in my body. I'm not sure where I am or, more precisely, where my mind is. I just feel separated from the physical sensation of making the music happen.

With the execution of the music completed, I am asked to approach the table. The Maestro introduces me to the panel, explaining that I am commuting from England in order to undertake the course. He puts me at my ease and I am grateful. I am asked the tuning of the Milanese mandolin.

"G B E A D G," I say aloud and then translate, "*sol, si, mi, la, re, sol.*"

They are satisfied and say that I am free to depart.

The Maestro greets me with the news that I have passed the exam and I am profoundly happy. To pass an examination in music in a foreign country fills me with a wonderful sense of achievement. It also means that I can continue with my studies. I am now promoted to the fifth year of the mandolin course.

2

My task for the November lesson is twofold. The first job is to find a suitable flight. This is easily achieved on this occasion; I purchase a ticket for Bologna after just a few phone calls. The second job is to acquire some new music, the sonatas of Robert Valentine, which proves to be altogether more difficult.

The Maestro reminds me that it is possible to view the published edition of these sonatas, printed in Rome in 1730, at the British Library. There is an Italian publisher who provides a facsimile edition of this work, but it is impossible to order a copy in England. Thus, the obvious solution is to obtain a photocopy from the British Library.

I don't have time to go to the British Library, but I do have a Reader's Ticket and I am familiar with their procedures. Instead I make a phone call to a very helpful lady in the Music Library, who advises me to put my request in writing. This, I do.

I write a courteous letter with all the required information. The full title of the work is *Sonate per il Flauto Traversiero, col Basso che possono servire per Violino, Mandola et Oboe*. It is curious that these flute sonatas, which may also be suitable for the Violin, Mandola (mandolin) and Oboe, were published in Italy over 200 years ago and composed by a man with an English name.

I consult my dictionary of music and find that Robert

Valentine was born in Leicester in c1680. He lived in Rome for over twenty years, returning to England in 1731 where presumably he spent his final few years. He was well known in his time as a flautist and a successful composer. The *opera* XII I am seeking is just one set out of fifteen sets of sonatas that were published in Valentine's lifetime. I am intrigued by the thought of a musician making the difficult journey between England and Italy several centuries before me. Equally, I am fascinated by the idea of an English Baroque musician assimilating Italian culture.

I remember to mention in my letter that my understanding is that the sonatas are already held on a microfilm and that it will be possible, therefore, to process my order without undue delay. I explain that I hope to be able to study this work before attending a mandolin course in Italy in three weeks' time. I put it in this way, inferring perhaps that it is a one-off course, because it is simpler and basically still truthful. I can't really go into detail about ongoing mandolin lessons. I think that would diminish my credibility.

Three days later, I receive a reply. The quote for a photocopy of the six sonatas is approximately £50. The cost is quite simply out of the question.

I decide upon a new plan. When I was in Padua the other day, I visited the music shop close to the *Conservatorio*. It is called *Musica Musica*. I had a little chat with the proprietor, explaining that I was studying mandolin with Maestro Orlandi at the *Conservatorio* and that I commute from London, visiting Padua once a month. The proprietor treated me like a celebrity and, although flattered by his respect and interest, I am getting used to the idea that this sort of behaviour is just normal good service in Italy. The proprietor said that he would be happy to supply any mandolin music that I required and I have decided to test out his service.

As I am in London at the moment and I am still a little apprehensive about using the telephone to speak Italian, I begin to put my plan into action by composing a letter that can be faxed. The only fly in the ointment is that I don't have a fax machine. Undeterred, I succeed in finding a friend who does have a fax machine and the plan is implemented.

Unfortunately, following three abortive attempts at sending the fax, my friend returns the letter to me. There is nothing else for it. I just have to muster up my courage and face the telephone.

I prepare carefully for the call. I rehearse my pronunciation out aloud. I underline the principal words and phrases of the letter in thick pencil. I also phonetically write out the letters of certain spellings, since the letters of the alphabet are pronounced differently in Italian. At last, I am ready to make the phone call. It goes much better than I had anticipated. The proprietor of *Musica Musica* isn't too fazed at my calling from London and he thinks it will be possible for the music to arrive in time for my lesson.

⁓

In Bologna, I have a pleasant surprise when Ette announces that her family are coming for lunch on Sunday. This is not a common occurrence, since they live a long distance away and there is always much work to be done on the farm. I am pleased that their visit coincides with mine.

Saturday is spent in the preparation of food. Ette keeps

referring to *polpettine* and finally I discover exactly what they are. After lunch and after the post-lunch sleep, Ette and I sit down at the kitchen table with minced meat and flour. Then, from the combination of veal and pork mince, and with a few other special ingredients, we fashion little balls, which will be cooked tomorrow in a tomato sauce.

I also have a lesson in making *tiramisù*. Its name sounds so exotic and means literally 'pick me up'. We dip Savoyard biscuits in strong black espresso coffee and line a dish with them. It is possible to add Marsala wine to the coffee, but it isn't essential. Egg yolks are beaten with sugar and then added to *mascarpone* cheese. The whites of the eggs are whisked until stiff and then folded into this mixture. The mixture is placed on top of the biscuits and the whole dessert is refrigerated until required. Just before serving, it is dusted with cocoa powder.

As we work in the kitchen, Ette asks me about the food and traditions of an English Christmas. She is anxious to know if I will be having a *presepio*. I am not entirely clear about what is meant by the word '*presepio*', a new addition to my vocabulary, since my friend has explained the recipe for baking a kind of dough. I am wondering whether it is a cake of some kind. When we emerge from our culinary preparations, Ette finds a photograph to show me the *presepio* she made last year. Perplexed, I find myself staring at an exquisitely beautiful nativity scene. Ette tells me that all the figures and animals are crafted from a kind of bread dough that is baked in the oven. I am astonished and enlightened.

It is midday and Ette's family have arrived. Her parents bring with them her aunt and uncle and the farmhand Gino, who is practically one of the family.

Immediately, Pina takes on her role as mother and homemaker. She inspects the preparations for food in the kitchen and then solicits Gino's help in visiting the *cantina* for wood and wine. The *cantina* is really an extra garage in the basement of the flats where Italian people store their wine, preserves and other junk which has no place in the living space. I keep my suitcases and old boxes in my loft, but Italian people keep theirs in a *cantina* or cellar.

In the contemporary square hearth, that I had previously thought to be ornamental, Pina builds a wood fire beginning with a cone of twigs arranged around screwed up newspaper. Then, small logs are arranged and quickly ignited. Soon, a good fire blazes and larger logs are added. The fire settles as the logs burn slowly. Glowing, they send out warmth and comfort which touches a deep eternal place within the human psyche. The clinical efficiency of central heating warms physical bodies, but is unable to nourish the soul in the way a wood fire can. I watch the flames for quite some time. They are at once both dangerous and destructive and yet also life-enhancing through their energy of warmth and light. Saint Francis thought of them with great affection when he spoke of Brother Fire in the *Canticle of the Creatures*.

During the meal around the extended dining table, I find the lively and humorous exchange between the men extremely engaging. Firmino stops, aware of my attention, and asks if I have understood. Embarrassed, I have to admit that I haven't understood. He explains that they were speaking in dialect, which accounts for why I vaguely understood that they were discussing a funny problem with salami but that was about all. Gino kindly translates for me their latest adventure in undertaking the autumn task of making their own salami, with graphic detail. I am relieved that my grasp of the Italian language hasn't mysteriously deteriorated. It is quite a strange feeling, like being a small infant again, to understand emotionally the sense of a conversation but not to understand it intellectually. The conversation had communicated the frustration and humour of their experience, just as other emotions such as fear, anger, sadness and joy can be communicated without being understood.

After dinner, we all go out for the traditional *passeggiata*. The air is cold but the sun is bright and Ette accessorises her winter wardrobe with sunglasses. I am beginning to understand more fully why they are an essential item even in winter and not just a fashion statement. Looking glamorous, like a beautiful model, my friend is really just being practical. The light is far more intense during the winter months in Italy than I have experienced in England. I make a mental note to remember to bring my sunglasses when I next visit.

Our party slowly meanders through the nearby residential streets, passing detached houses, set in their own grounds, behind fences and gates fabricated in metal. We chat in twos and threes, pointing out things of interest as we pass. Sometimes I withdraw, not feeling it entirely necessary to understand or even to notice every single word that is uttered. At these moments, I am aware of the vast expanse of duck egg blue that is the sky. As the light changes and fades imperceptibly, I notice a slight bruising of purple-grey clouds. I love the quality of the light. Pale, creamy yellow light illuminates the grey clouds from behind, giving them a halo effect. Later, in the distance, I notice the naked trees seem to scratch the apricot sky. I love the desolate beauty of November and the weeks leading up first to Advent and then to Christmas.

Gino points out a stunning tree, almost bereft of foliage, but adorned with glinting orange baubles. I wonder, in my innocence, if it is an orange tree, but Gino keeps repeating the word '*cachi*'. I don't really understand, but Gino is remarkably patient and doesn't seem upset at my incomprehension.

The road we are following runs out into open fields and countryside. Firmino spies a piece of land planted with grapevines. It is long past the harvest but Firmino walks between the vines inspecting them. He stops, finding a missed bunch of grapes disintegrating and still attached to the plant. He samples the grapes, some of which are naturally evolving into sultanas, and Gino joins him in the sampling. All at once, they are connoisseurs discussing the merits of the grape variety and the soil in which it grows. It is wonderful to see Firmino become so visibly relaxed and at home on the land.

On the way back home, I look, without success, for the lizards I had seen in the summer. I remember their movements, sometimes furtive, sometimes darting. They would flicker and flash with their luminescent lime green backs and their tails and feet of pumice grey.

Back at the flat, I am shown examples of the orange baubles. *Cachi* are in fact persimmons – a fruit that I have tried only once before and I had found to be disappointing, both in taste and texture. In fairness to the persimmon, I have heard that it must be absolutely ripe before eating, otherwise it can taste unpleasant. However, its decorative quality is quite exceptional.

In Padua, the Valentine sonatas have not arrived, but they will certainly arrive, I am told, in time for my next visit. In the meantime, I work on the Scarlatti sonatas.

3

When my spouse inquires about what I would like for my Christmas present, I usually say that I would like an item of clothing. This is because my budget for clothing is practically non-existent. The small income I earn from teaching the mandolin, violin and theory, and supplemented by occasional mandolin concerts, is barely enough to cover the cost of the expenses required to sustain my career and interest in music. Each year, I have a long list of expenses: instrument insurance, instrument maintenance, strings, music, Musician's Union subscription, professional journal subscription and so on. The list is endless and now I have to cover travelling expenses to Italy.

It is with all this in mind that I submit a request for this year's seasonal gift. I ask for a pair of jeans, not any old jeans though, a pair of designer jeans – in fact, a pair of Giorgio Armani jeans.

This seems a puzzling concept to some of my English acquaintances. They have the idea that jeans are both casual and sloppy. I, on the other hand, have been considering the idea for at least six months, if not a little longer, and I have come to an altogether different understanding.

In Italy, I have noticed that many young people, and especially the students at the *Conservatorio*, wear jeans. However, jeans are usually designer jeans and are part of a smart casual dress code. Usually they are worn with a jacket and good leather shoes, not trainers. Jeans are worn to college, for shopping, and for visiting friends and family. They are not worn for doing the housework, gardening, car maintenance and other messy chores.

Some people think that my desire for a pair of jeans is part of a mid-life crisis. It is true that I am approaching forty and that as a teenager I never actually owned a pair of jeans. In the early seventies, I remember cutting out triangles from scraps of cotton material and inserting them into the seams of wine-coloured cords to make them into fashionable flares. However, all this is to miss the point. In reality, a pair of Italian designer jeans, although appearing to be extortionately priced, are in truth an essential item in the capsule wardrobe of a European woman in the nineties. Together with my navy blazer jacket, I have an outfit that can be teamed up with a selection of blouses or other suitable tops to give a varied look that fits in with life in Italy at a minimal cost. I am, as every reader of *Vogue* knows, not being at all extravagant, but following the principle of dressing classically. The jeans are an investment that I hope will give me quite a few years of wear.

Needing no more justification, I persuade my husband to accompany me to choose the jeans. In a Covent Garden shop, during a dark Saturday afternoon in the hours before Evensong, I try on three different pairs of jeans. It is not difficult to understand the reason why Italians favour the designer product. It is not a shallow whim to display a name or a label. On the contrary, it is a question of being pragmatic. The reality is that the jeans are so well cut that they look amazingly elegant and feel extremely comfortable to wear.

In Padua, after the mandolin lesson, I visit *Musica Musica*. It is about half past four, which I have taken to thinking of as 'the *buona sera* hour' on account of this being the time of afternoon when everything returns to life again and the term of address changes from *buon giorno* to *buona sera*. The afternoon seems to be missed out altogether. I have never heard anyone say *buon pomeriggio*.

In the music shop, I am delighted to learn that the Valentine sonatas have indeed arrived. I am so pleased to take possession of my new music book. The peach and plum marble swirls on the cover are so attractive. Inside the facsimile edition, with its quaint eighteenth century writing, I look at the frontispiece with the composer's Italianised name 'Roberto Valentini' followed by 'Inglese' to acknowledge his English origin. Unfortunately, I now have to return to Bologna by train and tomorrow I fly home. This means that even with the best intentions, I won't be able to commence work on my new music until the January lesson. I already have music to study for the next visit, so in-depth study might well have to wait yet another month.

4

It is the depth of winter and my life has taken on a new rhythm without my perceiving it. It is measured in mandolin lessons and monthly trips to Italy. Each time I return, usually on a Tuesday, I spend the following morning arranging the next trip. I phone around looking for the most economical fare. I have a yellow cardboard folder, which contains the tickets and connected correspondence for my travel. On the outside of the folder, I have printed a list of telephone numbers of the airline companies who fly to the destinations I am interested in. In general, the pattern that has established itself is Milan if I am staying with Giovanna or Bologna if I am staying with Ette. When I have found the most reasonably priced ticket, I make a few phone calls to Italy to check my accommodation and to confirm the date of the lesson. I then make my reservation and I breathe a sigh of relief. I can settle down to practising the music for the next lesson and focus on my teaching, which will generate some money to cover the cost of the fare.

Just before my departure to Italy, I see an interesting advertisement in my music magazine. The Arts Council of England seeks applicants for the Artist's Research and Development Fund. I write at once for an application form.

On Tuesdays, I attend an Italian class during the evening at the University of London. Last summer, I obtained a certificate for reaching a certain level within the internally run Scheme of Proficiency. Now I am in the most advanced group and I have the opportunity to take another exam that is offered by the Institute of Linguists. The more serious members of our group are keen to take the exam and ordinarily I would be one of this subset. However, my commitment to the mandolin lesson means that more often than not I have to miss every fourth Italian lesson. It is a compromise, but I feel it is better to attend when I can than not at all. At least this way I am able to make some progress with refining my linguistic skills. I also like the structure of the homework that is set weekly, although sometimes it is a struggle to find sufficient time for it. The idea of another exam, though, fills me with horror. I just don't feel I have the mental space to afford it while I am studying music so intensely.

—◦—

When I get off the plane and my feet touch Italian soil, I have a strange sensation of taking on another role. I walk out of my life in England and straight into my life in Italy. It is as if I am walking onto the stage in a theatre wearing the appropriate clothes and carrying the correct props for my performance. I do not wish to give the impression that my experience is in any way artificial, unrealistic or pressured by expectations. I merely mean that one minute I am speaking English and being busy with playing, teaching, church activities and family responsibilities. The next minute, I am speaking and thinking in Italian, and totally bound up in the lives and concerns of the family that is looking after me.

In Bologna, I go shopping with Marco and Ette. Having had lunch and having taken a rest, we set off at about five o'clock – the '*buona sera* hour'. We visit first a shop that specialises in modern furniture. Inside, we see some beautiful bookcases constructed in cherry wood with glass-filled panels that lift and slide back over each bookshelf. I immediately fall in love with these bookcases and imagine them in my own home. My own bookcases are open and dusty. They are so difficult and time-consuming to keep clean that I have largely given up. These bookcases with the rich glow of cherry wood and their clean, simple lines are stylish and harmonious. My books and music could be displayed and stored neatly, free from dust, whilst at the same time contributing to an uncluttered look and a peaceful atmosphere. I have seen a number of similar bookcases in the houses of my Italian friends.

We move on to a lighting shop, which also thrills me. I walk around slowly, amazed at the high quality and diversity of fittings. This is only a little shop on the edge of Bologna and I would have to visit a central London shop to find anything approaching this selection. I suppose it is the sense of style that strikes me most. There are traditional fittings, although they are mostly Venetian glass chandeliers. But it is the contemporary fittings that really excite me. They have the power to transform mediocre rooms into places of exemplary design. Living space can be completely reshaped by just a little artful illumination. I stop to admire a cascade of tiny opaque glass cones suspended mid-air, as if drizzling, from thin pendulous wires.

Just as I am inspecting some up-lighters, we have a dramatic moment when everything becomes suddenly pitch black. A light flickers and steadies itself into a beam on the floor. A lady moves with a torch towards the front of the shop explaining that the lights have fused and she is going to the fuse box. I am a little confused for a moment and consider the possibility that it might be a power cut. Then, power is restored and the shop is once more alive with the intense energy of white lights, coloured lamps, coruscating chandeliers and the heat of all the bulbs.

During the evening, I spend time with Ette's other family – her in-laws. Each Saturday, Ette and Marco visit Marco's parents for dinner. When I am staying with Ette and Marco, I accompany them on their visit.

These visits are a great source of pleasure to me. We don't really do anything special; we just spend time being together. Marco's parents and particularly Marco's mother always make me feel so welcome and a part of the family. It is always very relaxed. Usually the television is on and Ette and I are given a pile of magazines to read. Marco's mother has a great interest in fashion and current trends in fabrics, probably as a result of her tailoring work, and has a good collection of magazines. Ette and I decide which ones we want to read and then sink into the cushions on the sofa for a quiet half-hour.

Every now and then, Marco's mother returns from her preparations in the kitchen and we have a little chat about something or other. Sometimes Marco's younger sister, Rosanna, also joins us for a little chat. Often the men retire to another room to discuss work-related topics.

The meal on Saturday always follows the same pattern. Marco's mother cooks a kind of soft bread roll using a device that looks like a waffle iron. These bread rolls, cooked in this particular way, are a Bolognese speciality. On the table is an array of fillings that can be placed inside the still warm rolls. There is *prosciutto*, salami, local cheese, artichokes and wild mushrooms, both preserved in olive oil. There is also salad of celery, chicory and bulbs of fennel. We each have a miniature pottery saucer in which to place a little olive oil and salt. Into this dressing, each individual dips pieces of a salad as required. The dinner is really an Italian version of English high tea. The sticks of celery arranged in a jug remind me of the suppers we had during my childhood on a Saturday evening. My mother would always have a wonderful spread of freshly baked bread, cheese, ham, pickles and celery.

My Italian meal concludes with a varied selection of desserts and fruit, followed by an espresso. Marco's mother makes an exceptionally good *tiramisù* and I have to indulge in a second helping.

I dip my biscuit thoughtfully in my tea. I glance up for a moment at the light filtering through the crochet curtain. In the distance, a bell tolls persistently. It is always the same note, enhanced with reverberations.

The tea, with the absence of milk, is translucent golden brown. The biscuit tastes rich and wholesome. Made with cream, it is called '*Macine*' and is thick and round with a small hole in the centre. On the back of the packet, it gives details of the calorific value of different breakfast combinations that include the biscuits. It seems that I am partaking of the 350 calories breakfast: four biscuits, a cup of tea and a fruit yoghurt. I look longingly at the other varieties of breakfast biscuit. There is the exotic '*Settembrini*', which contains the pulp of figs; the highly embellished *'Pan di Stelle'*, which is a chocolate biscuit studded with nuts and tiny white stars; and my personal favourite *'Ritornelli'*, which is made from almonds and cocoa.

On the side of the packet is a recipe for the biscuits I am eating. I am intrigued to know whether the recipe will turn out biscuits similar to the ones I am consuming with such relish. It claims that the recipe is genuine and simple, but it seems strange for the manufacturer to give away its trade secrets.

My flight isn't until lunchtime so I spend most of the morning helping Ette with the chores. I strip my bed of its linen and I take the sheets downstairs to be washed. Whilst I am there, Ette opens the door to the cupboard under the stairs and rummages around. She reappears and offers me a cardboard box, much like a pyramid in shape but with six sides and the top sliced off. I recognise the box: it contains *Pandoro di Verona*, a special kind of light sponge, which is traditional at Christmas time in Italy. I ask my friend if she is sure. She says that she has several of these cakes and there is too much for just the two of them. I remember that my son is particularly partial to this cake. It has a moist outer coating and the box contains an envelope of icing sugar that is to be sprinkled over the cake before serving. I waver for a moment, considering the extra item I shall have to carry. Then I hold out my hand, take the thin red ribbon handle on the top of the box and accept the gift with gratitude.

Towards midday, when I have finished my Italian housework, I put my mandolin, my overnight bag and the cake onto the back seat of Ette's car. It is quite cold and we close the car doors quickly. Ette puts the keys in the ignition, but she is unable to start the car. We both shiver, taken back by the sudden temperamental nature of the car at this inopportune moment. It is not a flat battery. The engine will not attempt to turn over. Quite simply, the ignition is somehow jammed. In a split second of panic, we decide to return indoors to make a phone call. A taxi is unavailable, but we manage to speak to Marco's sister who is free and leaves immediately to rescue us. We are only ten minutes by car from the airport, but without any means of public transport, we might as well be a hundred miles away. It is now past the check-in time of an hour before the flight and I feel very nervous about missing the flight. It seems an eternity before Rosanna arrives in her beautiful Fiat *Spirito di Punto*. I am so grateful for her kindness in my moment of need. At the airport, I thank her profusely, give Ette a hasty hug and run – mandolin in one hand and cake in the other.

Inside the terminal, I scan the departures and see with disbelief that my flight has been cancelled. I run back to the glass door of the entrance and see that my friends have now departed. I feel abandoned, confused and panic-stricken. I go to the check-in desk, feeling on the verge of tears. I explain my problem, how I came to be late and now my flight is cancelled. I don't know what to do. The lady behind the counter smiles and says that my cancelled flight is caused by an air controller's strike and that it has been transferred to Pisa airport. If I would like to return to outside of the terminal building, I would find a coach which was about to depart in five minutes' time. I run faster than I would have believed I am able to. I check that the coach is for my flight departing from Pisa and, trembling, I collapse into the first available seat near the front of the coach.

As we circumnavigate the city and I catch a glimpse between the buildings of the famous leaning tower, I can't help feeling that my disastrous homeward journey had brought about an unexpected pleasure.

On the tube in the rush hour, I am squashed and uncomfortable. Luckily I am sitting down, but I am having great difficulty protecting both the mandolin and the cake. At Knightsbridge, an elegant lady carrying a Harrods' bag and wearing a cream knitted suit gets onto the train. I judge at once that she is Italian and then I rebuke myself for being obsessed with Italy and all things Italian and making assumptions. Just as I am thinking all of this, the lady begins to converse fluently in Italian with the gentleman she is standing next to. I smile to myself. As I do so, I feel some discomfort in my hand. I look down and see that the red ribbon has cut into my fingers and left a deep imprint.

5

I am heading for the first free telephone kiosk in Brescia station. I have just arrived from Milan, after having flown into the airport at Linate. In my pocket, I have a small notebook with Giovanna's number and a handful of coins. The number is engaged so I try again and this time we are connected.

Giovanna asks me if I am tired or hungry. I am not sure what to say. I am not feeling too bad, so I politely say no to the question. I tell her that I'm feeling fine.

"Good," she says, "because we are going to a concert and the concert is at half past six. I am coming now to pick you up."

She hangs up and I walk to the entrance to wait the ten minutes it will take for her to arrive by car. I reflect upon our conversation. It is dusk and all around me there is the constant movement of shady characters. Outside, I stand near to the taxi queue because I feel it is the safest place. My decision to choose this spot as a place of safety is not based on any reason, but simply on intuition. It just feels right. The concert is only forty minutes away and here I am again just walking straight into my Italian life on a Saturday night. Within an hour of arriving, I shall be attending an unplanned concert. The unpredictability of what might happen when I am here is both charming and, at times, although not today, exasperating.

I look from my point of vantage for the arrival of my friend's car. I have a slight problem in that I can't see very far without my glasses and also I can't remember the exact details of the car I am looking for. I think it is a Fiat Panda in light, silvery, sage green, but I am not sure. This is because I don't pay much attention to cars unless they have a significantly beautiful shape. It is at moments such as these that I am subjected to irrational fears. A thought pops into my head: what happens if something prevents my friend from arriving and I am stranded at Brescia station for the night? I am tempted to give way to a ripple of panic. The ripple threatens to become stronger as car after car comes and goes, picking up passengers, but my friend drives none of them. I feel uneasy and vulnerable. Just then, I glimpse a movement, repetitive, soothing. A blurred image comes into focus. It is Giovanna walking towards me waving. I hadn't noticed her car arrive.

The venue for the concert is the church of *Santa Maria del Carmine,* which is situated in a road just off the *Via Battaglie* and is very close to the centre where the mandolin orchestra rehearse. It is not far away, but it is a struggle to get there through the busy traffic and it is difficult to find a parking space in the surrounding narrow streets.

The *Chiesa del Carmine* is reputed to be the most important example of Gothic architecture of the fifteenth century in Lombardy. From the outside, it is quite an impressive building with its countless spires embellishing the edge of the roof. Inside, the church is endowed with vast spaces. I am drawn to the intimacy of the side chapels. One of them, the *Capella Averoldi*, is frescoed by Vicenza Foppa. Almost at once, I am distracted by Giovanna noticing a friend. We walk over, arm in arm, to speak to the friend. We attract a few more people and I find myself mingling, listening and chatting. I am asked the purpose and length of my visit and where it is that I am staying. I so enjoy this pastime of chatting and being sociable. And now I feel even more pleasure as my Italian improves and allows me to express my thoughts and opinions more accurately and in more detail.

Just being here with my friend, chatting to Italian people in their own language and attending a concert of Renaissance music played in the setting of a Renaissance church is more than enough. I am living life, if only for a brief period at a time, as an Italian. The frescoes of Foppa, the depiction of the Annunciation by Floriano Ferramola and the newly restored cycle of pictures in the chancel, all recede into the background. Without any trace of disrespect, I can quite see why works of art become almost as wallpaper to Italian people. They are surrounded by so many great works in so many of their churches, galleries, historic buildings, and even by the exterior walls of frescoed edifices, that they become indulged.

A tourist visits a particular location to look at and to admire the treasures of historic interest and artistic merit. Sometimes it is difficult to appreciate the things that constantly surround you. In England I live near to Epping Forest, but I don't walk in it as much as I would like to. It is the same with central London. I am closely connected by tube to one of the cultural capitals of the world, yet I never make as much use of this convenience as I might by going to see concerts, films and plays. And so it is with Italy. I do not consume every detail or all the factual information, but I have an impression, a consciousness of something larger, if in places a little blurred. I have ceased to be a tourist and I am comfortable with my state.

Italians are not unmarked by living with the most beautiful wallpaper in the world. As if by osmosis, they know intrinsically, from the cradle onwards, what does and doesn't look beautiful. And this sense of beauty is in everything that is created in Italy. It is the same sense of beauty that is found in a Giorgio Armani suit, a piece of hand marbled Venetian paper or a plate of pasta cooked with the best fresh ingredients. And it is this sense of beauty that I have come to soak up into my music.

On Sunday, I attend the Mass with Giovanna at her local church. I love the way my friend touches my hand with holy water after she has dipped her hand in the receptacle near the entrance. She then crosses herself and I follow suit. It feels so natural and normal. It happens many times when we are visiting churches, but it is always the same. It is an outward expression of intimacy and spirituality that touches a very deep and private part of me.

The church of *SS. Trinità* is a modern church built in the round. Outside it is a concrete cylinder with little to commend it, except a modern campanile with five exposed bells set in a concrete framework. In the background, verdant hills soar, reminding me that we are on the edge of Brescia where the urban environment ends and is seamlessly joined to open countryside. Beyond the hills, to the east of the city, lies that exotic jewel of Italian lakes, *Lago di Garda*. My friend always refers to it as the big one; Lake Iseo – in the other direction – being the small one.

Inside the church, I find myself in a circular space, not unlike a contemporary theatre – perhaps reflecting the ancient Roman amphitheatre, in which unfolds a drama on several levels. Most central of all is the drama of the Eucharist that takes place around an altar just off-centre. In curving, tiered pews, the parishioners look on, sometimes participating in the drama.

"*Signore, pietà. Cristo, pietà. Signore, pietà,*" the onlookers murmur. "Lord, have mercy. Christ, have mercy. Lord, have mercy."

How deeply resonating these words, the *Kyrie eleison*, are in any language. They have a pleading quality, expressing a deep desire for a healed relationship with God.

Out of the corner of my eye, I am aware of flickers of movement. At the edge of the building, behind the highest tier of seats, people are wandering backwards and forwards. Around the walls are dark wooden wardrobes placed at intervals. These wardrobes, in reality confessionals, are constantly in use by visiting penitents even though the Mass is already in progress. I am sure that at home, in the Roman Catholic Church, it is usual to visit the priest to make a confession before the Mass. In the Anglican Church, the hearing of individual confessions is not obligatory and is seldom practised. Where it is encouraged, it is usually conducted on a more informal basis. The sight of individuals and families, some with small children, just milling around the edges, seems quite extraordinary to me.

I focus back to the words. I am amazed by how – in conjunction with the ritualistic choreography – easily comprehensible they are. I experience a slight time delay of a few seconds in the proceedings, because I must listen and then understand. Unfortunately, this church doesn't supply booklets or service sheets, so I am frustrated by not being able to follow the words. If I could read the words, I would be able to say all the words spoken by the congregation at the same time as everyone else. As it is, I have to hear the words and understand them. As I do this, I realise the words are identical to the words used in my own Anglican Eucharist at home. This delights me as it affirms my belief that there are more things in common that unite than differences that divide, when comparing the worship of the Church of Rome and the Church of England.

When we reach the point of going forward to take the Blessed Sacrament, I remain in my seat, as do quite a few others. This moment is poignant for me. Being christened as a Roman Catholic and then becoming a member of the Anglican Church in my adult life has left me feeling at times confused and hurt. I would dearly love to have membership of both churches in the fullest sense, so that I could also receive Holy Communion in the Roman Catholic Church. It is a bit like wanting dual nationality and perhaps mirrors my patriotic status. On the one hand, I am fiercely proud of being English and on the other, I am passionate about my adopted second home, Italy.

What is interesting is that no one in Italy quite understands my predicament. This is because in Italy, the Roman Catholic Church is the national church. Therefore, I am totally welcomed and accepted. Everybody – Giovanna, her parents, her friends, the priest – they all welcome and accept me enthusiastically. In England, it is not always the same because the Roman Catholic Church is a church in exile. As a result, it can sometimes become like an exclusive club. Today, Giovanna introduces me to her friends and the priest and I am made to feel included and special, even though I have not received the consecrated bread – the Eucharistic Host.

As the service concludes, I contemplate the three apsidal

icons. I think they are modern representations, pastiches of ancient icons found in the Russian and Greek orthodox churches. It is almost thirty years since the inauguration of this church, which was built to meet the demands of the expanding Brescian population. The centre icon is of the Trinity after which the church is named. I am not sure exactly who the Trinity are, but I think they are the three mysterious angels who appeared to Abraham in the desert. They are sitting together, under a tree, eating a meal. The composition is the same as the ancient icon of which I remember seeing a picture of in a book, but the buildings in the left-hand corner are more Byzantine in appearance and the *quercia di Mamre*, oak tree of Mamre, is more elaborate. The gloriously rich colours are bright and jewel-like and the gold leaf halos of the three figures are quite stunning.

Outside, Giovanna and I find *coriandoli* underfoot – tiny coloured circles, the size of the waste paper made by hole punching machines. The coloured circles are scattered everywhere. We have seen children dressed in fancy dress costumes for *Carnevale*, the Carnival celebration that heralds the beginning of Lent, and we saw them carrying plastic bags of the *coriandoli*, which they randomly threw about. It is the local custom and I only hope this confetti is biodegradable. It is everywhere. The word confetti is not used for this paper. *Confetti* means something else: the sugared almonds given at baptisms, weddings and other special family occasions.

Later in my room, I flick through a copy of *Grazia* magazine and I hear the plaintive bell of the local seminary being tolled. It has become a familiar sound. My mind returns to the angels visiting Abraham with a message that his wife, Sarah, will have an unexpected pregnancy despite her advanced years. I wonder whether angels only bring messages about births or do they communicate messages about other things?

―∾―

On Monday evening, after the mandolin lesson, we have dinner as usual but there is a special treat afterwards. We eat a kind of biscuit made locally to celebrate Shrove Tuesday, which is tomorrow. The biscuit is thin and wafer-like and very sweet. Giovanna's father asks me about our custom in England. He spent a little time working there as an engineer many years ago. I tell him about the making of pancakes, but we are both in agreement that these Brescian *biscotti* are *molto buono*, very good.

6

This month, I am preoccupied with my approaching birthday celebrations. Somehow I managed to agree to a party, suggested and organised by my husband. He is brilliant at organising things and comes into his own on occasions like this. He has printed an invitation card for my '*Forte* Party', which is a clever musical play on the word 'forty'. Invitations have been sent out to forty of my closest friends and colleagues. I am deeply troubled.

I can barely bring myself to speak of or write anything about these impending celebrations, since it seems an acknowledgement of my own mortality. I hadn't realised that I am so old, that I am possibly halfway or further though my life. In my mind, I am still twenty. I have an odd twinge in my knee occasionally and my health is a bit fragile if I get overtired or overstressed, but otherwise I feel fine. It is not that I feel no different exactly, more that my health hasn't deteriorated. And in terms of appearance, I am much better than I was twenty years ago. Now, I have blossomed. At twenty, I felt awkward and uneasy about my frizzy long hair and self-conscious about my complexion. I always felt slightly old-fashioned and behind the times. Now, I feel a sense of new self-confidence. I wear beautiful clothes that make me feel good. After experimenting with various different hairstyles over the years, my hair has returned to the shoulder length it was at the end of my teens. It is curly, and naturally so. At my very smart London hairdressers, the staff say I am lucky not to need a perm or colour. They think my hair is wonderful since others at my age seek all kinds of help. And where I once found it difficult that I looked so young and naïve, now I enjoy being mistaken for being younger than my chronological age. Perhaps I am like a vintage bottle of wine that improves with age.

Perhaps being a late starter has contributed to my state of mind. My childhood, up to the age of eleven, was lost to illness. I spent most of the time away from school as a result of a weak chest. I suffered with continual bouts of bronchitis and undiagnosed asthma. Sometimes I was quite ill and I spent a lot of time in bed. Nowadays, the advances in medicine have meant that asthma is more successfully diagnosed and treated. In addition, the efficacy of new medicines means that sick children are rarely so ill that they spend a prolonged time in bed. Ill children today are often up and playing with their toys, both at home and in hospital. Science and technology, as we are all too aware, has changed the world dramatically in the last thirty years.

Losing so many opportunities in the first quarter of my life meant that when I was a teenager I had to make up for lost time. My family spent a year in Canada when I was just twelve and during this period I taught myself to play the violin. I didn't realise that what I was doing was remarkable. I had begged my father for the violin. I was so desperate that the ukulele, given to me by my paternal grandmother when I was four and had first expressed my interest in a stringed instrument, was transformed into a violin. I made a crude bow out of wood and horsehair that I found in my father's shed, and then proceeded to make dreadful sounds on the ukulele with the help of my newly crafted bow. It was completely wrong, of course, because the ukulele has a flat bridge, unlike the violin, which has a curved bridge to accommodate the bowing. I was so disappointed but I held onto my dream.

My father asked around at work and found that a colleague had an old instrument in his loft. The violin came complete with case and bow and he wanted thirty shillings for it. My father, always with an eye to a bargain, thought it expensive. He hummed and hawed and I pleaded with him to purchase the violin. It is the only thing I remember wanting so much – the only thing I ever really made a fuss about.

One night my father came home with the violin under his arm and he also brought me a copy of a tutor entitled *Teach Yourself the First Step How to Play the Violin*. Thus, I began my journey.

In Canada, I took the violin everywhere with me. I remember hugging it like a security blanket. In a taxi at Montreal, my parents tried to persuade me to put it with the other luggage in the boot, but I insisted that I held it close to my body. In Winnipeg there seemed no opportunity for violin lessons, so I bought some pitch pipes to tune the instrument and set about work. As I had always heard music in my home, my father was a keen but nervous amateur pianist, I knew the sounds that I was aiming towards. I am enormously grateful that my father played the piano in the evenings when I had gone to bed. He would play popular tunes such as *'La Paloma'* and I remember creeping out of my bed and sitting at the top of the stairs, listening to the hypnotic rhythms. My mother would discover me and be cross with my father for disturbing my bedtime routine. I, however, was totally delighted with the beautiful sounds resonating through the floorboards. I would want to hear more and more and more.

When I returned to England, I found the opportunity I had been looking for and joined a violin class at a local Saturday morning music school. Within months of starting formal violin lessons, I had passed the first grade examination and then continued working quickly though all the other grades, skipping a few on the way, because I just didn't have the luxury of time in order to complete my studies by the age of eighteen. At the same time, I had to work hard on my academic studies to make up for lost time. One of my peer's parents asked me what I wanted to do when I grew up. I knew I wanted to be a musician but I was also realistic. Playing professionally is almost unheard of amongst late starters. I told the father in question that I wanted to be a peripatetic violin teacher. I was met with a puzzled response. No one was ever quite sure what the word 'peripatetic' meant.

This pattern of doing everything late and then with great urgency has been repeated time and time again in my life. Perhaps this explains my inner turmoil, the searching and questions now. Have I achieved everything I want to? The answer is certainly no. I think the problem is fear. Fear that I am running out of time. Fear that there will not be enough time for all the things I have still to accomplish.

There is a lot of cleaning to do in preparation for this party. I hadn't realised how dirty my house is. I start a little job and it becomes a major project. I wash all the lace curtains at the front of the house and I find I am embarking upon the washing of window frames. This leads on to skirting boards, pictures rails and so on. It is never-ending.

It is not just a question of cleaning my living room and breakfast room for the party guests. It is also a question of pride. Ette and Marco are coming to stay for a few days and the party will take place in the middle of their stay. It is the first time Ette has visited me in England and I want to give her a happy and comfortable stay. I would like her to find her stay as welcoming as I find mine when I stay with her. The problem is that her home is immaculately clean and tidy and I am discovering that it is difficult to maintain the same standards in English houses.

For example, there is the matter of carpets. English houses are usually carpeted, wall-to-wall throughout. Fitted carpets have become the norm – but to keep them truly clean, even with shampooing, is impossible. They are so unhygienic, always a trap for dust. In Italy, houses have marble, wood or tiled floors. A damp cloth, after hoovering or sweeping, or a bucket of water and a mop is all it takes to have a dust-free floor.

Then we rely on huge heavy curtains, another dust trap, unlike Italy where the windows always have a shutter to provide correct lighting and privacy. And I have also found that wallpaper attracts dust. I have a special wool mop to wipe the walls with, but eventually repapering is the only answer. In Italy, however, the plain white walls of houses can be repainted when necessary without too much fuss. I could go on and on.

I have found myself making numerous changes to my house since I began my trips to Italy. I have roller blinds at some of the windows. They are as dust-free as possible and allow the light to be more effectively controlled in each room. I have begun to remove carpets, replacing them with wooden floors. In my bedroom, I replaced our sixteen-year-old divan bed with an iron bedstead and a new mattress. This is easy to keep clean. It is possible to have access to the floor under the bed in order to clean and the iron framework can be cleaned with a damp cloth for a dust-free finish. The floorboards were not of sufficiently good quality to strip and seal with varnish. Instead, I scrubbed them clean and applied some floor paint specially formulated in bland, old-fashioned colours by a company for the National Trust. I am not really a do-it-yourself enthusiast – that is my spouse's department – but I actually felt so passionate about my solution for the bedroom floor that I undertook the whole project myself.

I have also attacked cupboards and wardrobes, completely reorganising their contents. In my room in Ette's home, an old-fashioned wardrobe much like mine stands between modern fitted wardrobes. This old-fashioned wardrobe in Italy, with a full-length mirror on the door, is a linen cupboard. I found my airing cupboard infested with moth larvae and was spurred into washing everything and beginning my own linen cupboard. In my Edwardian wardrobe, I have arranged towels, sheets and pillowcases. I was amazed when I first saw Ette's cupboard. It was a labour of love prepared for her wedding by the women in her family, who contributed all the items with their lace and embroidered finishes. I had hardly anything when I married, but now I find myself throwing out floral duvet covers and replacing them with plain white covers. I have also begun collecting white pillowcases with embroidery and other decorative edges. And I feel a great sense of peace and harmony in surveying my new linen cupboard.

I am rushing to get my grant application off to the Arts Council before my trip to Bologna.

I read the words at the head of the information sheet.

'The scheme,' it says, 'is designed to enable creative and performing musicians of professional status working in all areas of music.'

That includes me. I am a professional performing musician.

It goes on 'to research and prepare new and unusual repertoire, to explore new techniques or to pursue a programme of work, which will benefit their career in the music profession.'

All these criteria apply to me. I underline the words *'research'* and *'prepare new and unusual repertoire'*. I underline even more boldly *'to explore new techniques'*. The words are so appropriate. They describe exactly the work I am undertaking by attending the mandolin course. I am filled with a new sense of confidence that I might have, at last, found a source of funding for my project. It seems a realistic possibility.

I fill in the application form with details of my professional work, all my past and present performing work, and a brief description of my project. On a separate sheet, because the box provided on the form is too small, I write my description. I explain how the project is to visit on a monthly basis the Conservatoire in Padua in order to study, with Professor Ugo Orlandi, the Italian school of mandolin playing, which has a different approach to right-hand technique and interpretation.

I continue: 'I am the first mandolinist from England to study on this unique course and to study this method. As a result of attending this course, I will develop a new right-hand technique, which is central to the Italian school of mandolin playing. The right-hand technique with its different hand position allows greater contact with the instrument, better placing of the plectrum, and results in a greater resonance, accuracy and speed, together with a more relaxed and elegant style of performance. In addition, it affords greater clarity and precision in the ornamentation of Baroque music.'

I read over the words to myself. I feel I have encapsulated clearly my plan and my objectives. I am really quite pleased with my eloquence.

The form requires further details, so I have to explain how the project will help develop my career and I list ways in which I intend to use the experience gained from the project in my future work. It seems obvious to me that I will utilise the new technique in my performance and teaching. Similarly, it seems clear to me that the experience will help me in editing and publishing my own editions of Baroque mandolin music. It will help me in the performance of mandolin music, especially in historically informed early music, and, it will also help me in my teaching, which will focus on the Italian style.

By the time I complete the form with two references, I am fed up with forms and I hastily depart for the postbox.

7

The 'Forte Party' is upon us. Ette and Marco have arrived and Ette is surprised at how open houses in England are. By this, she means that the windows are without external blinds and shutters. It is difficult for her to sleep on the first night because she finds the bedroom too light. The orange glow of the street lighting pervades the room despite the lace curtains and roller blinds. In Italy, I always find the complete block of light and the consequent pitch black unsettling. Here, Ette is disturbed by the opposite. I find a solution in some eye masks, the kind provided on long-haul flights, which I borrow from a neighbour.

Although my husband has organised my birthday party, I still have an important contribution to make in cooking at least half of the food required for the supper. I am busy working on a huge casserole of lamb cooked with wine, garlic and tomatoes, and another huge pan of *calamari* cooked with the same three ingredients and with the addition of anchovies. I am also cooking large trays of roasted Mediterranean vegetables: aubergine, peppers, onions, tomatoes, courgettes and fennel. All of this is to be accompanied by a choice of pasta or rice and pieces of *ciabatta* bread, and is washed down with wine and water. The meal begins with a selection of cold Italian meats, such as salami and *prosciutto di speck*. After the hot dishes, it follows on with various desserts: mouth-watering meringues, prepared by my husband, fresh fruit salad and *tiramisù*, made authentically by Ette. This celebratory Italian feast is to be concluded with champagne and birthday cake.

I have a wonderful party. I so enjoy the idea of delighting some of my closest friends with a special meal, and I love chatting and sharing their company. I wear a short black dress, a new acquisition for the occasion, a classic piece, which I judge to be an investment. It makes me feel fantastically gorgeous.

Music comes after eating. Many of my guests are either professional or excellent amateur musicians, and the invitations had requested possible musical contributions. Sadly, my English friends are mostly reserved, probably feeling that they are required to put on a performance. My intention had been for some genuine music-making for our own amusement. In the end, only a few of us, including Ette and I playing mandolin duets, make music. This is perhaps the least satisfying aspect of the evening. It has become very much an audience and listener situation, instead of a few people playing and having fun in a corner, which might or might not attract the attention of other people. I suppose I have somehow managed to engineer a fairly formal component into the evening, when in fact I had desired a much more relaxed and informal situation.

I have received a number of thoughtful messages from friends and acquaintances counselling me not to be worried and saying that life gets significantly better from this moment onwards. When the room, suddenly darkened, is illuminated by only forty spindly candles on a cake, I feel unexpectedly empowered, for the first time in my life, to blow out every single flame with one breath. In this moment, I am focused. I take a deep breath and concentrate on extinguishing each and every light. To my utter astonishment, the room is dark and I have succeeded.

―◦―

In the Victoria Tower Gardens, next to the Houses of Parliament, Ette and I are occupied dispensing a picnic made up of the leftovers from last night's party. My family and I are spending a day showing my Italian friends the sights. With us is Ette's childhood friend, Chiara, who is presently working in England. I am so pleased that she was able to come to the party and that she stayed the night. It has been company for Ette to have another person able to communicate with her in her own language.

Like me, Ette is fond of the roasted *melanzane*, aubergines, and we both pile them on top of salami placed on *ciabatta* bread, making a kind of open sandwich. We look out across the Thames, mesmerised by the endlessly changing water. The sunlight throws silver sparks on the grey-green surface. It is not so different from Venice. The air is sharp. It is not a day that Italians would choose to have an outdoor meal. Ette looks at me and I wonder what she is about to say. She tells me that the *melanzane* is particularly good. This compliment fills me with a warm glow. It strikes me that yesterday's gathering had another function besides celebrating my life so far. It also brought together some strands of my life. It provided an opportunity for my Italian friends to meet some of my English friends and vice versa. It helped sew together the threads of my English life with those of my Italian life, and I am grateful.

A letter arrives this morning. It is dated April 22nd, the date of my birthday. It informs me courteously that the Arts Council has made 'no recommendation for support' of my grant application. They had a number of applications competing for a limited amount of money. They hope I will be able to obtain the necessary funding from other sources. I have heard it all before.

I don't feel disappointed exactly, maybe a little numb, or perhaps a little philosophical. I don't know really. I just know that I have to carry on visiting Italy, taking it one month at a time, one day at a time.

I have to forget the letter and practise my scales for the next visit.

8

Today is May 1st and Giovanna is arriving with her friend Eleanor to stay with me for a week. They hope to do some shopping in London.

Yesterday my son returned to boarding school after the Easter break and the day before Ette and Marco returned to Bologna. I am busy taking linen off beds, putting it in the washing machine, hanging out washing, airing the house, ironing only that which is necessary and making up new beds. I am seeing all sorts of other chores to do and I must consider some menus and find time to go shopping. I have no time for my pupils and I have no time to practise. Today, I am just in a frenzy of domestic activity.

Giovanna and Eleanor return to Brescia today and tomorrow I go to Italy to stay with Giovanna and to have my mandolin lesson. All this coming and going. Spending time with Italians even when I am not physically in Italy leaves me with the impression that I have not left Italy since my last visit.

In Brescia, I resolve to readdress an imbalance. Giovanna and Eleanor shopped extensively in London. They continually returned to my house with all kinds of bags and parcels containing their purchases. Inspired by their enthusiasm, I long to have time to shop in a relaxed and pleasurable manner, and I have decided that this time I will make a concentrated effort to have sufficient time for some serious shopping. I have saved up a little money and made a list of things I would like to buy.

High on my list is a good pair of sunglasses, which are so necessary for my time in Italy. On Saturday I walk about the Brescian shops in the late afternoon sunshine, feeling strangely carefree. I carefully study the windows of the clothes shops, looking at the styles and shapes, colours and textures, and making mental notes. I categorise all the garments, those that I would like if I had enough money, those that please me, those that would suit me, those that are indispensable. In the last category, I have to narrow it down to a handful of items. My budget will cover one blouse, a pair of shoes, a bag and a pair of sunglasses.

I find a cotton blouse, really a female shirt in design, with a tiny blue and white check pattern, which I purchase. I have seen other people wearing similar shirts at the *Conservatorio*.

The shoes I choose are a pair of tobacco-coloured loafers in soft leather. They are a delight to buy. The lady in the shop is so accommodating. I feel no sense of pressure, which might rush me into making the wrong decision. The shoes are flat and of a classic design. All my friends wear these with jeans or trousers and they will be practical for the long walk between Padua station and the *Conservatorio*. They are also half the price I would pay in London if I were able to buy the same shoes. My feet are unpredictably sensitive and I have found it difficult to find stylish shoes in soft leather.

My new bag is a designer *zaino*, a rucksack, which is made from a kind of exclusive canvas material. I have only seen these in Italy and I have noticed a lot of students on the train using them to carry their work. Giovanna also possesses one of these bags and I have admired it for some time. They are very practical because they can be slung over a shoulder or even worn on the back. I choose a colour called sand, a neutral taupe colour.

The purchase of my designer sunglasses mirrors the experience of my husband's purchase at Marostica during last summer. A handsome young man serves me and shows me every attention possible. He is so kind and helpful, but I think this reflects that he knows the product he is selling and that he lives in a culture where service is a pleasure and is considered normal. I choose the perfect pair and feel genuinely reassured by the assistant that I have made the correct choice. As he processes my credit card, I am aware that hundreds of designer specs are displayed openly all around me on the walls. I walked into an optician's shop at home, not my usual optician I am glad to say, and asked to see their designer frames. They only had six pairs, locked in a glass case. The assistant was extremely frosty and suspicious of me. When I tried on the second of two pairs offered to me, I placed the first pair on the desk in front of me and I was brusquely admonished. Apparently, although the shop was empty, my carelessness might have encouraged theft. Obviously the assistant felt vulnerable to the threat of crime, but there is something wrong when potential customers are made to feel so uncomfortable. Needless to say, I promptly left. Here in Brescia, all tensions are dispelled and I bask in the balm of trust.

The assistant smiles at me as he returns my credit card and receipt and the parting rituals begin.

"*Grazie mille.*" A thousand thanks. "*Buona fortuna con i studi.*" Good luck with the studies. I am always having personal conversations with perfect strangers. '*Buona sera*'. '*Arrivederci*'. Every time I leave a shop, there is always a sprinkling of these courtesies. I am probably a little old-fashioned, but I do like politeness and good manners. I leave feeling that I am walking on air.

My sense of elation has little to do with the material goods I have purchased, although they are all beautiful and useful and I am pleased with them. I am not experiencing a high as a consequence of participating in the modern leisure activity of consumerism. Rather I am filled with a rush of happiness, a result of life-enhancing interaction with the people I encountered.

At the bus stop in *Via G.Mazzini*, a stone's throw from the ancient *Duomo Vecchio*, the Old Cathedral, I see an astonishing sight. The bus stop has become electronic. A message moves past telling me that my bus will arrive in nine minutes. The Old Cathedral is sometimes referred to as the '*Rotonda*' on account of its round shape. It was built on the site of the Roman thermal baths and it is still possible to see some of the remains of these baths inside. It is literally only yards from the bus stop. I stare at the tiny flashing lights as they make their journey across the screen. I have seen so many examples of the old juxtaposed with the new. Somehow, they always seem to blend comfortably together.

The message now tells me that my bus will arrive in four minutes. There is a sign in music, a curved line like an eyebrow placed over a dot, which when placed over a note means stop and pause, giving more time to the note. This sign is often described as a 'pause' but is known technically by its Italian name '*fermata*', which translates as 'stop' and is also used for 'bus stop'. I often amuse my young pupils by explaining that they should think of a bus stop when they arrive at a note marked with a pause sign and that they should wait on the note, increasing its length, just as one might wait at the bus stop for the bus. Now that Italian bus stops have electric signs, I have a bit more to add to my analogy.

9

On the final day of May, I return to Bologna to squeeze in one final lesson before the end of the scholastic year. The weather is balmy in the opening days of June. I buy a new short sleeve cotton T-shirt in navy blue. It is not really a T-shirt in the usual baggy sense, it is a small top, which fits neatly under a jacket and goes well with jeans. I try to buy at least one new piece, even if it is something small, on each trip in order to build up my wardrobe. I remember how last year I didn't have the right clothes and Ette so kindly lent me a T-shirt so that I would feel more comfortable.

It seems incredible that this visit marks the end of the second year. Time has flashed by and already I am halfway through my time of planned study. And in all this time, although I never know from one moment to the next where the money is coming from, I always seem to find enough in my bank account. Somehow, even when things seem impossible, at the last moment I get a phone call and there is a new pupil or someone requiring some extra coaching. Unexpected things are always happening and somehow there is always sufficient for my needs. I am extremely grateful to have made it this far.

il terzo anno

i

"Two hours then," I repeat. I nod my head in agreement and I get out of the car. In front of me, soaring in the soft September light, is the magnificent dome of the Royal Albert Hall, one of my favourite buildings in London. Ever since, as a pre-adolescent, I watched the *Last Night of the Proms* on television, in black and white and with Sir Malcolm Sargent conducting, I have kept a special place in my affections for this concert venue. It symbolises something stirring, something patriotic and very English.

My husband drives away and I have just a couple of hours before he returns and I have to accompany him to Evensong at the cathedral. I turn away from the dome and I cross the road, walking towards the Royal College of Music. This weekend there is an exhibition of Early Music at the college and I am anxious to make the most of my precious time. I would like to have a complete day or even half a day free, but I don't, so I must make the most of my opportunity. As I walk towards the entrance, I privately declare my intention to myself. I silently tell myself that this time I will meet someone who will help me to achieve my desire of owning a Baroque mandolin.

This all sounds crazy. I have met many lute makers before and tried without success to interest them in making an instrument for me. When I completed the last day of the summer mandolin course last year, I remember thinking that I must have a Calace instrument – a different modern instrument from my own. I wanted to have the top-of-the-range concert model because so many people have this instrument in Italy, and I thought Ugo might like my playing better if I had the same instrument as he has. At Christmas I managed to sell one of my instruments, my first Pecoraro, but by the time I did so, I had already changed my mind about the Calace. The Calace isn't right for me for normal use. It is too heavy and I like the neatness of the cambered fingerboard of the Pecoraro or Embergher instruments. It was silly of me ever to entertain the idea that the choice of instrument would make such a difference to my playing. My perception was somehow temporarily clouded – the idea a fleeting whim. I know that I can make crude student violins sing and that skill is more important than choice of instrument. It is well known amongst violinists that a poor player will not sound any better just because he or she is given a Strad to play on.

So when I sold my mandolin at Christmas, another idea was born. I had for some time wanted a Neapolitan Baroque mandolin, but it is such uncharted territory. I only know of one luthier in Italy making these instruments. He has made two that I know of and the last time I enquired, there was a three-year waiting list. Clearly a simple solution would be to find a luthier here and now I have sold an instrument, I have some cash to plough into the project. In my final two years of the mandolin course, we have to study the performance of Baroque music in more detail and we have to be familiar with period instruments. Without experiencing such an instrument, I am not sure how this is possible, so I am determined to have my own.

I stand in the queue for tickets. In my mind I repeat my intention to myself again, affirming that I will meet someone that will help me to manifest the instrument of my dreams. It is like a prayer, but it is more positive and authoritative. I have been reading a lot of self-help books during the summer and I am very interested in the power of the mind and its ability to influence what happens to us. I have been reading about positive thought, affirmations and visualisation techniques. I have been thinking about this instrument that I would like to own, how it will feel to play and how it will sound.

It is my turn to buy a ticket. I also ask for an additional ticket to visit the historic instrument museum of the college, which is open today by special arrangement. I had read about this in a music magazine. I checked my books at home to confirm that the museum holds a number of mandolins, including those of the Neapolitan variety. I particularly want to view an instrument by Vinaccia, the most eminent of mandolin-makers in the Baroque period.

As I enter the museum, I am welcomed by the metallic throb of chords interspersed with wiry threads of decoration being executed on a harpsichord. I am excited to see so many people exploring the keyboard instruments and being allowed to play the exhibits. The museum appears to be accessible and friendly. The instruments I wish to view are, however, in glass cases in a viewing gallery reached by stairs to the left of the entrance. About halfway along the gallery, I find the mandolins. There are quite a few examples, some of the Milanese variety and some of the Neapolitan variety, including a Vinaccia. I spend some time studying the latter instrument and trying to fix every detail in my memory.

I return downstairs to speak to the custodian of the museum. I have quite a lot of questions about the Vinaccia mandolin. Sometimes, details of measurements and plans of instruments are available and can be viewed by special appointment. Sometimes, this information isn't available and it is possible instead to view the instrument outside of the glass case. Permission can be given for photographs to be taken and for measurements to be recorded in order to make a copy or a similar instrument. Without this valuable facility for research and the possibility of new instruments – replicas of the worn-out and fragile originals – these period instruments would decay until they became completely extinct.

As I am engaged in conversation with the custodian, she is distracted by several other enquiries. Suddenly, she disappears and I am left mid-sentence. For a moment, I feel the impossibility and hugeness of what I am embarking upon. I would like a copy of an old instrument that no longer exists except in a museum. It cannot be bought in a shop and I have not yet found a maker who will accept the commission to make such an instrument. Occasionally old instruments might come up at auction, but it is extremely rare and usually they are beyond being restored to playing condition. Makers on the other hand would have to take a risk in agreeing to construct a new instrument. A mandolin needs a mould, a carved piece of wood in the shape of a half pear, around which the ribs of the back are moulded. The mould is a pattern for the instrument and it is necessary to build one, from the dimensions taken from an existing instrument, before work can even begin. It might mean a great deal of research and the learning of new skills. I suppose the likelihood of finding someone interested today is minimal.

In the same moment, as all this flashes though my mind, a voice says: "I wonder if I might help you?"

I swing round to see a slim young man with long hair neatly tied back in a ponytail and melting brown eyes.

The young man continues: "I'm sorry, but I couldn't help overhearing your conversation and I wondered whether I might help you."

He introduced himself as Chris Allen, a luthier who specialise in lutes and hurdy-gurdies.

I begin to tell him about the Vinaccia and we walk up to the display of mandolins. Chris's face lights up when he sees the intricate mother-of-pearl inlay on the instrument I show him. His knowledge about instrument making is so interesting and he listens carefully and respectfully to everything I tell him. Soon I see that he is very enthusiastic about the instrument I would so love to own and he is expressing an interest in making it. We go for a cup of coffee to continue our discussion. We talk for well over an hour. I am elated at finding someone who is interested in my project, someone who is not afraid of a challenge, and who is both approachable and reassuring.

As I walk down the steps back onto the street, I remember my intention. I smile to myself.

"Yes," I whisper under my breath, "it worked."

Positive thinking really worked. Other people might dismiss it as a coincidence, but I believe it made a difference. I am filled with intense joy, confident that, whatever the obstacles, the new mandolin will somehow happen.

11

There have been some changes in Brescia during the summer. Giovanna now has her own flat; her father has retired and her parents have moved back to their roots in Treviso.

I can't wait to see Giovanna's new flat. It is in the historic centre of Brescia, in a little side street just off the *Piazza della Loggia*. It is situated over a dress shop. To gain access, my friend has to insert a huge iron key into the keyhole of the door at the side of the shop. Behind this door and stretching out in front of us is a long whitewashed corridor with a vaulted ceiling and an uneven flagstone floor. It feels as if we are entering a wine cellar.

"This is one of the oldest buildings in Brescia," my friend proudly informs me.

At the end of the corridor, there is an opening to the right. We struggle up some stone steps, turning sharply back on ourselves, and take care not to lose our balance with the worn-away middle part of the step. After the usual unlocking procedure, with many turns of the key, the thick and heavy door to the flat swings open.

Inside, the high ceiling is formed with dark brown planks of wood, which give it a rustic appearance. It is quite different from the modern plain plaster ceilings I have seen in other people's flats. It reminds me of rural buildings in Tuscany and I can well believe that the flat is part of a medieval building, which has been renovated and converted into flats. The walls are whitewashed and scattered with stylish music posters. The main room doubles up as a living room and a kitchen. The bedroom and bathroom are separate and self-contained. They open onto a tiny and thin corridor, which connects the entrance to the main room.

In the bedroom, Giovanna has prepared a guest bed for me and as I place my mandolin and bag on the bed, I notice her cat scurrying from under my bed. At the head of my bed, there is a little recess which gives way to a window. Giovanna opens the window to reveal louvre shutters painted in dark green. The shutters open to the left and right of the window. Down, far down, below is a courtyard. It is here on the window ledge that the cat likes to survey the world. He sits silhouetted against the light. Occasionally, I notice his head jerk as he reacts to a passing bird and then remembers that it is unsafe to move any further forward on the ledge.

In the evening, Giovanna and I prepare a simple supper of pasta with an olive and tomato sauce. The sauce, which comes straight from a jar, is a staple store cupboard ingredient and one of my favourite convenience foods. We add some grated *parmigiano* and accompany it with fresh crusty bread. It is followed with salad leaves, dressed with salt and olive oil. It is interesting that among my friends and acquaintances in Italy, wine vinegar and pepper are seldom used for the dressing of salads. Finally we conclude with an espresso, which we ceremoniously sweeten and take time to savour.

After we have washed up, we sit down to play mandolin duets. We spend several hours entertaining ourselves without realising it is getting late. Over and over, we play movements that we enjoy or are trying to improve. We are endlessly fascinated by the music and it feels enormously comfortable playing together.

At last we realise that we are tired and stop playing, but we find ourselves chatting about life. We sit at the kitchen table nursing large bowl-like cups of warmed, sweetened milk. It is comforting and a little nostalgic. During my adult life, I have rarely taken the opportunity to have a milky drink at bedtime. We continue our philosophical discussion until quite late and then we retire to our beds.

I am awakened on Sunday morning by the sound of a bell; the clanging of a single note, signalling the imminent start of Mass nearby, is full-bodied. The haunting reverberations tell me that I am truly in Italy, even though the room is still darkened by shutters. I fall asleep and awaken several times with other bells tolling. I love their sound. I snuggle further down under the embroidered sheet. I could listen all day, being constantly lulled to sleep and then awakened, lulled to sleep and then awakened…

Early Monday morning, I prepare myself quickly for the day. I have laid out the clothes that I need and I do the bare minimum that is necessary in the bathroom. Giovanna now has a job in an office and I don't want to inconvenience her by disturbing her usual routine. I can shower when I return this evening. After breakfast and rapid teeth brushing, we both depart for the day.

Giovanna gets into her car to go to work, but I am on foot today. Normally I would be going to the station to catch the train to Padua, but it is still October and the mandolin course hasn't yet started for the new academic year. Instead, this week, there is a special mandolin course in Brescia at the young people's music centre where the mandolin orchestra rehearse. It is the same location that I came to for the very first mandolin course I ever attended and it is the same place that I returned to for the summer course I took part in when I stayed with my family at Breganze.

I wave goodbye to Giovanna and walk towards the *Piazza Loggia*. I follow the path around the back of the *Palazzo della Loggia*. The billowing shape of the roof is so pleasing to me. It echoes Palladio's *Palazzo della Ragione* at Vicenza and I have read that Palladio was indeed a collaborator in the completion of the building. I have also read in the same guidebook, an English tourist guidebook that Giovanna's mother very kindly gave to me, that the lead roof was destroyed by fire in 1575, less than one hundred years after the first stone was laid in 1492. Amazingly, the restoration of the sixteenth century roof took place only relatively recently in 1914.

After the *Palazzo,* I turn immediately left out of the *Piazza* and into *Corso G. Mameli*. This takes me directly to the *Torre della Pallata,* where I must turn right into the *Via Battaglie* for the music centre. The whole walk takes about twenty minutes.

Corso Mameli is just coming to life and I am interested in the different shops I pass. I note a bookshop, which I will return to later, and a shop displaying ladies nightwear and lingerie catches my eye. I move invisibly between people going about their daily business. Elegantly suited businessmen stop for an early morning espresso at a bar. One glances over the headlines of the *Corriere della Sera* he is holding and another chats on his mobile phone. I remember once in Assisi seeing a Franciscan monk in a bar drinking espresso. As I looked down, I saw his bare toes peeking out of his brown leather sandals. When a mobile phone rang, I was utterly astonished to see that it was the monk who was answering. It was an incongruous sight, a religious who followed a life of simplicity and poverty using a symbol of contemporary technology and wealth.

An old lady walks past with a basket of green leaves spilling over the edges. Two teenage boys wearing the school uniform of jeans and trainers and carrying rucksacks on their backs walk to school. A man cycles past and greets a lady across the street. I notice a small dog running at the side and see that he is attached by a lead to the cyclist's hand. I enjoy this leisurely walk to work. There is so much to take in and I am grateful that I am within walking distance of my destination. It makes a welcome change to have short journeys.

Walking down the *Via Battaglie,* I remember the last mandolin course and my curiosity about the people who live in the apartments high up and hidden away within the buildings on either side of the road. I am taken back even further to my first visit to Brescia. On the Sunday, I spent the day being a tourist. I visited the *Duomo Vecchio*, the Roman ruins, and the art collection at the *Pinoteca*. It was a difficult day. I didn't realise everything would shut down so completely for lunch. I had managed to get a sandwich and a coffee just before the bar closed, but then I found myself in the courtyard outside the *Pinoteca* waiting for an hour and a half for it to open for the afternoon session. I sat on a bench in the shade, listening to the echoing voices of a family emanating from an open window high up. I could hear the clutter of cutlery on the table, the chatter and the laughter, and I so longed to be up there with them, to experience their life, to see the rooms they lived in, to taste their food, to talk with them. It seems so strange that now this is exactly what I am doing. I am living with my friend in rooms high up above the ancient streets of Brescia. I am living only a few streets away from that family I overheard all those summers ago.

Another experience clouds my memory, dark and humiliating, a secret I have only shared with Giovanna. I remember waiting later that same day to be collected by Dorina with whom I was staying. As I waited for her car, a stranger stopped his car and after some confusing conversation, I sent him on his way. I realised with burning cheeks that he mistook me for a prostitute. I felt so ashamed. In time, I came to understand that it was because I was wearing a long flowing floral dress of the kind that was so fashionable in England during the eighties. I just had no idea that to classically-minded Italians, my dress would seem bizarre, even outrageous, and might give the wrong impression. Now, I look at other women in the street, the jackets, the trousers, the designer sunglasses, and they reflect back the image I now have. I move about unseen and untroubled, and I am content.

The mandolin course is dedicated almost exclusively to the music of Giacomo Sartori. I am not acquainted with Sartori. I know nothing about him or his work, but this is about to change.

"*Ciao*," Deborah cries out from across the room, "*come stai?*" How are you?

She comes to me smiling, gives me a big hug and kisses me on both cheeks.

"*Bene,*" I reply, "*sto molto bene, grazie.*" I am very well, thank you.

We are the only females at present and we sit tribally together, tuning our instruments carefully. The Maestro places a piece of music on the stand in front of us. *'Pianto di bimba'*. 'Tears of a small female child or baby'. The letter 'a' at the end of the word *'bimba'* denotes the gender of the tiny child or baby. It is an intimate title.

We begin to play. It is an old-fashioned waltz, just like the tunes my father used to play on the piano. The window near us is ajar and a warm breeze comes through the iron railings – the security grate that protects the window. We stop. The Maestro talks. He has a great deal to say about the music and its interpretation. He always has a lot of opinions and I enjoy listening to the sound of the discourse as much as its contents. The rhythms of speech and the rise and fall in pitch of the words are as interesting as the ideas conveyed. The Maestro makes music even as he speaks. Young children's voices from the nearby school float in with the breeze. They punctuate, comment, blend and disappear.

We play the piece again, better this time.

Giacomo Sartori was born during the latter half of the nineteenth century, in 1860, at a small town called Ala in the Trento region, not far from the Austrian border. His family ran a perfume and barber's shop, in which he was required to help. However, Giacomo was more enamoured with music than with cutting hair and he devoted himself to musical study, beginning with the violin. Later, he taught himself mandolin and guitar and he also developed keyboard skills; a harmonium was kept in the back of the shop. But his greatest love, and what he considered his real work, was composition. He composed prolifically for the mandolin and guitar, turning out at one stage in his life compositions every fortnight, which were published in the Turin magazine *Il Mandolino*.

I love the fact that, like me, Sartori began his studying with the violin before graduating to the mandolin. I also learn that he taught violin privately and was interested and active in the education of young children; further connections between our lives. I am beginning to build a picture of his character.

We go onto other pieces. *'Non ti vedrò più'*: 'I will not see you any more', an elegy dedicated to his mother. *'Sorrisi'*: 'Smiles', a small *'serenata'*, a serenade, with the dedication *'Ai miei nipotini'*, which could refer to nephews and nieces but probably means grandchildren. *'Ai Bagni'*, another waltz with a title that translates as 'at the baths', presumably of the spa variety so popular in Italy, and is written for his three children. There are many personal dedications and the titles frequently record moments and people in the life of the composer. It is as if we are looking at Sartori's personal photograph album and experiencing the images as sound.

Sartori's music reflects the lyricism of Italian *bel canto*, combined with the dance music of Viennese tea-rooms. Sometimes I find it a little too syrupy and at other times I relax and enjoy its old-fashioned charm. The notes are all comfortably under the fingers and it is good fun to play.

I have a wonderful surprise when the Maestro presents me unexpectedly with a book, *Il Periodo d'Oro del Mandolino: The Golden Age of the Mandolin*. The book is a collection of nineteenth century Italian writings about the mandolin that are brought together and republished as one work under the editorship of my teacher, Ugo Orlandi. Sometime in the last two years, I've forgotten exactly when, the Maestro consulted me about the English translation of various excerpts. Now the book is published and there is a printed mention of my name, thanking me for my 'precious contribution'. The Maestro has also signed my book with his name and the date and a personal *'Grazie, per tutto!'*: 'Thank you, for everything!' It is a small token of appreciation, which I value enormously. It is both strange and fantastic to be acknowledged in an Italian book.

Deborah and I climb the steep stairs onto the luxury coach. We are accompanying the Brescian Mandolin and Guitar orchestra on a concert trip to Ala. Being from Piedmont, Deborah is not familiar with the members of the orchestra, but I have met them many times before, so I find myself introducing her to various people and telling her who is who. It is really lovely to be greeted by Talia, Anna, Fiorella, Lorella, and others with such genuine warmth. They always make me feel part of the crowd.

We leave the urban environment of Brescia by joining the autostrada that runs across the top of Italy, connecting Turin with Venice. We head towards Venice, sweeping through the open countryside of Lombardy and skirting the lower side of Lake Garda. Just before Verona, we change onto another motorway, heading north to Rovereto and Trento. It takes us parallel along the east side of Lake Garda and also follows the course of the River Adige. We pass signs for famous wine-growing regions; Bardolino, one of my favourite red wines, on the left and Valpolicella on the right. As we reach our destination, I am aware that we are making a considerable ascent. To the left is Mount Baldo and to the right are the Lessini Mountains.

We alight from the coach at Ala, a short walk from the historic centre. I breathe the thin sharp air. It is very cool and heavily scented with wood smoke. When we reach the narrow street at the side of the theatre, I can't help thinking that the character of the town is just like other mountain resorts I have been to. This isn't a ski resort, but I can imagine a sprinkling of snow and people milling around in their padded ski suits, woollen hats and snow boots. I am really excited by the transition from being in a city to, within a couple of hours, being in a mountain town on the way to the Austrian border. It is a completely different landscape and unforeseen treat. One of the things I love about my mandolin lessons is that I constantly get to see new locations that I would never have dreamt of visiting as a tourist.

Inside the *Teatro Giacomo Sartori,* preparations are in progress for the concert. It is being recorded for television and there are technicians with wires and cables. The concert doesn't start until a quarter to nine and there has been no opportunity to eat so far. Feeling hungry, I ascertain that we have time to pop out for a snack. Deborah and I, and Deborah's mum, who is also with us, decide to take a walk to see what we can find. Our investigation culminates in the only open bar. There are no sandwiches left, so Deborah and I stave off hunger with cappuccinos and chocolate-covered biscuits.

The Maestro has rehearsed a Sartori work with the two of us called '*Maliziosette*'. I am not sure if I like the title of the 'mischievous seven'. It can also mean 'malicious', but I feel certain that the composer didn't have that interpretation of the word in mind. It is dedicated to the female mandolinists of Ala. The Maestro has the idea that we should join the ladies of the orchestra for this unscheduled item that will be announced. We don't know when it will be announced, but I imagine it will be an encore item. However, the idea gets abandoned because the television cables make it impossible to add further chairs to the stage and I am relieved because I feel that I am not wearing the correct clothes. I didn't bring my concert dress to Italy. When the idea was sprung upon me, I didn't worry because I thought it was a relaxed concert, but I don't want to appear, even fleetingly, on television wearing clothes that don't blend.

The concert is a wonderful celebration, not only of Sartori's music – it is the fiftieth anniversary of his death – but also of other composers from his era such as Raffaele Calace and Hermann Ambrosius. Afterwards, we are invited to an adjoining room where an excellent supper is laid out for the orchestra and hangers-on like me. There is all manner of finger food. I feast on wedges of cold pizza, topped with olives, anchovies, capers and mushrooms. Feeling restored by the food, I chat with my friends from the orchestra and we drink freshly made espresso. There is a marvellous feeling of euphoria after the concert and I am caught up in it. I feel energised, animated and happy, just as if I had been playing with them.

iii

Backwards and forwards, I slip effortlessly between my Italian life and my English life.

In the beginning, I had wanted to play the mandolin more beautifully. This entailed studying the mandolin in its native country and required me to travel there to learn new skills, a different technique, in order to be able to play more beautifully. Then, after technique, there was the question of aesthetics: what is and what is not beautiful? This is a fundamental aspect of, and intrinsic to, Italian culture. I found myself not just making physical journeys to and around Italy, but also learning about and assimilating the culture. I thought I had gone to learn to play my instrument better and I ended up being changed profoundly.

I have refined further my already well-developed ideas about food, I have changed the way I dress to a more classical European style and I have made adjustments to harmonise the interior of my home. I move between the two languages, talking, reading, thinking, and even dreaming in a mixture of Italian and English. My garden has acquired pots of pelargoniums, herbs such as rosemary and even a fig tree. Everything about my existence is touched by Italy.

So absorbed am I in all things Italian that some friends quite genuinely think I will move to Italy permanently. Some joke that I have a secret Italian lover. They are mistaken. Others still think, quite wrongly, that I must be making a fortune, simply because of an assumption that frequent trips abroad equates with business and making money. I must be giving concerts and earning huge sums of money. But it is quite the reverse. I am making a great sacrifice in terms of money, energy and time, not to mention taking a risk by taking time out of my career in England and all this in order to achieve my objective of playing more beautifully.

There are a number of things troubling me, and in my third year of study, I realise that my journey is not just about music. Neither is it solely about the huge impact a different culture has had on both my music and my life. The journey is no longer a physical journey at all. Instead, it has become another journey, one in which I travel deep within. It is an interior journey, a private and intimate exploration.

Sometimes, people cannot understand what it is I am doing in Italy. I often find it best to say that I am doing research, which in a way is true but is also a bit misleading. By saying that I am researching, and I am finding out about the Italian method of playing and new repertoire, I give people something they can relate to. It is consistent with the status of a professional musician who has a Master's degree. However, to say I am starting all over again and relearning something in a different way seems incomprehensible in our materialistic society. People say, "but what are you are getting out of it?" I often hear myself saying that I will obtain a diploma, a certificate, or a piece of paper at the end to prove my proficiency as a mandolinist. This is easier, because people understand that I will get something. Some people think I am already proficient and don't understand the point of learning a foreign way of doing something. Many people miss the point altogether. I just have to do whatever is necessary to play more beautifully. Through music, by playing expressively and by teaching effectively, I touch the lives of other people. I have to do the best I can and I have to follow this path. I have to do this to be true to myself and to honour my spirit.

―⁌―

I am walking along the *Via del Santo*. At the end of my lesson, I told the Maestro that I had an important errand to run. He probably thinks I am shopping, but I am returning to the tomb of St Anthony. I have not seen it since my first visit to Padua many years ago. We were staying as a family in Venice and my son was very small, still being pushed in the buggy. Recently, I saw a documentary at home on television that highlighted the tomb of St Anthony as an important place of pilgrimage and the site of many healing miracles.

The shops of this street are filled with religious paraphernalia. There are all manner of statues, mostly of St Anthony, appropriately, and the Virgin Mary, as well as crucifixes, rosaries and icons. There is something for every purse and every taste. I notice a restaurant where we once had dinner. It doesn't seem to have changed much. In the *piazza* in front of the *Basilica di Sant'Antonio,* there are a number of souvenir stalls selling garish plastic statues of the Madonna and rosaries, as well as postcards and miniature wooden models of Pinocchio.

At the site of the tomb, I stand in the line of pilgrims waiting to pass and to touch the sarcophagus of St Anthony whilst saying a prayer. As we file slowly round, passing through the sumptuous chapel, I find myself touching the cold marble of the tomb with my fingers. Previously, I had been preoccupied with my thoughts, desires and prayers. Suddenly, my mind is completely blank. I cannot utter the words I want to. I cannot even form the words in my mind. My fingers slide over the silky stone. All I am aware of is being enveloped by a feeling of great peace and stillness. It is as if everything stops for a few seconds.

I place some paper money in a box and I choose a large candle, which I place on a pile to be lit at a future Mass in the Basilica. I hear the chanting of a priest celebrating a Mass in progress. The sung liturgy is evocative and timeless. I wish I could join them, but I have to return to the station to catch the train back to Bologna. The chanting haunts me all the way back to the station. I can still feel the moment at the tomb when I had the sense of momentarily connecting with eternity. I was not in the past and I was not in the future. I was in the moment and conscious of an overwhelming presence, a feeling of acceptance, of contentment.

iv

Just before Christmas, I find myself in Brescia whilst my son is far around the other side of the world in Brazil on a concert tour with his choir.

We have only just become used to the idea of my spending time in Italy whilst he is still at school in England. Now I am still in Europe, but he is in South America. Despite the thorough preparations and the elaborate security procedures in place, Brazil suffers from the tensions of great poverty and great wealth co-existing. I am worried. It is the nature of mothers to worry about their offspring. I try to focus on the wonderful opportunity he has, possibly a once-in-a-lifetime opportunity, to see a new and exotic country.

This month, I make a new friend from another faraway place. She is called Miki and she has come from Japan to live in Italy, whilst studying the mandolin at Padua.

On Saturday, I attend another Sartori concert given again by the Mandolin and Guitar Orchestra *'Città di Brescia'* – this time at the *Teatro Colonna* in Brescia. Afterwards, Talia, Giovanna, another non-musician friend of Giovanna's and I all go for a pizza.

Talia works in the family-run music shop in Brescia. She is wonderful at keeping an extensive stock of mandolin music. I am always popping in to look through to see if there is anything I haven't got and she always has time for a chat.

This evening Talia and I are quite hungry, but Giovanna and her friend are less so. They decide to share a pizza. When the waiter comes to take our order, we ask for three pizzas and an extra plate and drinks. The waiter doesn't bat an eyelid. In fact, he is most obliging. I have seen this before in Italy. It is so normal to provide whatever the customer requires in a restaurant. Often a request to remove or add an item to a dish, or to provide a simple basic dish not on the menu, such as *ragù* for a child, is met with pleasure and without fuss. In England, many restaurants are over anxious to press unwanted food on you in an effort to make more money. Cooking something that doesn't appear on the menu is unheard of. This probably has something to do with a deep cultural difference. Until recently, eating out in a restaurant in England has been seen as something of a luxury – a treat, rather than a necessity.

Travelling affords me time to myself. I have time to reflect on life and its meaning. I am enormously fascinated by this subject. It is a fascination that goes back to my infant years. I remember my maternal grandmother telling me at a very tender age that I was 'philosophical'. I have never been philosophical in a dry, academic sense though. It is much more practical, like my teaching. I want to know how the life process works and how we can achieve success easily and more effectively.

Like everyone else, I want to be happy, and on the whole I am happy and content. Through music, I have achieved enormous pleasure and joy. Practising privately in the seclusion of one's own room can be meditative, therapeutic, restorative, healing. Teaching is deeply satisfying because it is possible to communicate all of this to my pupils. I watch them grow in confidence and joy as they progress, knowing that I am enabling them in the process.

Performance is quite different. It is risky, precarious and unpredictable. There are great highs and great lows: elation when things go well, and post mortems, guilt, blame, anger and sadness when things go badly. Performance can be competitive, open to analysis and therefore criticism and judgement, rather than just being and celebrating life.

The Maestro has a sensible didactic approach. He says we should practise technique by itself and then we should play music. When we play music, we should think about the musical interpretation only, enjoying the music for itself, and forget about technique. In other words, it is no use worrying about my right wrist movement whilst I am trying to make the music sing. It is confusing to think about both things at once. Eventually the technique will become second nature and it will just happen, leaving the mind free to concentrate on art, on making the music sound beautiful.

However, it is sometimes difficult to achieve. In the lesson, anxious to please, I find myself conscious of the right hand and distracted from my art.

I start work today on the first of six partitas by Filippo Sauli. I am working from a newly published edition, in which my teacher has transcribed the partitas. The first partita is in D minor, which after G minor is my favourite key. I sometimes worry that I adore the melancholy of minor keys. I hope it doesn't mean that I am a sad person. I just find they resonate with me. They are so expressive, reflecting not just sadness and suffering but also tenderness, intimacy and a sense of spirituality.

I also love the names of the Baroque dance movements that make up this suite: *Allemanda, Sarabanda, Corrente, Bourée, Giga, Minuetto*. The *Sarabanda*, my preferred dance, is to be played lightly. Apparently, I play it too heavily. Also, I have to play the *Corrente*, the *Giga* and the *Minuetto* much faster. I hope I will be able to manage this next month.

V

Occhiali da Sole. Sunglasses.

This is our first day in Cavalese and I am engaged in buying yet another pair of sunglasses. This time they are for my son, who has just returned from the *piste*. After an awkward moment skiing, he fell over and crushed the glasses in his jacket pocket. I have to sort out the problem as I am the 'language expert'. It is my main function to be useful as an interpreter.

I have long given up any hope of finding pleasure in skiing. The boots feel like lead and I am afraid of injury to my hands. I am happy pottering around the town, window shopping and stopping for a leisurely *cioccolata con panna*, hot chocolate with cream. When I have had sufficient of these pleasures, I return to the hotel for a rest or a spot of undisturbed practice. I am quite happy during the day being left in peace, knowing that my husband and son, who are always energetic and fidgety, are being occupied by something they enjoy. In the evening, we come together for delicious food and a glass or two of local wine. It is an excellent arrangement.

This week I plan to go to Padua for my lesson on Wednesday, since Monday, being January 6th, is a public holiday. Epiphany, or Twelfth Night, celebrates the successful conclusion of the journey of the Magi and brings the Christmas festivities to an end. On this day, many Italian children receive presents from *Befana* – a kindly witch.

I locate the only travel agency in Cavalese by looking through the *Yellow Pages* and I make an early visit only to find it shut for the holiday. On Tuesday, I go first thing to ask about trains to Padua. There is a connecting bus from Cavalese to the nearest station, but I need to arrange my train ticket in advance. It seems that I am able to take a train, originating from Bolzano, from Egna-Ora to Verona, where I will have to change for the train to Padua.

The helpful young lady behind the counter is a little flummoxed when I tell her that I want to go tomorrow. She speaks with her colleague and then she comes back to talk to me. I elucidate the importance of my trip to Padua and the difficulty I had in coming any earlier since they were closed for the holiday. The young lady speaks again with her colleague. After some deliberation, she tells me that if I return at six-thirty this evening they will make sure they have the ticket ready. The agency usually requires a day or two's notice to make a booking. I hadn't appreciated how small Cavalese is. The agency is a branch of a bigger organisation with the main office elsewhere. People come to Cavalese for skiing holidays in winter and rarely require assistance to travel to other towns. Normally, once they are stationed in the mountains, they stay there.

During the early evening, we join the exodus into the streets for the customary *passeggiata* before dinner. It doesn't seem to matter that it is dark and icy cold. The town is in festive spirit. Tree skeletons sparkle with pinpricks of white light. Inside the stable of the life-size nativity scene, the three kings are paying homage to baby Jesus. Outside the *presepio*, in the snow-covered sunken garden, there are other visitors dressed in local period costumes and bearing gifts. The female pastoral figures wear long skirts, scarves and shawls. They are at the other end of the social scale from the kings. The rustic theme is continued in the building, which is adjacent and at right angles to the stable. It is decorated with dangling sheaves of wheat and maize.

Nearby, the street is offered a magnificent display of art. The illuminated exterior of the *Palazzo della Communità* is covered in colourful frescoes. Once the palace of the bishops who held the power base of the practically autonomous *Val di Fiemme,* it is still a symbol of power and authority. Today, local affairs are predominantly run from this building.

I take a few photographs of the *presepio*, the *Palazzo* and the majestic *campanile*, which is also dramatically lit up. I am using a tiny discreet camera that uses advanced film. A Christmas present, it is supposed to be the latest in technology and almost idiot proof. Despite the minimum of fuss in preparing to take a picture and the miniature size of the machine, I still feel self-conscious and uncomfortable taking photographs. It is a new experience for me, trying to capture moments of interest and importance. Whether I will manage to distil the essence of a feeling or an emotion is another matter. Here, I am trying to catch something of the atmosphere that will remind me and set off a chain of thoughts. I am so much more at ease with music and words that I am not convinced that this will be anything other than an occasional experience.

At a quarter to six in the morning, I leave the Hotel St Valiér by an emergency exit door in one of the recreational rooms. None of the staff are on duty yet and I arranged with the headwaiter yesterday that I would leave by this door as the front entrance is still locked from the night. I walk through the garden and around the side of the building to reach the road running at the front of the hotel. I turn right and walk towards the bus station. It takes only a few minutes, but it is eerily quiet. The only sound is my feet crunching the snow underfoot. I tread carefully, deliberately, but with a new confidence. No longer am I afraid of sliding and slipping, falling and hurting myself. I always used to concentrate on what might go wrong and I was terrorised by a walk in the snow. Now, instead of thinking about the possible icy patches, I focus on placing each foot firmly and I imagine it sticking there. Thinking positively seems to influence my feet. I feel secure and I am secure.

The bus station is deserted. I am alone and it is dark and silent. I look around uneasily. It could be a set in a thriller film. It could be the scene of one of my anxiety dreams. I try to think of how the bus will look when it comes. I was expecting it to be parked here already. I hear the murmur of an engine. It isn't a bus. It is a dark saloon car. It stops. I feel very uneasy. The passenger door at the front opens gingerly. My heart races. A teenage girl wearing headphones and carrying a rucksack slowly emerges. I begin to feel calmer. A bus arrives, but it isn't my bus. I begin to feel anxious again. I am also feeling quite cold. Another bus arrives. This time, it is my bus.

The bus is really a coach. Inside, it is warm and comfortable. I sink into the generous seat. The descent down the mountain to the valley where the nearest local train station is takes about an hour. The bus driver has the radio on softly. It is a strange sensation being driven in comfort around the slow bends which wind though snow-laden woods, whilst listening to Italian songs and chatter on the radio. The skiers, Italian and foreigners alike, are not yet out on the slopes and I am slipping into the everyday routine of Italian life – only this time, I am commuting from the most extreme rural perspective I have witnessed so far.

Occasionally the bus stops and people climb up the stairs at the front to board. There is always the exchange of some greeting with the driver. "*Buon giorno.*" "*Ciao.*" "*Salve.*" Some of them are young and obviously on the way to school. Sometimes we stop and we are surrounded only by the woods, and people seem to appear from behind the trees. I am not sure where their homes are. Some must have a long walk to the bus stop.

In the valley, we are on the flat again, but I am mystified at first by all the name signs. I am looking for the station of Egna-Ora, but I see signs for Ora-Auer and Egna-Neumarkt. We are in Trentino – Alto Adige, Sud Tirol, and the Austrian influence is everywhere. All the signs display the German equivalent. In Italian, Egna and Ora are two different places, but the train station is positioned between them and is, therefore, called Egna-Ora. However, the German equivalent would be Neumarkt-Auer. With all these possibilities, I am confused and I check with another passenger to see whether we have arrived at the station I require. I am told that we are just five minutes away.

At the station, shortly after seven, the ticket office is closed and there are no staff to be seen. I feel in my pocket for my ticket, checking I have it safely. I am glad that I arranged it in advance. I wait till almost the last minute before I leave the relative warmth and shelter of the station building. On the platform it is bitterly cold and I hear German being spoken by a family standing nearby. Everyone else looks dressed for business.

The journey to the Veneto takes us through the stations of Trento, Rovereto and Ala. I look eagerly out to view the winter landscape of Sartori's life.

At Verona, I have just missed the Venice train that will take me to Padua and I have to wait almost an hour for the next one. This is the problem with travelling. A journey may theoretically only take a certain number of hours, but all the extra time waiting for connections adds to the total journey time. I do not arrive at Padua until midday. My journey has taken approximately six hours.

At the *Conservatorio,* the Maestro and the other pupils are all amused to hear of my journey this time. My account is prefaced by the fact that I did not even fly to Italy. I flew instead to neighbouring Austria. From Innsbruck, I transferred by coach to Italy and the last leg of my journey to Cavalese was undertaken by taxi. I look around and watch the smiles and looks of incredulity as I explain that I have travelled today from a ski resort in the mountains. This time, it was expedient to combine a family holiday with the mandolin lesson. I have the impression that they think I am quite a character. Maybe I am.

I enjoy very much playing the Sauli partita and I am given the next one, in F major, to prepare for the next month. After only three hours in the class, I have to make my excuses and begin the return journey to the mountains.

It is a very long and tiring journey home. I read a bit. From Verona, I close my eyes and try to rest. A female doctor sitting opposite is interrupted by her mobile telephone. I hear her giving advice about a sick child. The phone is cut off and she waits a bit before continuing her conversation. Why do return journeys drag so? This morning I was so excited to be going to the *Conservatorio* and now I can't wait to get home.

At Egna-Ora, I have half an hour to wait for the bus and the lacerating cold is unbearable. There are no refreshments at the station, which is isolated, but a small road leads into the station and there are a few buildings at the beginning. One is a bar and I order a cappuccino. It is the wrong time of day, mid-evening, for a cappuccino, but I am frozen and I need a warm milky drink. I mention this to the lady behind the counter and she is most hospitable. I sit down and read the local paper provided, whilst I drink slowly to while away the time and keep warm.

When I finally reach my hotel at just after nine, the evening meal has finished. The headwaiter has kindly saved me a plate of cold meats, cheeses, grilled vegetables, salad and bread, together with some wine. I am grateful for this feast. I sit in the empty restaurant with my family, sharing the day's events whilst I hungrily devour my supper. I am absolutely exhausted and it is no time before I am soundly asleep.

vi

On the train to Padua, I am sitting opposite Ugo in a compartment of six seats. We met on the platform at Brescia whilst we were waiting for the train.

Ugo is very chatty this morning, asking me lots of questions about the mandolin scene in England. I don't feel completely awake yet for detailed conversation. Suddenly he stands up and takes down his briefcase from the overhead luggage rack. He rummages around inside the case for a moment and takes out a booklet.

"Have you seen this before?" he asks me.

"No," I tell him, "I know of this and strangely I have been trying to trace it."

The booklet, a photocopy of the out-of-print original, is entitled *Mandolin Memories* by Samuel Adelstein – a nineteenth century American mandolinist. I know this document is of interest to me, but I'm not exactly sure why.

"*Leggi, leggi,*" Ugo encourages. Read it, read it.

I settle back in my seat and begin.

The language is old-fashioned, sometimes rambling and a little clumsy to my twentieth century ears, sometimes beautifully crafted and exquisitely evoking the charm of a long-forgotten era. The text rumbles along, describing the rise in popularity of the mandolin in America during the close of the nineteenth century. Previously the mandolin had been almost unknown outside its native country, Italy, and even then it had been dormant for some time.

In fact, Adelstein is describing the renaissance, the first renaissance, of the mandolin. He doesn't mention that during the Baroque period it had enjoyed great popularity, which had extended far beyond Italy to other important European cultural centres: Paris, Stockholm, London and so on. This has all become known only recently as part of current research undertaken by mandolinists and musicologists during the last twenty years. I am part of a second renaissance of the mandolin, which is happening now and taking place a hundred years after the first.

I look out of the window. We are edging along the southern shore of Lake Garda. The late winter sun shines brilliantly. I love the houses: blocks randomly stacked together in ice cream colours of strawberry, pistachio and lemon, and sensuous villas in the pale creamy yellow of old ivory. I try to take in and hold every detail; the ravishing light, the water shimmering and its colour changing like mother-of-pearl. The water is always a perpetual source of fascination to me. I could stay here and watch forever; the whole scene is so ineffably beautiful.

My eyes return to the text and I am startled by two sentences:

> *'From the beginning the writer had applied the down and up bow of the violin to the mechanism of the plectrum movement on the mandolin. Not being satisfied with the result of this self-taught style of playing, and at that time there being no one of acknowledged authority on this most important point (of which*

more will be said later), the writer determined to go to Italy, the home of all true knowledge pertaining the mandolin.'

So, here is the connection. Here is the importance. History repeats itself. Adelstein was originally a violinist and travelled to Italy in 1890, just over a hundred years ago, in order to find out more about how the mandolin should be played. He travelled all the way from America, making his way to Italy via Paris. In Italy, he met the leading mandolinists of the day, including Carlo Munier and Raffaele Calace. He attended their concerts and studied under their supervision. Of these great exponents, Adelstein says that they *'were astonished and expressed surprise that one should come so far for instruction.'* How many times have I heard the other students at Padua say exactly the same thing?

Here I am walking in the footprints of Samuel Adelstein.

Ugo tells me that he is editing a book in which *Mandolin Memories* will be republished along with two translations of it, one in Italian and the other in French. The Italian version has been translated by my friend Giovanna and the French version by Didier Le Roux, who I met on my very first trip to Brescia. Ugo has written a preface to this book and he has a special task that he would like me to undertake. He would like me to translate the preface from Italian to English.

I am silent for a moment. I am both thrilled and daunted by the prospect. It is yet another connection. I am walking in Samuel's footsteps. I have no option other than to accept the task.

'*A Night in Tunisia*'.

No, I have not suddenly been transported across the Mediterranean Sea to the shores of North Africa. I am joining the Mandolin and Guitar Orchestra for the Monday rehearsal and we are playing jazz tonight. We are trying a Papparelli/ 'Dizzy' Gillespie number called '*A Night in Tunisia*'.

Claudio Mandonico, the conductor, looks up and greets me. He is always pleased to see me, even if I am the most infrequent attendant of rehearsals. The orchestra meets twice a week to rehearse and I only visit when I am in Brescia.

This evening is strangely nostalgic. We are upstairs in the room we rehearsed in on my first ever visit. I ask why we are using this room and it soon becomes obvious. The extra percussion instruments required are already set up here.

I am tired from an exacting day in the mandolin class and also from the journey to and from Padua. Now I am sitting next to Miki, Giovanna is sitting further forward, and I am struggling with crazy rhythms and a style I am not used to. Curiously, though, instead of becoming exhausted, I seem to be growing more and more animated as each moment passes.

I am quickly intoxicated by the repetitive quirky rhythms. They swing and dance provocatively around the same spot. The hollow sound of a traditional drum echoes behind me. A modern drum kit increases the tension. All these elements combine to generate infectious energy, raw and urgent.

―♪

On the commuter train from Brescia to Milan, I have a sticky moment. I take my ticket from my bag in preparation for the ticket inspector. Ticket inspectors invariably visit, usually several times in a journey. I place the ticket in my pocket, but as I do so, I realise that my return ticket to Milan has been validated twice. I remember putting it in the punch machine this morning at Brescia station. I look closer and notice that the other hole with time, date and place refers to Padua, yesterday, late afternoon.

I look in disbelief. I can't believe I have made a mistake. I thought I was so organised this time buying a return ticket for Milan to avoid queuing at Brescia station when I returned. I flick though the other bits of paper in my handbag. The return ticket to Padua is unmarked. There is definitely no hole, no stamp. Obviously, I validated the wrong ticket yesterday.

I take a moment to consider my predicament. I devise two plans. The first is that I will erase all knowledge of what has happened from my mind and act as if nothing has happened. The inspector, despite it being unlikely, might overlook the other marking on the ticket.

The second plan is that if he or she notices, I will act surprised and explain the truth, as if I am only just becoming aware of the mistake. If I have to pay the fine, so be it.

To my absolute delight, the ticket inspector takes my ticket, punches it, and with glazed eyes returns it with a '*grazie signora*'. I am relieved not to be the centre of conflict and attention in my carriage. I am grateful that I am not a protagonist in the kind of drama I have seen so often before.

In Milan, I have the whole day free until mid-afternoon, a rare treat, and I intend to make the most of this opportunity. Ugo has told me of some interesting early mandolins in two different museums. I take my mandolin and overnight bag to the left-luggage office, taking care to remove my umbrella from my bag as it is raining. Then, I head for the newspaper stand, where I purchase a map and some tickets for the *metropolitana* – the underground train. I spend five minutes sitting down in the waiting room whilst I study the map and memorise the salient details. I don't want to wander around looking like a lost tourist. I then fold the map up and put it in my pocket and make for the *metropolitana*.

As I approach the entrance of the *metropolitana* at nine o'clock in the morning, I am met with a terrible disappointment. Officials are closing the entrance with metal shutters. For the second time this morning, I stare in disbelief. I ask an official what is happening. Apparently, the *metropolitana* is having a strike and no one seems to know when services will be resumed. I walk back to the waiting room upstairs in the mainline station and have another look at my map. I have such a long stretch of time before me that I have to press on with my plan. I noticed that there were hundreds of disgruntled commuters waiting for buses and taxis outside the station. My only realistic option is to walk.

I study the map carefully and check the position of the stations before the *Teatro alla Scala*, Milan's famous opera house. On the number three line from the Central Station, the stops are *Republica*, *Turati* and *Monte Napoleone*. There seems to be an almost direct overground route, with just a slight twist to the left and then to the right in the middle, between here and the opera house. It doesn't look too difficult and it doesn't look too far on the map, although maps can be deceptive. If the distance between *Milanese* stations is roughly the same as the distance between London tube stations, then I have to walk perhaps a distance equivalent to the length of Oxford Street. After Tottenham Court Road station, there are three stops: Oxford Circus, Bond Street and Marble Arch. It seems feasible. I put up my umbrella and set out into the inclement weather, heading towards Milan's historical centre.

I have never seen the heart of Milan, even though I am frequently moving through the city. I often fly to Linate airport and take a bus to the station. It is a very convenient service, running frequently and taking only twenty minutes between the airport and the station. I see the suburbs and unknown Milan. I see old-fashioned trams and interesting shops. I always notice a street called *Via Stradivari* as we approach the station from the north-east of the city. I think it is wonderful to have a road named after a violinmaker.

Standing in front of La Scala, Milan, I feel humbled. This is an important moment in my journey. All my life I have heard of the prestigious reputation of La Scala, one of the great opera houses of the world. My friend, Maria Cleofe Miotti, plays mandolin in performances of Prokoviev's *Romeo and Juliet*, as does Dorina Frati who was so hospitable to me on my first solo visit to Italy. And I feel another sense of connection because I sometimes play for the same ballet in London at the Royal Opera House, Covent Garden – another of the world's great opera houses.

I enter the *Museo Teatrale della Scala*, The Theatrical Museum of the Scala, by a door on the left of the main façade. As I buy a ticket, I am warned that the theatre itself is closed for a rehearsal. The price of admission to the museum normally includes a peek at the opulent splendour of the interior. I am not bothered by this news because I have come specifically to see the mandolins in the museum collection.

I wander through the glass cases, looking at scores, conductor's batons, pictures and other memorabilia. I see a charming eighteenth century porcelain figurine of a mandolinist.

I see an early flute and various Baroque keyboard instruments, but I see no sign of the mandolins. I check carefully as I return through the displays to make sure that I haven't missed anything accidentally in my excitement.

At the custodian's desk by the exit, I feel quite let down. Clearly there are no mandolins, but I feel that Ugo wouldn't have given me incorrect information. In the past I probably would have accepted the situation and departed, puzzled and frustrated. Today, something stirs within me. I find myself mentioning the mandolins to the custodian. I tell him that I had understood that the museum contained a collection of early mandolins. I tell him that I was advised by Maestro Ugo Orlandi of the *Conservatorio* at Padua to visit the museum and that it was a matter of some urgency because I have a flight to London that I must take later in the day.

All at once, the custodian is taking headed notepaper from the drawer in his desk and he starts to write a letter. He tells me that the mandolins have been moved to the nearby *Palazzo Clerici*, just a few minutes' walk away. He says that if I take the letter with me and present it to the reception, I will be allowed to see the mandolins that are of such interest to me. I thank him profusely, hardly believing what has taken place. In a split second, I summoned up the confidence and language to pursue what I wanted, and against the odds a door has been, quite literally, opened for me. So many times in Italy, what seems impossible suddenly becomes possible.

At the *Palazzo Clerici,* I walk up the steps into a building which seems to be mostly for business. I hand over my letter and I am asked to give up my coat and umbrella. A uniformed security officer carrying a huge bunch of heavy keys is summonsed and he takes me up in the lift to a higher floor. He unlocks the door of a huge white room housing various glass cases. Then he hovers at the door whilst I have my own private viewing of the mandolins. I have the impression that the collection is not quite ready for the pubic and I feel enormously privileged to have this opportunity to view it.

Outside in the rain again, I feel a huge sense of achievement at having found the mandolins. I abandon the idea of visiting the instrument collection at the *Castello Sforzesco* as the custodian at La Scala museum informed me that the castle was closed for restoration. He has saved me an unnecessary walk. Instead, I relax by going to the *Duomo*.

The cathedral is the largest and most complex Gothic construction in Italy. It has 135 spires that stretch towards heaven like stalagmites. It is hard to comprehend the time that skilled craftsmen have laboured to produce such an intricate structure. It is eternally incomplete. My guidebook explains that after six centuries it is still not really finished, owing to the continuing maintenance and restoration required.

I stroll through the *Galleria Vittorio Emanuele*, an impressive arcade, just off the *Piazza del Duomo*. It is shaped in the form of a cross with a glass dome over the central octagon. The high vaulted roof and the dome, both constructed of metal and glass, afford light and space. The patterned tile floor and the mosaic pictures in the lunettes of the octagon give a richly furnished feel to this covered stretch of beautiful shops and smart restaurants. The arcade, with its many coffee houses, has a reputation as a meeting place for artists, scholars and politicians. No wonder it has been dubbed the 'sitting room of Milan'.

I walk on through the *Piazza della Scala* and back the way I came along the *Via Manzoni*. At the *Piazza Cavour,* I stop at a Brek restaurant that I had noticed earlier on my way to the centre. I have a nourishing lunch of pasta with *zucca*, pumpkin and *prosciutto di speck* – an unusual but excellent combination.

A quick detour though the public gardens on the opposite side of the *piazza* brings me almost to the next *piazza*, the *Piazza della Republica*. From here, after a delicate negotiation of the tramlines, it is just a ten-minute walk in a straight line to the entrance of the Central Station. I shall collect my belongings and wait for the bus to the airport.

vii

Work has begun on my Baroque mandolin.

I suppose, in a sense, work begun on the first day that I met Chris with the idea that it might be possible. After that, we found it difficult to arrange an appointment to return to see the instrument at the Royal College of Music. They were very busy with numerous enquiries and the arrival of computers. Instead, we managed to secure an appointment to view a similar instrument in the Victoria and Albert Museum. We were able to view the instrument in an office away from the public viewing area, and we were allowed to take both measurements and photographs.

In the weeks that followed, Chris phoned me saying that some of the detail of the decoration hadn't come out well enough in the photographs. The V and A Museum were unable to provide a further viewing as they too were installing new computers and now lacked the space. There seemed to be only one course of action open to me. I returned to the museum's public gallery on three successive occasions, the first two with my spouse, in order to take further photographs. With my husband's state-of-the-art photographic equipment, we had a good chance of obtaining photographs without reflection caused by lighting and the glass case surrounding the exhibit. Unfortunately, not one photograph was good enough.

By the third and last visit, I was fed up and struggling with negative thoughts that my idea to have an early mandolin wasn't going to materialise. Alone, I made a hasty visit to the musical instrument collection late one Saturday afternoon in early spring, with my idiot-proof camera in my pocket.

Furtively, I removed the camera from my pocket and quickly, guiltily took the required photographs. I am not really sure if one is supposed to take photographs of exhibits, although tourists do it all the time. Nevertheless, I felt I was only trying to recapture the image that we had had permission to capture previously and had failed to achieve. I tried to focus on the idea that, despite it being unlikely, the photograph would somehow be good enough to be useful to the mandolin-maker.

Outside my kitchen, the fig tree is covered in green buds. I am filled with childlike wonder that what looked like a dead twig last week is now alive and growing. Inside, I feverishly unpack my new photographs from their box and arrange them on the long table in the breakfast room. I stand back and take a deep breath. Somehow, the photographs look as if they might be good enough.

viii

The Alsatian held on a lead by an armed officer ignores my mandolin case and bag. There is nothing to sniff at. I walk unimpeded through the *dogana*, the customs, at Marco Polo airport. The Venetian light is bright and the warm air is humid and body hugging. It is wonderful to be back.

I am thinking carefully about what I have to do. I need to purchase a bus ticket for Treviso and when I have found out the time of my arrival, I must phone Giovanna's parents so that they can meet me. I am visiting Treviso for the first time, so I am a little anxious.

"Frances."

Someone is calling my name. I look up automatically, but without thinking that it refers to me. I realise that I am looking into the face of Giovanna's father. He smiles and I smile in recognition at the same time; we are both pleased to see each other. I wasn't expecting him to collect me, so it is a lovely surprise and a great relief.

As we walk to the car, he introduces me to a family friend, a young lady in her twenties, who is studying English and has come along for the ride and a bit of English conversation practice. I am more than happy to oblige.

I am always being looked after in Italy. The mums are especially concerned with nourishment. On one occasion, Marco's mother pulled a homemade frozen lasagne out of her freezer, at the last moment before my departure, to save me having to cook after a tiring journey when I returned home. Another time Ette's mum pressed a jar of her own *passato* into my hand, so that I could cook my son's supper easily on my return. So many little acts of kindness.

When it is necessary, Italian families are very good at pulling together and rallying round. Once, I had arrived at Brescia station and was unable to make contact with Giovanna by phone. I just kept getting the *segretaria telefonica*, the answering machine. On the third try, I heard her father's voice. He had just popped into her new flat to collect some post. He gave me the phone number of Giovanna's brother and told me to ring it. When I did, immediately afterwards, Giovanna's mother knew of my predicament, as if by telepathy, and told me that she and her son were coming directly to the station to collect me. I found out that Giovanna and I had our wires crossed and I was expected on the following day. The family gave me supper and looked after me until Giovanna was able to pick me up.

After lunch and a little rest, I am off to explore the sights of Treviso with Giovanna's parents. We walk past the site of the Fish Market and into the *Piazza dei Signori*, the heart of the city. Here many people are gathering to meet friends, to do a little shopping and to take the customary *passeggiata*. We continue our *passeggiata* viewing the Venetian influence, canals, narrow streets, over hanging houses, some with exterior frescos. Apparently, half the city was lost in bombing during the Second World War. At the beautiful *Porta San Tomaso,* Giovanna's father shows me the heads of the winged lion, the symbol of Venetian dominance. He points out a faint crack at each neck. This, he says, is because the heads were damaged during the occupation in the war. They have since been restored.

At six o'clock, we conclude the sightseeing by attending Mass at the Duomo, a Venetian Romanesque cathedral dating from the twelfth century. I take great pleasure in the tranquillity of this quiet hour of ritual and prayer. The Saturday evening Mass counts as an attendance for the following day and is very popular with those who need or wish to have the whole Sunday free.

A blackbird is singing on the horse chestnut tree outside my balcony window. I am busy practising another Sauli partita, this time in G minor. I am glad of the bird's company. I have always loved the sound of birdsong. When I was sick as a small child, I would lay in bed listening intently to the birds and their music. It was an endless source of delight and fascination to me. As I grew older, I used to make my own little manuscript books and I tried to notate the sound that they made. For a while, the blackbird and I make music together.

Outside, the vegetation is alive and growing prolifically. The plants are always a few weeks, sometimes as much as a month, ahead of the same plants in England. It feels like summer to me, but it is only April. Yesterday we managed to squeeze in a quick visit to Giovanna's aunt, her mother's sister. She lives in the country just outside of Treviso. It is only ten minutes in the car, but suddenly I found myself walking amongst the lettuce and tomato plants, and observing how advanced everything was in comparison to our allotment at home. A short while before, we had been in the city centre. One of the things I have noticed about Italy is a greater connection between town and country. I remember seeing once, in a Tuscan market town, a lorry completely laden with artichokes for sale. It is quite normal for a farmer to bring for sale just one type of vegetable or fruit – the one that is currently in season. And so many people who have their own piece of garden devote a part to growing vegetables, salad items and herbs, and everyone with enough room has their own vine. All this reinforces the sense of season and the rhythm of nature.

I have also seen that in the most remote hilltop town in Umbria or Tuscany, it is possible to find a small clothes shop selling stylish, if basic and practical, garments. And the food shops sell the best quality produce, together with local specialities that we might consider a gourmet treat if bought in some smart London delicatessen. Even in the country, it is possible to buy specialist goods of high quality. And everywhere, it is easy to find something good to eat, in the most isolated of places, in the most unpromising locations. A sense of the land, a sense of nature, intermingles comfortably with the sophistication of culture and an urban environment. It is reflected everywhere in art and architecture: the bucolic fresco on an exterior wall, the mouth-watering bunch of grapes dangling in the decoration of a building and carved from stone.

⁓

In Padua, the Maestro is very keen that I should take part in the *saggio* next month – the end-of-year recital given by the students of the *Conservatorio*. He hands me a copy of the music we are going to play, '*Tramonto*' by Raffaele Calace. I am really flattered to see that my part is for the first mandolins. '*Tramonto*' translates as 'Sunset' and is a descriptive piece for a plectrum quintet with the addition of flute, oboe and piano. The quintet comprises first and second mandolins, mandola, mandolincello (or *liuto*), which is the mandolin equivalent of the cello, and the mandolone (or *arciliuto*), the mandolin equivalent of the double bass.

We spend some time rehearsing the piece and I feel so happy that I am able to make the notes sing and breathe with an even tremolo. Today, I know that I am among equals. I know that my tremolo is good enough and I play with a wonderful confidence. The notes soar up high, and higher still. Sometimes they are full of emotional intensity and other times they are pure and ethereal. It is soul-nourishing food.

⁓

In London, I have some engagements playing the mandolin again in *Otello* at the Royal Opera House. It is strange being a professional player in one country one moment and a music student in another country the next. But I am grateful for a new sense of ease in my playing. I don't wonder nervously whether the tremolo will be wobbly and unsteady. I just do it. It is just there.

I always find it hard to switch off after I have been playing professionally. It is difficult to go home on the tube after the opera and just go to sleep. Adrenalin pulsates around my body and I feel energised. To relax, I have been reading a facsimile edition of the journal of Dr Charles Burney's tour through Italy. It makes excellent bedtime reading. He meets so many interesting characters in his travels and describes both the encounters and the music with such attention to detail that it is easy to imagine actually being there. The language is so graceful and harmonious that it is a joy to read, both for its sound as well as its content.

I find several references to the mandolin and one in particular that astonishes me. Burney describes an impromptu concert for a famous castrato, Luini Bonetto, staying at the same inn as him in Brescia. He says:

'He is a native of Brescia; was welcomed home by a band of music, at the inn, the night of his arrival, and by another the night before his and my departure, consisting of two violins, a mandoline, french horn, trumpet, and violincello; and, though in the dark, they played long concertos, with solo parts for the mandoline. I was surprised at the memory of these performers; in short, it was excellent street music, and such as we are not accustomed to; but ours is not a climate for serenades. (Thursday, July 26th 1770)'[1]

So the tradition of mandolin music in Brescia goes back two centuries before my visits there and a century before Samuel Adelstein's voyage to Italy. And we have evidence, an eyewitness account, that it was of the highest quality. Mandolin concertos played from memory. I wonder which ones they were or if they were concertos that have now been completely lost. I also wonder about the variety of instruments in the ensemble. The idea of two brass instruments consorting with a mandolin seems preposterous. Then, I remember the Renaissance concert I attended in Brescia last year – the programme being a mixture of pieces for brass instruments and pieces for mandolin. Perhaps they can exist alongside each other.

It seems extraordinary to me that an Englishman should travel so far, so long ago, when travel was an even more arduous exercise than it is now, to learn about music in Italy. And that he should visit a city that I have become so familiar with and find there an exceptional performance by a mandolinist is even more remarkable. History repeats itself time and time again: Burney, Adelstein, myself. It is as if I am standing with two mirrors either side of me and, as I look into one, I see my image repeating itself into infinity. Who was there before Burney?

ix

On the motorway heading in the direction of *La Serenissima*, the strains of '*A Night in Tunisia*' and other familiar jazzy numbers come from the car speakers. I remember the rehearsal in which we practised these pieces three months ago. Ugo takes his right hand from the wheel and gives me the cover of the new CD. It is entitled '*Musica per un Momento*', 'Music for a Moment', and is dedicated to the memory of Lorenzo Bianchi who tragically died prematurely last year. An active member of the Brescia Mandolin and Guitar Orchestra, he was distinguished by being the first student ever at the mandolin course in Padua when it was initiated in the mid-seventies with Giuseppe Anedda as the Maestro.

I think of a photograph I have at home – my own memory of Lorenzo. He was playing the mandola after the rehearsal of the orchestra had finished. He had been interested in the nature and details of my visit. He didn't seem to think that it was so crazy to be travelling such a long distance to find out about mandolin playing. I asked him and some others if they would mind if I took some casual pictures. It was one of my early trips before my formal study at Padua. I nurse my memory for a while, before being jogged back to the moment by the start of '*Tramonto*'.

'*Tramonto*' is the final track and we listen intently in preparation for our performance today at the *saggio*. We listen repeatedly to the same track, mentally rehearsing our playing. It is only mid-morning but I am troubled by the sun. Despite air conditioning in the car and my *occhiali da sole,* I find little protection from the heat. The bleaching light of the sun, unremitting and relentless, scorches my forearm through the window. I place my cotton cardigan over my raw skin to prevent further injury.

I look at the final pages of the CD booklet. It lists members of Lorenzo's family, friends and musical colleagues. I find the names of my mandolin friends. All my friends and acquaintances are here. They have contributed by playing in the recording. I am moved by this expression of love, this fitting way to honour the life of Lorenzo B.

—⁂—

'Click'.

Deborah has taken a picture with my camera of me standing in the corridor behind the auditorium of the *Conservatorio*. The moment is captured: the black understated jacket and trousers, me playing a few notes, in a relaxed posture. We are well rehearsed and now we are looking forward to our turn in the concert. I want some more tangible evidence of my playing in Italy, to nudge my memory in years to come. My enthusiasm takes me outside into the courtyard, where the Maestro is smoking and talking to three of the male students. I want to take a group picture but Deborah is reluctant. With some difficulty, I persuade her to overcome her shyness and join the others.

'Click'.

Hopefully, I have distilled the essence of another moment.

We hover near our open mandolin cases, cherishing and comparing our instruments as parents do their children. Emanuele, the youngest pupil, is playing a solo with piano accompaniment in the concert. He is quite chatty and wants to try out the English he has been studying at school.

From stillness, our music begins. Notes drift here and there, soft and fine, like gossamer threads floating in a gentle breeze. Softly, neatly, smoothly, passionately, we create a seductive pink and golden glow. The sun is set. The light fades. Our music fades. The notes become stillness once again.

We celebrate the success of the concert with supper at a local *pizzeria*. Being part of this group of mandolin students feels like being part of a family. There is a feeling of warmth between us; everyone looks after each other, a bond we share because of our commitment to a tiny pear-shaped instrument. I love this sense of belonging. I love being part of this family.

I have a pizza with *melanzane*, aubergines, which I am partial to, but I notice that Ugo chooses a pizza topped with *rucola* and raw tomatoes. When the pizza arrives, it is swamped by a huge mound of salad and Ugo asks for the *condimenti* and proceeds to dress his salad with olive oil and salt. I decide I will try this variety the next time I have an opportunity. I also notice that everyone seems to drink beer with pizza in Italy. I imagined that people would enjoy a good glass of local wine with their pizzas, but time and time again, I see people imbibing Italian beer instead of *vino locale*. I try the beer and find that, strangely, it does seem to have an affinity with pizza.

"Tonight I will stay in Padua in a hotel and tomorrow I fly home from Venice," I tell someone.

Another question is asked.

"I arrived yesterday at Milan and I stayed last night as a guest of the Maestro's family in Brescia," I continue. "Midweek. Two nights. Arrival at one destination, departure from another. Yes, it sounds glamorous and expensive, but I saved coupons for a whole year from my supermarket, and then exchanged them for this special ticket. It is amazing what a person will do for the love of our instrument, for the love of music."

X

Although the academic year has drawn to a close, I find myself unexpectedly back at the *Conservatorio* in the second week of June to take an exam. The rules have changed and I am required, along with three other mandolin students, to be successful in an examination in order to pass into the next year of study. It is probably only a formality, but I am unnerved by yet another test, especially when I thought there would be no more assessments until the final diploma.

The Maestro confirms that I should present the first two movements of the G minor partita by Sauli. I love these movements and the whole work they come from and I play the piece fairly well in the lesson. However, I am suspicious. It all seems too straightforward and simple. I start to fret about what exactly the examiners will be listening for.

The day is hot and interminably long. We are unable to escape to take any substantial refreshment because we are on standby for the exam. We are unable to find out an exact time for the exam and we receive a number of vague and conflicting messages. Eventually, we are asked to wait downstairs in the corridor leading towards the examination room. We distract ourselves by chatting and joking, but I notice that my head is swimming. It must be the heat and lack of food, combined with a little pre-performance stress.

When it is my turn to enter the examination room, I feel strange and weak. I sense the impatience of the examiners. I had thought there would be some conversation as in other examinations, but they are anxious for me to start. I adjust the height of the music stand and lightly touch the strings to re-check tuning. I had already tuned carefully before entering. To my horror, my feet do not touch the floor. I have been given a piano stall to sit on instead of a chair, but I do not feel able to adjust it. Under the beady eyes of the examiners, I start the music and immediately regret doing so.

Without proper contact between my feet and the floor, I am uncomfortable and unable to support the mandolin adequately. Worse still, I cannot establish a secure sense of pulse. I am unbalanced and insecure and the music reflects this. It is clumsy and awkward. I tense up and hit the strings too hard, which results in one of the A-strings becoming flat and making everything sound even more dreadful. I can't think of a word to say in Italian when the music is finished. My mind is blank and confused.

After a shower back at the hotel, my body feels a little more comfortable but my mind is still uneasy. The silence of the room is punctured by the squeal of the phone. There is someone to see me in the foyer.

It is Gianluigi. The Maestro is in the car outside and we are about to depart for a rehearsal of Vivaldi's *Juditha Trumphans* in Venice. I had been very much looking forward to this opportunity. I have not heard this oratorio before and tonight there is a rehearsal for a concert to be given by *I Solisti Veneti* in the *Basilica di San Marco*. The Maestro is playing the mandolin accompaniment to the aria '*Transit aetas*': 'Life passes'. Gianluigi and I are really just hangers-on.

In the car, the Maestro informs me that I passed the exam and can continue into the seventh year. However, my mark was not that good and he thinks I should delay taking the final diploma. I can take it whenever I am ready as an external student. I sense he is perplexed that I play well sometimes and not others. I need time to let this all sink in. I should feel relieved, but at the moment I feel disappointed.

On the bridge to Venice, we park the car and change to a bus. At the *Piazzale Roma,* we proceed on foot. The Maestro races ahead, sure of the well-worn route to the *Piazza San Marco*. Strangely Gianluigi is uncertain, as this is his first time in Venice. I, on the other hand, have already rehearsed this walk with my husband. Gianluigi and I follow the Maestro like two young ducks following their mother. We are always a few paces behind, but as we reach each corner I always remember the way we should go, left or right, or straight ahead. I chat to Gianluigi, telling him the things I remember from my last visit and pointing out things of interest. How odd: here I am, an Englishwoman, giving a young Italian man a guided tour of Venice.

As we walk through the Campo S. Margherita, I long to linger. The warm evening air, drenched in golden light, is laced with cooking smells mingling with the fragrance of summer flowers. I am so hungry and I think how lovely it would be to stop for supper and a glass of wine, to sit at one of those outdoor tables, but no, the Maestro continues on tirelessly.

In the Basilica, Gianluigi and I find a kind of natural bench, made from stone jutting out of the posterior wall. We sit and watch what is happening. I feel the cold, damp Venetian stone against my back and I gaze up at the ceiling. It is quite incredible. The beautiful mosaic pictures with golden embellishment are illuminated exquisitely by powerful lights, which are being adjusted in rehearsal for a television recording of the concert. The lights are positioned on towers of scaffolding. There are no chairs and no pews in the space of this Holy place. There are no tourists, just an orchestra and some singers going through their paces at the front. It is absolutely extraordinary. All the times I have previously visited the Basilica, it has been crowded and dark and hurried. Now, I have a precious gift: light, space and time to view the mosaics in the cupolas, and all this accompanied by the most marvellous music. My attention is drawn from the plumage of an angel to the theorbo. I adore the deep purr of the strings.

Outside, in a brief break, there is still no talk of food, but I am able to buy a soft drink. I am astonished to see my companions choosing a sloppy *granita* of garish fluorescent green colour.

At about ten o'clock, while we are still waiting for the magical mandolin moment, Ugo advises us that the rehearsal is badly behind schedule and that he thinks we should make our way to Venice station. Gianluigi has the overnight train to Naples to catch and I must return to Padua by train. We are both sad not to have heard the mandolin, but we cannot risk being stranded in the watery city.

Again, Gianluigi is uncertain, but I manage to steer us to the correct stop for the number one *vaporetto*. We buy the tickets and we are soon aboard the *Accelerato,* which, despite its name, chugs deliberately along the Grand Canal. Sluggishly, we move past the tapestry of *palazzi* with their intricate lace balconies and embroidered windows, and facades of richly coloured threads – some gilded and some faded.

At the station the ticket office is closed, but Gianluigi is feeling more at home. He takes me to what looks like a cupboard full of cleaning materials, where an assistant sells me a small green cardboard ticket. It doesn't mention Padua, it just records the distance in kilometres, but Gianluigi says it is normal for a ticket out of hours. Then he takes me to a local bar, where we satisfy our hunger with toasted cheese and ham sandwiches. Finally he insists on accompanying me all the way onto the platform, making sure that I get the correct train and that I find a suitable carriage with other people. I am touched by his gentlemanly concern.

I have a five-minute walk from Padua station and I walk smartly through the groups of girls working the streets. Curiously, I feel no sense of unease. They are just doing what they do. I neither judge them nor fear them. I just walk safely to my hotel.

xi

Italy comes to England in July in the shape of Sergio Zigiotti.

Sergio has completed the mandolin course, but is still studying at university to finish his degree. He needs to spend a few weeks in London perfecting his English for an exam he must pass, in order to conclude his work for the degree.

The two weeks of Sergio's stay are an extremely happy period, in which life takes on yet another different rhythm. Sergio attends a language course in the mornings and some afternoons I travel on the tube to meet him and we spend the rest of the day together at the British Library looking at old printed music. One day, we are able to make photocopies of duets and other music by Antoine Riggieri as it is already on microfilm. We are extremely pleased with our find. On the train home, Sergio points to an article in someone else's *Evening Standard*. The young man reading, noting my interest, gives me the paper as he leaves and I read a feature about an author called Louis de Bernières who has written a novel entitled *Captain Corelli's Mandolin*.

On the days that I stay at home, I am usually teaching the violin or attending to various chores. At about six o'clock, when Sergio arrives home or we arrive together, we ritualistically make a cup of coffee and sit in the garden for a while and chat about music. The weather is unusually and consistently good at present. Then, I prepare supper. Sergio seems to know nothing about cooking, so I always send him away to relax. This works perfectly, because I am happy to be left with my thoughts and preparation while Sergio retreats to the sanctuary of my music room. Then as I prepare the vegetables, freshly picked courgettes or peas, to go in a risotto or a sauce for pasta, I am serenaded by the most beautiful music. Sometimes, it is the sound of my new Baroque mandolin with which Sergio is very much enamoured. It is such a joy to hear someone else playing the mandolin in my home, to hear the cascade of different patterns filtering down to the kitchen. I am utterly enchanted.

At supper, my young Italian friend is appreciative of my food and eats up every morsel, but he is unconvinced that it is truly Italian. It is different food from the food that his mother cooks. I am unconcerned because cooking changes so much from region to region and even from family to family. I know that some of my recipes are interpretations. For example, I often use more than one vegetable in a risotto and although I might use traditional risotto rice, *arborio*, *carnaroli* or *vialone nano*, on occasions I am also frequently prone to using Italian brown rice for reasons of health. Much discussion on culinary matters ensues each evening. One day, Sergio announces that my food is truly delicious, but not, in his opinion, strictly Italian. He concludes, with a twinkle in his eye, that it is *'la cucina di* Frances', which ends the discussion and I take as a huge compliment.

At the end of each meal, Sergio gets up without fail to make the coffee. He excels at making an espresso. My husband then clears away the table and washes up, whilst Sergio and I withdraw to the music room for an hour or two of playing. Every evening is brought to a close in this way. We play duets a great deal and Sergio helps me enormously with my playing, giving me advice and encouragement. Sergio also trained initially as a violinist and he has brought Bartók's violin duets along for sight-reading, which really tests me out. Otherwise, we spend all our time playing original music for mandolin.

Sergio is so grateful for the hospitality I have afforded him, but I feel it is little recompense for the way in which he has so greatly enriched my life through our mutual study of music.

il quarto anno

i

It is late September and I find myself driving in the dark, down a tree-lined drive in search of a Baroque mandolin.

The mandolin is going to be played by a friend of mine, Alison Stephens. Like my friend Sue, she studied at Trinity College of Music and sometimes all three of us play together at the Opera House.

I have brought my mother to the concert at Finchcocks, an early Georgian manor set in unspoilt Kent countryside. The manor is home to a remarkable private collection of historic keyboard instruments that are displayed and demonstrated on specific open days.

Living some distance from my parents, I don't often get the chance to take my mother out to a concert. However, Finchcocks is reasonably local to my parents' home and is a convenient location for an outing. Tonight is a special occasion. So often I have wanted to share my music with my mother and it hasn't been possible. Although this isn't my concert, it is very close. It is my friend playing and it is exactly the kind of mandolin music that I play.

When Alison joins the ensemble, *Fiori Musicali*, to play the Vivaldi mandolin concerto, I am surprised to see my mandolin's twin. Alison is using an original 1764 Vinaccia. She is extremely fortunate to own such an instrument. They are difficult to find and usually fragile, requiring careful restoration. I am struck by how my own modern copy of a Vinaccia appears to have the same design and similar markings to the one my friend is playing.

In the interval, I make contact with my friend and discover that her mother is also here for the concert. Our two mothers make friends whilst we discuss mandolins. Upstairs, some of the rooms containing instruments are open for inspection and whilst Alison retreats to prepare herself for the second half, I accompany the mothers on a wander round.

In the second half, we hear the Paisiello mandolin concerto. It is stunningly beautiful and my mother and I are both very much taken by it.

―○―

Just a week after the Baroque mandolin concert, I am playing with Alison and Sue in *Romeo and Juliet* for the Royal Ballet. We are playing at the Apollo, Hammersmith since work on the modernisation of the Opera House has now started.

Everything is strange and cramped at the Apollo. All around the side and back of the theatre are temporary buildings to house costumes, toilets and so on. After the interval, as I return up some concrete stairs backstage with my mandolin in hand, I come face to face with two female ballerinas wearing the most flamboyant make-up and provocative costumes. They smile and I allow them to pass by, carefully protecting my instrument with my right arm. All at once I am back in Padua returning from Venice, walking from the station to my hotel.

Another rhythm, another pattern, is initiated in the autumn – one that I hadn't anticipated. My son's organ teacher has moved to a new post and in order for my son to continue his studies with the same teacher, I find myself accompanying him to a new place of worship. On Thursday afternoons, having rearranged my own teaching to another day, I travel by tube to collect my son from his boarding school. We then travel together on the underground, across London, to St James's Park and take the short walk to the *other* cathedral. When I walk over the threshold of Westminster Cathedral, the Roman Catholic cathedral, I feel at once as if I am walking into a church in Italy. It is an emotional moment.

There is holy water to bless oneself with, just as I do with Giovanna, and there is a plethora of candles to light. There are side chapels, one with exotic mosaics, and there is a lady who sits quietly waiting for enquiries and usually a nun to welcome people. A man pushes a long broom handle, polishing the floor. Everyone moves in silence or with hushed whispers. There is an atmosphere of stillness and respect. People come here to pray, to worship and the tourists mingle inconspicuously. There is no charge to enter, although there is a small admission fee for the lift in the tower.

Every week I offer prayers and light candles, and some weeks, after a trip to a nearby bookshop, I return to strands of plaintive organ notes wafting like incense, only to find that it is *my* son who is playing. I feel a great sense of joy.

I do not return to Italy until November and I am happy to be able to stay once again with Giovanna. She has had a lodger, a girl sharing her flat to help with the expenses, who has now departed.

Everything continues much as before: Brescia, Bologna, Cervinia for skiing with a train ride from the west side of Milan to Padua and two nights at my usual hotel, Bologna again. I visit Bologna three times in the spring.

I am exhausted. It is hard to keep the pace up. Travelling. Practising. Attending lessons. Teaching my own pupils. Performing. Looking after my family and coping with endless chores. And this isn't the whole list of activities to juggle. Sadly, I have long since stopped going to Italian lessons. I decided that I have enough practice whilst I am in Italy. In any case, the language is a matter of confidence. If I think I can do it, I can. When I tell myself *I can't, I haven't practised enough, I will forget everything I have ever studied* and so on, then I am tongue-tied. When I give myself a mental pep talk, when I say to myself *you will have the words you want just as you require them, they will come to you*, then the Italian words and expressions complete with hand signals just flow like lava from an erupting volcano.

And so it should be with my playing in the Italian manner, but somehow that is more elusive.

I decide not to worry about the exam – the final diploma – any more. I have to accept that, for whatever reason, it is just too much pressure, too much stress. I decide that I just have to get through the final year and that I have to try to enjoy it as much as possible. I am not one to give up easily and it seems to me that commitment, attending the full length of the course, is the essential thing.

What I actually learn and take away with me is also important, not the piece of paper, the certificate that I had hoped for to confirm that I had been through this course and met the required standard of accomplishment. Whether I get the piece of paper or not, I will still be judged by what I accomplish in giving good concerts and by passing on my knowledge to others through teaching.

In fact, I didn't begin the course with the idea of obtaining another qualification. I had only wanted to improve my playing. The qualification is a thing to have, a material possession. I have quite a few of them already. The playing, the ability to express oneself, the creativity to arrange something, in this case notes or sounds, beautifully and in a pleasing manner, is something far more ephemeral. It is something spiritual.

Nevertheless, I am niggled that some lessons are better than others; that I seem to be getting more uncertain about my playing when I am under the spotlight. When I give concerts in England or when I play in relaxed circumstances with my Italian friends, I am fine. But when I feel I am being analysed in the lesson, it touches a raw nerve and I am mystified by it. I thought I had done so much to rearrange my thinking, to process my past, to heal old wounds. What is it that so disturbs me?

Sometimes, I am accompanied to the lessons by a ghost. I never acknowledge her but I feel her presence.

I have the impression that she is a teenager at first, but then I realise that she is much younger. She misses a lot of school because she is ill. She only attends occasionally. The illness makes her feel weak, her chest is often sore and wheezy, and sometimes it is difficult to breathe. When she returns to school, her illness, her weakness, seems synonymous with stupidity. She is slow and often criticised by her teachers. When she returns, those she thinks are friends have made new friends. Everything is confusing. Everyone knows about new things that have been explained whilst she was away. She feels as if she is on the outside looking in.

Misunderstandings occur. She feels powerless, unable to express herself. She feels worthless and unattractive, lonely and sad.

She increasingly bothers me, even though she doesn't exist any more. I don't understand why, but a casual remark, a look, a circumstance can set off vibrations and I feel her feelings again. *But she doesn't exist any more.* I am not the same person. I have come a long way. I have taught so many children to play the violin and I have done so with a sense of humanity that has healed those painful memories.

I need to go within and look deeper. Healing doesn't always get dealt with in one treatment. Sometimes further work, further refinement is needed. However, my existence is hectic and I am irritated by my weakness. I don't give the matter sufficient attention. I respond by throwing myself further into my work. I continually contort myself trying to arrange the notes in this way or that way, always trying to find the perfect arrangement in order to please. The harder I try, the further I get away from succeeding.

Sometimes, I need the Maestro to be more appreciative than analytical. Sometimes, I feel as if I know nothing. I know this is about me and not about him. Then, if I acknowledge that it is not true about myself and that the truth is that I do know something, I blame myself instead for creating the situation in the lesson where I displayed my lack. I blame myself for not focusing my thoughts in a positive way sufficiently to bring about the outcome I desire. What I desire is that the Maestro will be pleased with my playing and in turn pleased with me. At all costs, without even being conscious of it, I blame myself instead of accepting the situation. I am so unkind to myself that it is impossible to move on.

Constantly, I am searching for answers. Constantly, I am reading, thinking, praying and meditating.

In my final year, everything around me is so beautiful and I want to enjoy it, yet it is tarnished by my inner turmoil. I cannot believe that I am having this struggle. I am supposed to be a professional. I have so many well-received performances to my credit. I have obtained so many academic objectives in the past. I had thought that the achievement of my Master's degree had finally vindicated the humiliation and healed the deep hurt of failing my eleven-plus exam. I had forgotten all the illness and missed schooling that preceded it. The structure of tuition in the *Conservatorio* is quite old-fashioned, just like my early school days. It seems to have set this old pattern off again, this pattern of feeling unworthy and not good enough. I forget to consider that what I am doing is special and remarkable. I am the first foreign student, the first English student, to study mandolin at the *Conservatorio* in Padua. It really doesn't matter if I am the worst student in the world, since what

I am doing is unique. It is quite an achievement in itself. It is something worthy of celebration.

It suddenly occurs to me that when my closest friends used to say that it was nice to see me at church, my reaction was connected to this old wound. I always, if not openly, felt offended by their remarks. I never thought that they were pleased to see me. Instead, I assumed that they were criticising me for my frequent absence. The internal monologue would say, *They just don't understand the difficulties of my life. They don't realise that I often attend church in Italy when I am not here and sometimes I am also at the cathedral for my son.* In reality, in every return to church after every absence, I was reliving my return to school after each illness. I felt disapproved of.

And in Italy, I have the same problem of continuity and the same fear of disapproval. I just drop in once a month whilst everyone else is going at least once a week to the mandolin class. Now Kim from Korea is taking the class. He has a wife and child and has taken a two-year sabbatical from his job and has brought his family to live in Milan so that he can attend the class each week. Miki from Japan lives in Brescia during the academic year and is also able to attend weekly. Two Croatians also visit the *Conservatorio* to explore the possibility of joining the class. They are hoping to commute from Croatia on the train. The class has become quite international.

The Maestro is a good teacher. He is a consummate musician. His playing is beautiful and expressive, but also filled with energy and excitement. But his true gift, his genius, and perhaps this is why I am somewhere deep down so in awe of him, is that he truly understands how the playing of his instrument works. He has an intimate and profound knowledge of its technique, which he explains to his students with eloquence and clarity. He tells me that he only really understood some of the finer points when he began teaching and had to communicate his skills to others. I have always thought that the process of teaching helps the teacher to better absorb the knowledge he or she is trying to impart. I remember this being true for me with the violin and perhaps now this is what I need with the mandolin to consolidate my playing of it.

One Sunday morning in England, I am at church. Near the beginning of the service, the minister says some words which are described as the summary of the law. Basically, these are the two commandments given by Jesus.

"You shall love the Lord your God with all your heart, with all your soul, with all your mind, and with all your strength," the booming voice of the minister declares emphatically.

How often have I heard these same words repeated?

He continues with the second commandment, "Love your neighbour as yourself."

Something strange happens. These familiar words startle me. It is as if I am hearing them for the first time. They seem to jump out of the text emboldened. They seem illuminated, highlighted in fluorescent rainbow colours in my mind.

A thought comes into my head. *But what if you don't love yourself? What if you don't know how to love yourself?*

The people around me blur and the continuing words of the service fade into a low background mumble. Why hadn't I seen these words in this way before?

In a moment of perception, I realise that you cannot love other people effectively if you do not first love yourself. If you are unkind to yourself, if you don't forgive yourself easily, if you don't accept yourself just as you are, if you don't appreciate and value yourself one hundred per cent, then you will not know how to, let alone be able to, achieve the very high ideal of loving unconditionally.

I had always understood that love meant putting other people's needs before your own. Now, I realise that it is impossible to put other people's need before your own until you have first seen to your own needs. It is a paradox. Love is a paradox.

ii

I am on the number ninety-four bus from Zola Predosa going into central Bologna. It is a journey I have done many times. It is the journey that takes me within walking distance of the train station.

The elderly gentleman next to me asks me about my instrument. I explain that it is a mandolin and we have a little chat. He seems very friendly and genuinely interested. Eventually, to satisfy his curiosity, I have to explain that I am not really living locally and that I am just staying with my friend. I had thought that it was all a bit complicated telling him that I am travelling to another city for my mandolin lesson and on top of that I don't even live here permanently. I only volunteer the information when it becomes absolutely necessary.

The man falls silent and thoughtful and I think we have finished our conversation.

"Your Queen Elizabeth played the lute," he suddenly continues, "not the present Queen, but Elizabeth I."

I am taken aback and have to agree. Our conversation moves in a new direction. Whilst I am having an in-depth discussion on Renaissance music and the connection between the lute and the mandolin, I notice, rather uncomfortably, that the bus takes a wrong turning. It is going completely the wrong way. I remember another bus ride a long time ago, almost twenty years ago. It was during my first ever visit to Italy.

―⁕―

Cento cinquantadue: 152.

I had found the correct bus stop amongst the myriad of bus stops near the central station in Rome. It was the departure point for the number 152 bus: *il numero cento cinquantadue*, which was to take me to the outskirts of the city in order to collect the mandolin I had commissioned. I clutched my instructions: a detailed hand-drawn map, together with notes on Italian public transport. I had purchased the bus tickets in advance and I held a large spray of flowers, which I had bought that morning in the market of the *Piazza Vittorio Emanuele II*. The flowers, intended for the mandolin-maker's wife as a token gesture of gratitude, were already beginning to feel cumbersome. The huge, happy *Signora* at the flower stall had, with customary Italian charm and generosity, insisted on arranging together roses, carnations, lilies and other flowers. Instead of a modest posy, I had accepted a lavish floral display beneath cellophane and curly satin ribbons that needed to be cradled in upturned arms like a small sleeping child.

The bus arrived and I mounted at the rear, placing a ticket in the clipping machine. Then, I found a free seat by the window. I was almost smothered by the flowers and thought how fortunate it was that I had found a single seat. I was able to rest the flowers against the window without causing anyone else discomfort and it was good to be sitting down with such a weight to carry.

It was just after ten and the April sun was beginning to get hot. I had no idea of the length of the bus journey, other than I must get off the bus when it reached its destination. I would know this because the bus would make a U-turn and come to a rest facing the direction in which it was originally travelling.

In the meantime, I had decided to enjoy the journey, taking in everyday Italian life as I passed it by. The bus was bumpy and uncomfortable as it bounced over cobblestones: the seats were made of moulded plastic without upholstery and the long single deck bus seemed devoid of suspension. As I moved from the tourist centre into the suburbs, I became aware of the adrenaline racing around my body. I was excited by the reality of achieving a long cherished ambition to visit the eternal city, and also by the thought of meeting the master luthier, Pasquale Pecoraro, who had agreed to construct a concert mandolin for me. At the same time, I was beginning to feel a little isolated and anxious. I glanced at my watch, half past ten. At the *Colloseo,* I had inquired in Italian about the opening times. The attendant replied in perfect English. Obviously, he had detected my English accent.

"*Questa fermata è per…?*"

The question was repeated and although I didn't catch the final word, the name of the place, I realised that I was being asked if this was the correct bus stop for a particular destination. At once, my fears were confirmed and panic surfaced for a moment. It was like the emerald lizard I had seen the day before at the *Villa Borghese*; suddenly you notice it and then it is gone. I collected myself and with English coolness explained that I was a foreigner and didn't know.

Outside the bus, buildings of sand, apricot, rose and ash moved by, their peeling walls blistered by sunlight. Modern blocks of flats interspersed with the older buildings, each dwelling complete with its own balcony decorated prolifically with herbs and pot plants. All the windows were protected from sunlight by the characteristic green or brown shutters or rolled canvas blinds. The women congregated together in small groups; the younger women in yellows, blues and other bright colours with matching flat shoes; the older women in black garments and carrying heavy shopping bags.

Occasionally, the bus stopped close enough to see inside a shop. Black olives, cold meats, cheeses, *tortellini* and other filled pasta were displayed on red and white chequered cloths behind the glass. Bottles of local wine stood in the background. Further on, there were shoes and bags in colours and styles that looked as if they had spilled out of the pages of *Vogue*.

Once again, I felt excited. I felt rapturous that I would soon possess an instrument of superior craftsmanship. I would soon meet the man who could construct the Stradivari of the mandolin world. I felt like an intrepid explorer or a pioneering television reporter; I was joyous and strong. My appointment was for eleven o'clock and the bus had made the expected U-turn. It had come to a stop facing the direction from which it came. I got off the bus.

I began to walk in the direction that the bus had originally taken. The road was wide and straight, stretching miles into the distance. On both sides of the road, there were blocks of flats. In the distance, there were many more buildings. One of these buildings was crowned with a dome that appeared glass-like and gleaming in the sun: a modern church or a futuristic public building perhaps. The map indicated that I would pass a small chapel on my left and after this I would reach a T-junction at which I must turn left. A little way further and I would notice a supermarket. By walking through the car park of the supermarket, I would arrive at the block of flats where *Signore* Pecoraro lived.

Quite straightforward, I thought as I passed a number of shops. I perceived a gathering of large, threatening local men who were taking their morning coffee at a café. Their Mafioso appearance made them seem unapproachable.

In a few moments, I had reached the T-junction and was surprised to discover that although a railway line travelled parallel with the road that ran at right angles, the road along which I had been walking continued. I was also aware that I hadn't passed the important landmark, the *cappella* or chapel. I wasn't sure at first what to do. I decided to err on the side of caution and follow the map exactly. I must find the *cappella* first before turning left and I felt sure it could only be a little way.

I passed fields, which were amazingly green and intended, I thought, for the Italian passion of football. The road was dusty and the sun hot. It was now half past eleven and I felt uncomfortable: already I was late for my appointment and the flowers were heavy to carry in the heat; I felt I should have passed the *cappella* by now. I approached a young lady with a small boy and asked her the way to the address. The lady eventually understood the request, but didn't know the answer. I continued to walk on. There were some more shops ahead and perhaps someone there would know. I had walked out of one district and into another. I had left behind one group of buildings and now approached another group, which included the beautiful glass dome. The road sign said *Napoli* straight ahead. I was consumed with panic; the emerald lizard gleamed in the sunlight. No one knew the whereabouts of *Via Francesco Secondo*. I was tired of approaching strangers and having difficulty with communication; no one expected to converse with foreigners in the suburbs.

Suddenly, I saw a bus station in front of me. I took *Signore* Pecoraro's letter from my pocket and showed the address once more, this time to a group of bus drivers. One of the men smiled at me and explained that I required the *cento cinquantadue*. *Surely there must be some mistake*, I thought. But no, the bus driver insisted that I must take a bus from across the road as far as the *piazza*-something – a name I didn't catch – where I must change and take the 152 bus that I had already taken earlier in the day.

The bus came and I travelled to the *piazza* – whose name I hadn't grasped – where I once again mounted the 152 bus and retraced part of my earlier journey. Again, the bus made a U-turn and halted. I descended from the bus and walked past the café where the Mafioso men were still drinking coffee. (The emerald lizard flashed its tail.) I had no alternative but to approach them. Trembling, I showed them the letter. They smiled sympathetically and one of the men disappeared and returned with a map of the area. It was straight ahead and left in front of the railway line. Stunned by their kindness and generosity, I continued along my former route, this time turning left at the crossroads. After some minutes, I saw the supermarket and its car park.

Signore Pecoraro pointed to my letter and laughed. He had expected me an hour earlier: perhaps I would like to stay for lunch? I apologised and tried to explain what had happened, but I couldn't find the vocabulary. I was bursting with emotions I was excited to meet the master luthier and to see my beautiful new instrument and yet frustrated by my inability to communicate. I hoped that I hadn't seemed rude.

I smile to myself. We are in a supermarket car park. The bus has come to a halt. The bus driver is having an altercation with a driver who has carelessly parked a small fiat and impedes the progress of the bus. The car driver is confused to see a bus in the supermarket car park. He doesn't know that the bus is on a detour. The passengers on the bus are also confused. They don't know what is happening and they chat excitedly amongst themselves.

In the October of the following year, I arranged a second trip to the mandolin-maker in order to collect another instrument for a colleague. I sat on the *cento cinquantadue* and felt tranquil and triumphant; this time, I knew exactly where I was going. Everything was in order: the flowers for *Signore* Pecoraro's wife, the bus tickets purchased in advance, and the hand-drawn map. When the bus arrived at its destination, it made the customary U-turn, but incredulously I saw a wonderful Roman viaduct spanning out in front of the bus. The destination was somewhere completely different to that which I had travelled to in the same bus the previous year. Indignant, I told the bus driver that last year when the bus had reached its journey's end, there had been no viaduct. It was useless. The bus driver didn't understand. No one seemed to understand or know the whereabouts of the address I showed them. I couldn't believe it was happening to me again. (The green lizard blinked.)

In desperation, I asked where the supermarket was. There

was an immediate response of understanding. It was further along the road continuing in the direction that the bus originally travelled, and left at the T-junction. As I approached the T-junction, I saw a small chapel on my left. *Of course*, I thought, *this is exactly like the hand-drawn map.*

Signore Pecoraro laughed. Eighteen months earlier, the bus had been diverted for a few weeks whilst traffic works were being carried out. I laughed with the master luthier and noticed the decoration on the mandolin; for a moment, I thought it was a mother-of-pearl lizard, but then I realised it was something quite different. Although it looked like a reptile, it was in fact a creature of mythology; a winged monster, a fiery dragon.

It is strange how patterns repeat themselves. It is strange how different I feel now. No longer am I afraid of being abandoned. Things still happen from time to time which test me out, but I feel an increasing sense of calm. And I even find myself helping other people in difficulties.

The old gentleman bids me goodbye and wishes me good luck as he exits the bus. I think how privileged I am to have met Pecoraro before he died. The fountain at the end of *Via Marconi* is enlarging through the front window of the bus. I too must dismount at the next bus stop and walk briskly towards Bologna station.

iii

Sitting in my music room, I am playing Vivaldi. It is in my beloved G minor, a key, a colour in sounds, which resonates deep within me. I am engrossed in the beautiful patterns, the sequences, and also by the clarity of harmonic progression, intrinsically implied in the melody. Even though I am alone, the music is potent: it is not necessary to be with the other musicians required by the piece to feel its strength.

The piece is comfortable; all the notes are under my fingers. The music stills me; it is like a meditation.

Outside in the garden, a blackbird sings to his heart's content. He sings lustily, raucously, sweetly. It doesn't matter how loud he sings, what he sings or how he sings. He just sings. He is not worried by what I think about his singing, or by what anyone else thinks about his singing. And he is certainly not worried about disturbing people. It is of no concern to him. To be a blackbird, he has to sing. He has to sing to be. He has to sing to his heart's content. He has to sing joyously.

It is a paradox. Love is a paradox.

I have struggled with this for a long time: the idea that enjoying my music, giving time to my music might in fact be self-indulgent; a selfish act, a bad thing. For so long, I have known in my heart that this is what I must do. And yet, I have heard conflicting voices: voices that say I should put other people's need before my own. Piece by piece, I discover that it is alright to be who I am and that we each have different ways of expressing love.

I don't need to feel guilty any longer for enjoying myself when I play. In fact, if I don't enjoy myself, then no one else does. If I play the notes with fear, fear that they will not be liked, that they will not be good enough, then they will sound dreadful and no one will want to hear them.

If I desire approval instead of thinking that the notes are already beautiful, then I am also lost in fear. The notes, if it is a good composition, will be beautiful. Whether the listener discerns this or not is not my concern. I know they are beautiful and all I have to do is deliver them confidently without fear.

If I desire approval for myself, then the audience is the wrong place to look for it. Those who listen are fickle and praise is transitory. The only approval I need is my own approval, approval of myself.

I know I still have to deal with all the other doubts that come to test me from time to time. Thoughts like, *music is not a real job.* Thoughts like, *I am a late starter and in some way deficient, a cheat, a fraud.* When someone starts at an early age and quickly acquires sufficient skill to play professionally, no one says this. No one says they haven't studied for a great period of time. Instead, they say that because they are young and have studied only for a short period of time, they are gifted. It is no less remarkable being older and studying for a short period of time with excellent results.

My whole life has changed during the last four years in ways that I couldn't have foreseen at the outset. I have increased in self-confidence in my everyday life: I feel as if I could take on any challenge. I have also developed a deeper faith in humanity: a belief in a safe compassionate world. I am a lot more positive and I have learnt to appreciate and enjoy life instead of seeing it as one long struggle. And all this is in addition to improving my skills as a musician and gaining an insight into another culture, another way of thinking.

However, I still have one final hurdle. I cannot return to Italy until I know that I can play for the Maestro without fear.

On one of my frequent book shopping expeditions, I found a copy of *The Prophet* by Kahlil Gibran. It is a much-quoted book and amongst its gentle wisdom there is a particular line, which encapsulates my thinking.

Gibran writes: *'Work is love made visible.'*

In other words, we have to do everything with love. Every note must be crafted with love, with joy, with care.

All day, every day throughout June, I play the music of Vivaldi. I am not playing the mandolin concertos, rather the violin repertoire, which is also suitable for my instrument. I am trying to get back to the essence that I have somehow lost. I have been so concerned with style and technique that my vision has been obscured. I need to remember how good it feels to play music. I need to feel the pulse of the music within my own body. I need to feels its energy, its life. I need to be absorbed with it and to be happy creating it. I need to forget about playing things in a certain way and fretting about how it will be judged. I need to play music simply, for my own enjoyment, and I need to enjoy it.

It was so easy to see it as work and to forget its joy. It was so easy to forget that the idea is to create and to live. Now, I have to rearrange my thoughts. Now, I have to remember that it is easy to feel the joy, the creativity and the life in music.

It is easy.

iv

Maria Cleofe Miotti, my friend Ette, makes a visit to England in July. She and her husband stay with my family for a week's holiday. During the week, we give a concert of Italian music for two mandolins at my church. We play sonatas by Barbella, Scarlatti, Gervasio and others, all with the accompaniment of harpsichord and cello. I am relaxed and happy and we both enjoy our music-making. The concert is a great success and a significant moment in my work of bringing unknown Italian repertoire to England.

Somehow, the *Conservatorio* had precipitated a crisis of confidence within me, at the same time as being the catalyst for my evolution as a mandolinist and as a human being.

People are endlessly fascinated by artists, including those who are musicians, because they are involved in the creative process and in doing so they touch upon divinity. But creativity isn't just about performing music, painting pictures or even writing a book. Creativity is not the prerogative of artists. Creativity is available to each one of us in each moment: we can choose to be happy or we can choose to be sad. In each moment, we are free to choose our reality. We can choose love or we can choose fear. I have decided to choose love.

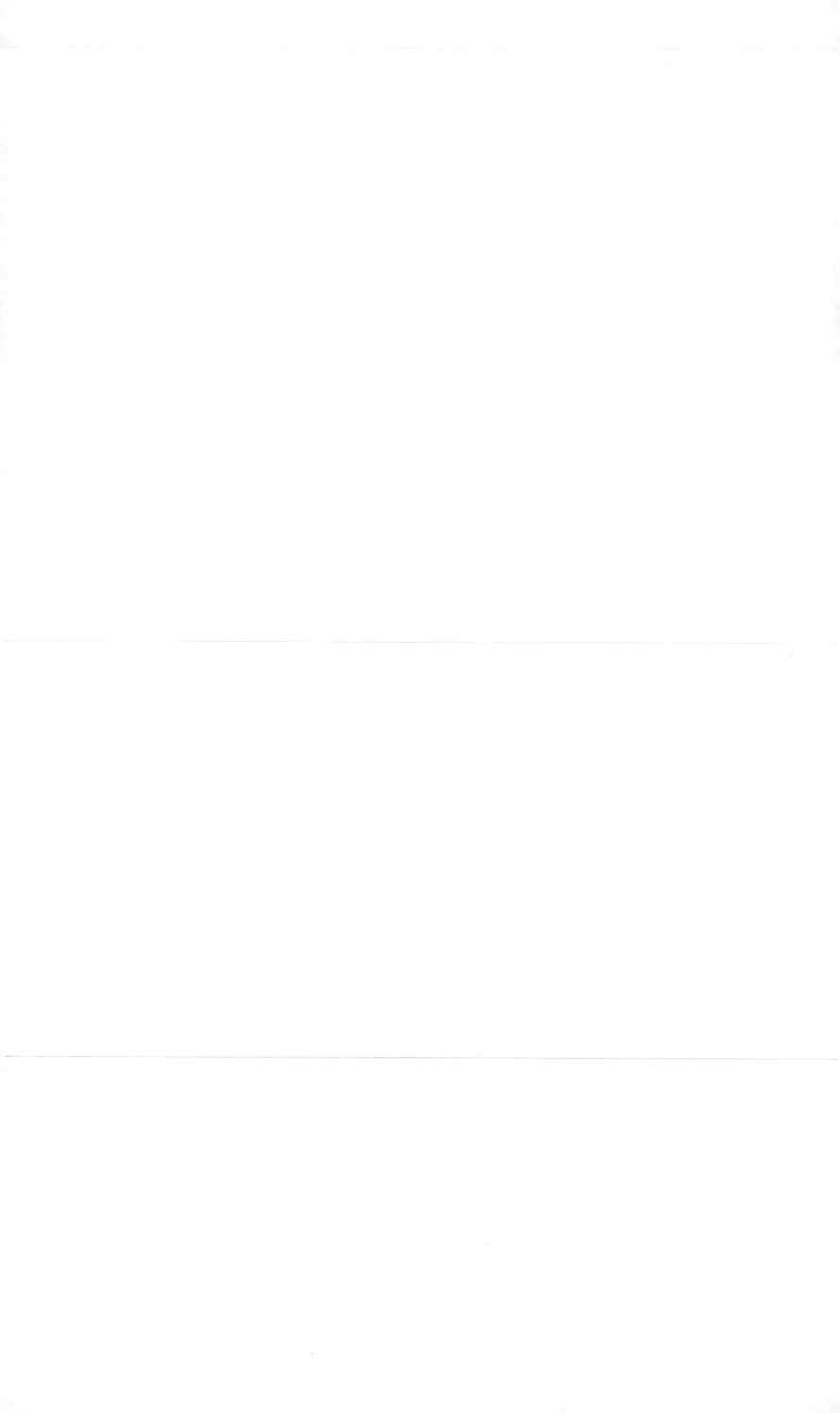

epilogo

I arrive at Venice airport one Saturday afternoon in spring with just over two hours before the concert at the *Conservatorio*. I know it will be a miracle if I arrive in time. I have managed to keep my overnight bag with me as hand luggage in addition to the mandolin. This is a good start as it allows me to walk through passport control and straight out of the airport, although passport control is very slow today.

Before leaving, I find the *biglietteria* and ask if there is a direct bus to Padua. I haven't tried this route before but I have a feeling that it is possible. For a moment I feel unsure, but then the official says that it is about to leave in five minutes. The ticket costs just 6,000 lire and the bus stop is outside the door and 200 metres to the right. I find it easily.

The bus is a joy. Firstly, it is almost empty. Secondly, it takes me on a detour to *Piazza Roma*, the entrance to Venice, which means that I have a wonderful view of *Venezia*, entering across the rail and road-bridge that joins the islands to the mainland. The sea is exactly as I remember, turquoise, beautiful turquoise, contrasting with shot grey clouds. On one side of the bridge, against the backdrop of the industrial area, young men practise windsurfing. On the other side, other young men are engaged in a more traditional pursuit: learning the skill of the gondolier. I see several boats, each with three gondoliers silhouetted against the sea.

Eventually, the bus delivers me, almost door to door from the airport to the *Conservatorio*, in approximately an hour. I am in plenty of time for the concert. If I had taken the bus to Mestre station and then taken the train to Padua, my usual plan, the journey could have taken hours. It is a matter of missing connections and there is also a long walk from the station to the *Conservatorio*.

As I walk down the little side street to the *Conservatorio*, a voice calls my name. I look up and it is Ugo's wife, Marina. It is a lovely welcome. Then, as we go inside talking together, I begin to meet other friends. One by one, they come up to me, kiss me on both cheeks, hug me and ask the appropriate questions. How are you? When did you arrive? How long are you here for? It is absolutely wonderful. I feel as if I have arrived at my party, a special Italian party in my honour, as I meet my friends and companions from the past four years. I have not seen or been in communication with some of them since last summer.

I play two pieces in the concert. They are both group pieces. In the first, *Sinfonia* by N. Piccinni, a Baroque piece, I play sitting next to Ette. In the following piece, Scot Joplin's *The Entertainer*, I sit next to Sergio. I am delighted to be able to play with friends who have played an important part in my Italian life.

The concert is a celebration of twenty-five years since the foundation of the *cattedra di mandolino*, the teaching post of mandolin, at Padua. It is therefore a great privilege to be included in the pupils, past and present, playing in this concert.

The Auditorium *Pollini*, the concert hall of the *Conservatorio* and our venue, has tiered red seating. The surrounding walls are white and the stage is of natural wood and is spacious. Behind us stands an organ, which I always think is a bit strange, being mostly covered in white painted wood with occasional golden coloured trumpets exiting from spaces around the console.

The concert is well attended and much appreciated. Giovanna is in the audience and we meet up after the concert. We go to the *Caffè Eremitani* for a drink with Sergio and Cristiano. I have tea *al limone*.

Next, Giovanna and I meet Sandro, who I had helped in the summer when he attended a language course in London. He is accompanied by two other friends, a married couple, and we all go to another café. This time, I have an apricot juice. Sandro hands me a present, a beautifully wrapped gift, large and heavy. A struggle with thin curly ribbons combined with some delicate tearing of paper reveals a huge round dish, the type used for serving spaghetti or other pasta at the table. It is a brownish-red colour with white decorations of mandolins and musical notes. It is a one-off, handmade dish. It is truly beautiful, unique and special, and more than was necessary for my kindness. I am quite touched by this gesture of gratitude.

We return to Giovanna's flat. This is my first visit since her relocation to Padua. I have a simple, comfortable room with white walls and a wooden floor and a view of *Santa Giustina* between the apartment blocks opposite. We go out for a pizza and then return for an early night.

―⁕―

Sunday is a quiet day. We sleep late and have a civilised breakfast of cornflakes, fresh milk and tea. I am always grateful for the cereal and milk to settle my stomach for the day. It is just a matter of what you are used to. The biscuits and *brioche* aren't always sufficiently filling to last me until lunchtime. Also, I am glad to have proper milk. So many times UHT milk is thought to be equal to fresh milk, although I have to admit that Italian UHT milk is better than English UHT milk for some reason. What the reason is I don't know.

We visit Giovanna's new flat. It is the one she will move into after her marriage in May. It is a brand new flat and at present the builders are adding finishing touches. The outside is primrose yellow and yellow ochre. Inside, there is a spacious living/dining room with a connected kitchen space in the corner. On one side, a wall is being increased to create a partition and prevent the whole area being open plan. The other side is a workspace, which is open to the living space by virtue of a half wall.

On the same level, there are also two bedrooms and two bathrooms, one of which is small and doubles up as a utility room. In addition, there are wooden stairs to a second floor with an attic type room, with a slanting ceiling, which might provide space for a study or a guestroom. Both floors have a balcony.

The wooden floors are very dusty and Giovanna explains all the alterations and extra work yet to be achieved. Then, she and a friend will clean the flat ready for moving in. She is not sure about the shutters for the windows. They are the traditional kind like wooden doors, which necessitate opening the glass window in order to close the shutter. Giovanna is used to the kind made of many horizontal strips of wood or metal, which is adjusted by means of a thick tape that is positioned internally at the side of the window. I think the flat is wonderful and my friend is extremely fortunate to have found such beautiful accommodation in which to start her married life.

We take a walk before lunch and we visit *Prato della Valle*, which I had never managed to see before. It is apparently the largest *piazza*, public space, in Europe and the second largest in the world, Red Square in China being the largest. I'm not sure about these claims. My guidebook only says it is the largest *piazza* in Italy. There seems to be a lot of green grass and statues in the centre of this *piazza*, hence the name *Prato*, which means grass. In the centre, there is a fountain and there are beautiful *palazzo*s all around. There is one with Moorish influence in its design which I particularly like.

I become a tourist and take some photographs. Somehow I have never got into the habit of taking photographs, despite my camera being so very tiny. I am always trying to blend into the surroundings. I am always trying to look and appear Italian, but now I have a conflict. I want to record so many memories as I have a sense of a phase in my life drawing to a close.

We visit the Basilica of *Santa Giustina*. We are dwarfed by the hugeness of the empty space within. We visit the side chapels and feel the heat of the many candles as we pass. A Mass is in progress in the little chapel under the main altar. My friend says that the cupolas of the roof look beautiful from her apartment when there is a pink sunset. It is amazing that such an extravagant piece of ecclesiastical architecture is only a short walk from the famous Basilica of *San Antonio*. It is especially so when one considers how the exterior of *San Giustina* mirrors *San Antonio* with its clump of domes.

We also visit the Basilica of *San Antonio* on our way home. The Mass is just finishing and the unaccompanied singing which brings the service to a close touches me deep within and I feel the slightly giddy feeling of my emotions surfacing. There is always something special about this place. There is a pervading feeling that I notice when I am in this building. Despite the internal opulence, there is a sense of being somewhere pure and holy.

Outside, we return to the world of street stalls selling all the usual religious and tourist trinkets. This time I notice candles of every size, small religious images, statues, icons, postcards, plastic cameras for small children and the ubiquitous Pinocchio pencils.

At home, we lunch on chicken breasts cooked in a griddle pan on top of the stove and a salad. This is followed by light sponge cake similar to *colomba* or *pandoro*, and coffee. We are both ready for our siesta and we have a luxurious two hours for our afternoon sleep.

In the evening, we meet up with Giovanna's fiancé and go to a big cinema complex just outside of neighbouring Vicenza. The cinema complex is situated next to a shopping mall and I remember the pyramid structure after which it is named as being a landmark when we took the journey to Breganze. The film is booked up, so we buy tickets for the next performance.

In the meantime, we decide to eat and the fiancé takes us to a country pub he knows. As usual in Italy, the pub is really a *pizzeria*. It is a restored farm building constructed from local thin, long bricks. These bricks are arranged in various patterns and the beautiful designs are visible internally as well as externally. We are delighted by the architecture. The *pizzeria* is very busy, but after about ten minutes we have a table. There are lots of rooms inside, but we seem to be near what looks like a monastery cloister in which the openings onto the courtyard are glazed.

The menu is extensive offering traditional and special pizzas, as well as various kinds of local bread with fillings or salads served separately. I have a pizza with a salad of *rucola* and tomatoes added on after the cooking. A touch of salt and a drizzle of olive oil perfectly complements the generous salad placed on a pizza base that is crisp, light and wafer-thin. In my five-star rustic ambience, I muse upon the fact that pizzas in England are positively stodgy by comparison.

The Walt Disney film *A Bug's Life* is great fun to watch in Italian. It is not a film I would have chosen for myself, but I am nonetheless greatly entertained.

Monday, 8th March, is *Festa della Donna*. Today certainly feels like a festival or a celebration. I am out of the flat at eight o'clock with all the other Paduans. Giovanna has to go to work and her flatmate has not returned from her weekend with her parents. Giovanna only has one set of keys and Italian front doors all seem to require being locked from the outside. If you examine the hinged side of the door it is possible to notice up to seven metal bars, several centimetres in width, which move into the door frame with the turn of the key. With doors that lock like prison doors and sturdy wooden or metal shutters at all the windows, it seems that Italians are very security conscious when it come to their homes. I remember Ette being surprised how open English houses are without shutters and with windows looking onto the street.

I walk for about twenty-five minutes into the centre of town. It is fresh, but any chill is psychologically dispelled by the sun illuminating everywhere it is able to penetrate. *Via Facciolati* is a big main road leading towards the centre. I have left the tranquillity of a simply furnished white room behind me and stepped into the world of feverish activity and loud traffic noise. I notice the side streets with wires strung across between the buildings, supporting and powering streetlights. Sights such as these, a lone light shade with a single bulb, high up in the street and attached to a wire, reminds me that I am somewhere very different, somewhere far away from England.

I stop for some traffic lights at an intersection. I feel already in such a positive mood. It is something I have long been cultivating within. But it is also something that is actually happening around me now. The quality of Mediterranean light provided by the sun is perfect. I feel so lucky that it is good weather today. The buildings, apartments and villas are radiant in their pastel shades. There is one villa painted in pale lemon, with decorations picked out in white, standing between palm trees in a garden overflowing with exuberant vegetation.

I smile at the policewomen on duty at the intersection. She smiles back. An old man on a bicycle, also waiting to cross, asks me about the mandolin case. Was I an amateur or a professional? I say that I am a professional, but not here, in London. He asks me if am playing in a concert. I am able to say yes, that I have already played in a concert given at the *Conservatorio* on Saturday. He asks if it was with the *Solisti Veneti*. I say no, it was a special concert of present and past pupils of the *Conservatorio* to celebrate twenty-five years of mandolin teaching there. He is impressed and rides off happily as the lights change to green for pedestrians. I am also happy, deliriously happy.

I walk across *Via San Francesco* and glimpse views of the domes of the *Basilica* of *San Antonio*. I am in a state of constant delight looking in all the shop windows and taking in the various features of the architecture. I notice the tall rectangle shape of windows, the green wooden shutters, the wrought iron design of balconies and the arrangement of potted plants on those balconies. I notice a Venetian looking *palazzo* and I read the plaque, which mentions the building's association with Dante. I don't remember this building from my previous visits. I stand for a moment to take in the detail of the quatrefoil tracery motif that embellishes the windows, a feature commonly found in the architecture of Venice. So carried away am I by my vision of delight that I completely forget to turn right into the *Via Zabarella,* which leads directly to *Via Eremitani* and the *Conservatorio*. Instead, I go straight ahead and suddenly realise I am in the *Piazza Erbe* with the distinctive landmark of the *Palazzo della Ragione*. It is only a five-minute detour that I have taken and I am soon at the *Conservatorio*.

Breakfast is at the *Caffè Eremitani*. Sitting at a small round table draped in an apricot damask cloth, I order a cappuccino and a *brioche marmellata*. As I look out of the window at the *Chiesa Eremitani*, its brickwork bathed in sunlight, I feel happy and relaxed. Today being *Festa della Donna*, Ladies Day, everyone is buying and giving sprays of mimosa, a plant covered with tiny yellow fluffy balls. Two ladies at the next table are each given a spray by the waitress. The stems are covered with silver foil, giving them the appearance of flowers worn in buttonholes by wedding guests in England. On the counter of the bar is a huge turquoise ceramic vase. Branches heavy with pink blossom are arranged in the vase, giving the message that spring has finally arrived. After I have breakfasted, I too am given a spray of mimosa. I feel cherished and special.

At the *Conservatorio,* I decide to go straight up to room eighteen – the mandolin teaching room. As I arrive, I hear the vocal scales and arpeggios of a female singer. I did wonder at the entrance whether I should enquire from the porter if the room had changed. Knowing how easily confusion has happened in the past and knowing that I hadn't attended the *Conservatorio* for almost a year, I was aware that I might find some change. I enter the room and speak with the singer. She says that it is still the mandolin teaching room and that she is just practising whilst the room is free. I agree to wait outside.

I am not expecting Ugo to be on time and I would rather like to warm up before he turns up. I am refreshed from my stimulating walk from just outside the historical centre into its heart. No long train journey from Brescia or Bologna this morning. No long bus ride at Bologna before even beginning the train journey and no tedious walk from the station in Padua.

I hope to play through my music and I have brought the other parts of the score in the hope that the other students will arrive early and we can play together. Whilst I wait, I look out of the window onto a courtyard and I take a few photographs. Suddenly, a party of schoolchildren arrives. They are accompanied by two female teachers and a male administrator from the *Conservatorio.* They go into the adjoining room for a talk by the violin professor.

Michelle, the new French student that I met on Saturday, arrives. The singer departs saying that she has finished. Michelle and I reclaim the mandolin room. Michelle begins to play the piano, whilst I get my music and mandolin ready. I persuade her away from the piano, suggesting that we play the Barbella concerto together. I have the solo mandolin part and I show her that I have the first violin part for her to play on the mandolin. She hasn't seen this piece before and she is delighted with it.

Miki, the Japanese girl, arrives and I find her the second violin part to play on the mandolin. All three of us play happily together. It is a good start to the morning and I feel the best prepared I have ever been for the mandolin lesson. The door swings open and it is Ugo, grinning. I sense his surprise and pleasure that his students are all using their time usefully.

As we sit down to begin the lesson, Ugo is laughing again at me and I ask him why. He says that I appear so English and organised with all my music parts, neatly printed by computer and arranged in various folders. He still writes out scores by hand and tries to fit all the parts in a compact score, with as much as possible all on one sheet of paper.

I offer him the bass part, so that he can accompany me on his mandolin. The notes would naturally be transposed an octave or two higher since the mandolin is a soprano instrument, but the two parts should make sense. He says thank you, but he doesn't require the music as he knows the music already. I expected him to say this. I knew he would know the music from memory but I was really asking him to play with me. I felt it would be more comfortable if we both played. I felt it would take some of the pressure off and it would be less intense. Instead of me being the object of the critical ear of the Maestro and the other students, I would just be making music. So often I have felt that instead of making music I was being judged. So easily, the element of fear had been present. Where there is fear, there can be no love and no creativity. Then, there is no joy.

We play the Barbella together. My playing is relaxed and confident and we both take great pleasure in its execution.

"*Ha migliorato molto*," the Maestro tells me: it has improved greatly.

I sense that he is happy and I am happy, too.

The Maestro notices a mistake I have made in copying the manuscript. I have mistaken a sharp sign for an appogiatura. The appogiatura is written as a small note and is a note intended as a decoration to the normal size note it is attached to. He notices a second mistake of the same sort. I think it hardly surprising that mistakes like this occur sometimes, because the manuscript is so messy and confusing. Some manuscripts are legible and the scholar has only to become accustomed to the style of elegant Baroque handwriting. Others leave a great deal to be desired with messy pen work, careless copying mistakes, scribbling out, corrections in miniature and scattered ink blots. In fact, whole sections may be obscured.

This particular manuscript was difficult to reproduce in photocopy from the microfilm for various technological reasons. Firstly, the microfilm was in negative and the machine at the public library was without the attachment to convert it back into a positive image. Thus I had black paper and white spots for the notes, instead of the other way around. Secondly, the size of each page of the manuscript didn't seem to correspond to the size of paper available from the library machine that particular day. It transpired that in order to capture everything on a single page of the manuscript, I had to take four photocopies. I had to shift the magnifying lens of the machine to the left and right, top and bottom of each page, so as not to miss any corrections and scribbles at the edge of the page.

When I came to examine the manuscript at home, I had to cut and paste the sheets together as if I were creating a montage. So complex was the procedure that, in this case, I wrote a score out by hand before feeding the information into the computer. It was impossible to stand by the computer and know what the notes were. I had to compare all the parts and make decisions about the composer's intentions.

Thus, I am not unhappy that mistakes in my work have been pointed out. On the contrary, I am pleased and rather excited. I love the ensuing discussion. I am fascinated by comparative opinions and the evidence presented to support those opinions. It is exactly for this that, in the beginning, I pursued meetings with Ugo. I wanted to know his ideas and reasons for those ideas. I also, from the outset, wanted especially to study the concerto repertoire. It is only now, at the conclusion of my studies, that I have finally reached my objective.

Ugo finds two other separate short notes in the first movement that he thinks are incorrect. I protest saying I have copied them precisely, but Ugo says that I must use my ears. He cups his ears in his hands to emphasise the point. It sounds rude, but in this case he is right. What he might say if he were to put the matter more delicately, is that it is a matter of harmony. The two notes in question are most probably erroneously written, as, in each case, other notes provide a more satisfactory harmonic progression.

The musicological discussion comes to an abrupt halt with a knock at the door. The administrator that I had seen earlier asks for a word with the Maestro. The Maestro returns after two minutes and asks me and the other two students to accompany him to another room. He tells us to bring our instruments.

In the new room, I see the party of schoolchildren I had encountered earlier this morning. They look about twelve or thirteen years old.

Maestro Orlandi is introduced by the administrator and then proceeds to embark upon an improvised talk on the mandolin. He introduces me and the other two students as three of his female pupils, which he thinks is appropriate as today is *Festa della Donna.* He also thinks it is appropriate because the mandolin has so often been associated with female gender. Historically, women, rather than men, have been painted with this instrument. The instrument is full of beautiful curves, he explained, like the shape of the female body. Finally, the generic word from which the Italian word for mandolin, *mandolino*, is derived is *mandola,* which is a feminine word.

I am fascinated by this thesis. It sounds sexist and at odds with the politically correct society with which I am so familiar in England. I listen carefully to the Italian words, which I no longer translate in my head; I just understand them. I think this idea is being explained as an historical concept, but it sounds, with the use of the present tense, so definite that the mandolin is a feminine instrument now. I would like to qualify this statement by saying that, for various reasons, the mandolin has traditionally been thought of as a feminine instrument. Maybe that is what he means, too. Perhaps it is just a matter of emphasis. I am reminded how difficult it sometimes is to understand people when talking in English. Being well acquainted with one's native language does not provide immunity from misunderstanding.

I am asked to play some music to illustrate the sound of the instrument. I play the opening of the Barbella concerto I had been working on earlier. The notes sing out from the instrument. Michelle is asked to sound the open strings of her instrument to demonstrate the tuning and Miki is required to perform some notes with tremolo technique.

The commentary is at times simple and entertaining. At others, it is comprehensive and complex. I notice that the schoolchildren are in their outdoor jackets. They are padded and brightly coloured. They all look like ski-jackets and most of them are done up. Outside, the sun is shining and its light streams in through closed windows. Inside, the central heating is on. I notice how hot the room has become and I am sure the schoolchildren are too hot in their ski-jackets. They have been mostly enraptured by the talk, but as we discuss the mandolin's connection to the lute family and other ancient plucked instruments from around the world, I notice some fidgeting. I am not surprised. They have been attentive for a long time and they must be feeling the excessive heat.

Our talk and demonstration is so successful that we are later called upon to give a repeat, if abridged, performance to another group of schoolchildren.

My lesson continues with a second concerto. This time, it is by Luigi Lamberti. We play the first movement happily. Ugo points out another small note that is erroneously written. I have copied it exactly from the manuscript, but the harmonic sense suggests the Maestro is right.

In yet another place, another wrong note which I have again reproduced exactly from the manuscript. I don't argue. I will reflect upon the correct solution later.

When we play the second movement, I am stopped and told that I am touching only one of the two strings with the plectrum. This is true. It is a little nervous thing I sometimes do when I am playing softly and become distracted. It happens imperceptibly without me noticing. We start again and now I am stroking both strings at once to create maximum volume, whilst, at the same time, maintaining the *dolce*, sweet, sound of the slow movement. The quality of sound is melodious and tender, but also powerful and penetrating.

In the final movement, there are a couple more tiny alterations to be made to my edition. Again, notes erroneously written in the manuscript and meticulously copied by me.

I am very pleased with today's work. I have discovered many new things about the two manuscripts I have studied. It has been a musicological discussion that I had hoped to have last year, at the end of the spring. When I last visited, my playing was so nervous that we never reached the intricacies of today's discussion. Today I played well and instead of discussing playing technique, we were able to discuss the music itself.

I am asked about my next visit. I don't know when I will come again. Probably I will come for Giovanna's wedding at the end of May, but that is only for a few days. Also, lessons at the *Conservatorio* end at the beginning of June. Between now and then is Easter. I do not think I will return for the mandolin until the autumn. I am told that 'more concertos are good' and I am happy with that plan.

I have a list of music at the British Library, which Ugo would like me to find for him. I was given the list at the concert and now we discuss his requirements. I mention that there is something I too require: my *certificato della frequenza*, certificate of attendance. In the absence of the final diploma, it is quite important that I should have some official record of my attendance. Ugo is at once putting on his jacket and asks me to accompany him to *la segretaria*, the secretary. I tried to arrange this certificate in April last year, but, despite various enquiries, events had conspired to prevent me either attending to collect the piece of paper, or receiving it by post or personal messenger.

The secretary thumbs her way through the mandolin folder on her desk. I am mentally admiring the rose pink colour of her cardigan, when, halfway through the pile of papers, she finds my paper. It is dated 21st April 1998. It has been waiting almost a year in that folder for me. I mention that I also haven't received the *pagina scholastica*, which is an official document I had received in my first two years. In the sixth and seventh years, my third and fourth years, I had received no such documentation. I was told that the Italian government has changed the law stopping the issue of the *pagina scholastica*. The certificate I had just received was in place of it. Today's certificate with its official stamp and signature is on see-through computer paper. Its appearance is disappointing, but I am pleased to have it finally.

Then, as an afterthought, the certificate for the *diplomino* is mentioned. The *diplomino,* or little diploma, is an exam which I had successfully passed at the beginning of my second year. I had never received a certificate and when I had enquired, I was told it was not possible. A certificate was just not issued for this diploma. Now I am told that it is possible and that I can have a certificate, probably tomorrow, all being well. However, I must buy a *marca da bollo* for 20,000 lire, a type of stamp as excise duty, from the nearest tobacconist's shop. I have just five minutes in which to achieve this, since the secretary's office will then close for lunch.

I run all the way down the marble stairs, out into the street, through the little arcade opposite and across the next road, taking care to avoid a bus and a cyclist. I go through another small arcade and turn right. I see the white T sign on the black background and head immediately for it. Luckily, I remembered the tobacconist's position. I quickly buy the stamp and return by the same route. I am astonished by my speed. I am so excited by the thought of having the certificate I thought I couldn't have, that my body's movements are accelerated to a new height. I am also fearful of missing this five-minute deadline and I am aware of the consequential surge of adrenaline pulsing though my body. I excel myself and return at exactly half past twelve, just seconds before the office is locked close.

Back at the classroom, I find that someone has arrived with a mandola to show the Maestro. An interesting discussion ensues but it mostly washes over me. The morning has been so happy and fruitful in so many ways, but also intense, that I need a pause. I feel jubilant.

After a while, the mandola player departs. Kim, the Korean mandolinist, begins his lesson and he is also studying the Barbella concerto. He hasn't studied the manuscript and is playing from a photocopy of a handwritten edition prepared by the Maestro. The score is quite different from mine, with lots of musical shorthand to speed up the process of writing by hand. After just one movement, I find I am at saturation point with mandolin music and, in particular, with Barbella. Miki and Deborah have both had an early lunch and are now at their history of music class. Ugo has decided he is too busy to eat at present. Michelle awaits her lesson. It is nearly two o'clock and I haven't had anything to eat or drink since breakfast, not even a cup of coffee. So I decide to excuse myself and go for some lunch.

I go to the Caffè Eremitani, since it is close and convenient. I can have a good lunch at a very reasonable price and at this time of day, I will be assured of a seat. I am not unhappy to be alone. In fact, I am very pleased to be able to rest my mind for a little while. I would equally have been happy to eat with some of the other students, but I feel just as comfortable with or without other people. The only thing is that I would have liked an opportunity to catch up with Deborah's news. She wasn't at the concert on Saturday and I haven't spoken to her for over a year.

I order *tagliatelle al ragù*. I had seen the dish downstairs behind the glass counter as I entered. There are usually two varieties of pasta, which change daily and which are heated up as required. This is in addition to the many different types of sandwiches and salads available. I know I will not be eating until quite late this evening so I choose a wholesome pasta dish, only I am told that it is called *paglia e fieno*. That is fine, I agree. I have learnt not to be fazed by anything. I suspect the dish is called *paglia e fieno*, straw and hay, on account of the two colours of *tagliatelle*, yellow and red. The amusing fact is that usually the 'straw and hay' name of the dish refers to yellow and green *tagliatelle*. The dish also usually has peas, cream and ham as the ingredients for the sauce. My sauce is definitely *bolognese*. Typical Italian confusion, which is at times frustrating and, at times, quite charming.

Instead of a salad, I also choose a delicious dish of chargrilled vegetables, *peperoni*, *finocchio* and *melanzane*, peppers, fennel and aubergines, all drizzled in extra virgin olive oil. For me, this dish is gastronomic heaven. It is fresh, simple and so good. I drink water with my meal and complete my lunchtime treat with an espresso.

For the second time today, I receive a sprig of mimosa. I will give this one to Giovanna this evening. From my table, I can survey the whole café. I am in the corner of the upper floor and at the balcony edge. To my right side is a balustrade filled with glass. Over the edge is a sheer drop to the bar below and a small number of tables. To the left of this balustrade is the descending staircase. The back wall of the establishment is covered with a mirror that reflects light and amplifies the space. Thus I am able to enjoy a view of everything that is going on, both downstairs and upstairs.

My attention wanders from one little drama to another and provides me with constant entertainment. These people hadn't ordered water: they had ordered something else. That lady has waited an inordinate length of time for her sandwich and confuses the waiter by asking for a cappuccino with it – and so on. There is always something to watch, something to amuse. I feel relaxed and happy. I feel a contentment I have long desired and never quite achieved before.

Back at the *Conservatorio,* I meet a new pupil, Anna, who is in her early teens. She has been to school this morning and, like Emanuele, comes for her lessons in the afternoon. I manage to speak with Deborah. She is suffering with a cold and not feeling her usual cheerful self. I find out that her father has retired and they have moved from the family-run music shop. Deborah gives me her new address and explains that she now has her own smaller business, selling music accessories. I promise to send her a postcard from London.

Deborah and Miki depart to catch trains. Anna and Michelle have their lessons in turn and also depart. The lessons are completed for the day. Ugo begins to pack his belongings away and I take my leave.

I stop for a cup of tea at the Bar Pollini, which faces the entrance of the *Conservatorio*. I meet Michelle there and we talk about her life in France. I am interested to know how she finds living in a foreign country. A graduate in philosophy, she tells me that she misses her family.

We follow our refreshment with a visit to the music shop, *Musica Musica*, which is just around the corner. Last time, I visited with Sergio and found some useful newly-published Italian Baroque music for mandolin. Today I find five new pieces, which have been published since my last visit. I find a solo mandolin sonata by Giuseppe Giuliano, and sonatas for two mandolins by the same composer, as well as by Giovanni Battista Gervasio and Prospero Cauciello. In fact, I find two works by the last composer. I am really pleased with my find.

Next, I visit the flower shop to fulfil my obligation to buy vegetable seeds for my husband. I buy packets of the *Genovese* variety of courgette, plum tomatoes and wild rocket.

I return home to Giovanna's apartment after a highly successful day. On the way, I notice how many more shops are open this evening than there were this morning. A Monday phenomena; many shops remain closed on Monday morning as their half day. Somehow in my euphoria, and with the distraction of so many interesting shop windows, I walk straight past Giovanna's road and miss my turning for the second time today.

―◦―

Tuesday morning is a bonus. Normally, I have to spend the morning of my return day travelling. Very often, I have had to take trains and buses to connect with my flight. Sometimes, because I have been involved in other people's lives, the time has been lost time. It might have been spent just being at home – my friend's home. Often I was grateful for the lost time, because although I didn't do anything special, I was glad to have the rest, the slowness of pace, after a period of intensity.

Today, however, is different. Today I am in Padua and only an hour away, by bus, from Venice airport. Between now, eight o'clock, and midday, when I take the bus, I have four hours of free time. I intend to enjoy myself and to use this precious time being a tourist. I ardently desire to see a number of things that I have never had the luxury of time to see. I have always been too busy studying music and travelling. Although I hope to continue visiting Italy occasionally, to maintain my contact with the mandolin culture here, I want today to celebrate the conclusion of a period of formalised study of the mandolin.

Giovanna has a plan. She takes me with her in the car on the first part of her journey to work. She drops me near the hospital and tells me to keep walking in a straight direction. Eventually I will arrive at the bus station where I can check the bus times and buy my ticket for later. Giovanna is sure this will save me time as I have a heavier 'magic' bag now to carry (Giovanna has always referred to my canvas overnight bag as the 'magic' bag, since I always manage to fit so many things into it). Yesterday, I only had music to carry in my bag. Today, I have my overnight things as well. In addition to my bag, handbag and mandolin case, I also have the big plate to carry. It is now wrapped in newspaper and placed in a strong cardboard carrier bag with red rope handles. Nevertheless, it is cumbersome to manage.

I am not entirely convinced that Giovanna's plan is any better than the route I took yesterday. I suspect my perception is coloured by the weight and awkwardness of the items I am carrying, together with the onset of rain. This road is a busy main road flanked by twentieth century urban and industrial sprawl. It is a completely different world from the historic centre and yet it is the same city.

Finally, I reach the bus station. I easily purchase my ticket and obtain a timetable. There is a departure at five minutes to midday. If I miss that bus, there will be another half an hour later. I make a mental note of bus stop number eight, from where the bus leaves. Everything is organised – well, almost organised.

A five-minute walk brings me to the *Conservatorio*. I place my mandolin case, bag and the carrier bag down in a space near the porter's office. It is possible to leave luggage at our own risk; a very useful service that seems strange and outmoded to me, living with excessive security precautions in London. I chat with the lady porter, explaining that I have an appointment with the secretary to collect a certificate and then I will be returning to England via the bus and Marco Polo airport. I mention the fragile gift and she finds a safe corner for it. She is so kind and accommodating. I was afraid that she and the gentleman porter might be confused by my appearance as today is not a mandolin teaching day and also because I haven't visited the *Conservatorio* during this academic year. However, they recognised me from yesterday and from the concert on Saturday. Everything is fine and I am properly organised for the morning.

After breakfast at the *Caffè Eremitani,* I head for the *Musei Civici Eremitani*, the *Eremitani* Civic Museums, which are just across the road, next to the *Chiesa Eremitani*.

This collection of museums comprises of an archaeological museum on the ground floor and two art museums on the first floor. All three museums are brimming with enough treasures to last a day's viewing. I have only an hour to spare on my itinerary, so I immediately look for directions to the *Cappella degli Scrovegni*, a chapel that stands in the museum's grounds, and is the real object of my visit.

The *Cappella degli Scrovegni* contains a series of frescoes on the life of Christ and of the Virgin Mary, painted by Giotto. These frescoes are said to be Giotto's finest work and people come from all over the world to view them. The small chapel in which they are painted is situated in a cordoned off area of the public gardens, which I passed each time I walked from Padua station to the *Conservatorio*. Entrance is only possible through the collective museums. I had walked past this building dozens of times and, when I had stayed at my hotel, I had slept only a few hundred yards away from it, yet I had never found the right moment to visit. My visit today is the fulfilment of a long-held wish.

I by-pass a group of Japanese visitors with their guide and find myself alone on the path that leads to the chapel. The path is divided by rope and there are directions for visitors entering to keep to the right-hand side. I breathe in the cool, damp air. It is a luxury to be without crowds of people. Often, as I had passed the entrance to the museums early in the morning on my way to the *Conservatorio*, I had noticed several coaches parked in front of the Church of the *Eremitani*. Sometimes, the coaches contained parties of schoolchildren. At other times, they heralded an influx of tourists.

I open the door of the chapel and step inside. It is empty, except for the custodian. I am immediately struck by the beauty of the celestial blue, vaulted ceiling, jewelled with gold stars. The splendour of the heavens is intensified by the stillness of the building. I am filled with a sense of awe and wonder, which makes my body move slowly and reverently.

I begin to examine the frescoes one by one. I notice how effortlessly the angels seem to float over the *Nativity* scene. There are five of them and they are preoccupied in different ways. The central one is giving its attention to the crib. I say 'it' because it is difficult to know whether angels have gender. Recently, it has been the subject of much discussion in the letters page of the *Times*. Three other angels are looking towards heaven with gestures of praise and thanksgiving. An inverted angel at the right side of the group is greeting the shepherds with peace.

In the next scene, *The Adoration of the Magi*, I cannot help thinking how sultry Mary looks. This is not in anyway a disrespectful thought. She is a truly beautiful women who, had she lived in our times, would appear on the cover page of *Vogue*. I wonder who the model for Giotto's painting might have been. Perhaps an unobtainable Paduan noblewoman who he had viewed from afar at the Mass in the Basilica of St Anthony.

I am quite amazed by the realism of the pictures. I think of the style as Renaissance, but I read that the pictures were painted between 1303 and 1305, which means that part of Giotto's greatness lies in the fact that he was ahead of his time. Well ahead. Approximately one hundred years, in fact.

I particularly like the *Baptism* scene, in which the water is a muted emerald green. The bottom of Christ's body, but discreetly not his most private parts, together with some swimming fish are discernible most clearly through the water. It reminds me of another favourite fresco of mine, Jesus walking on the water, in the *Duomo* of San Gimignano. That fresco, painted seventy-five years later by Barna da Siena, also depicted fish in the water.

I love all the colours of these pictures. The reds, sometimes burgundy, sometimes terracotta and often a soft salmon pink. The blues and greens, opaque jewel colours, softened and subdued. Radiance is provided by the gold halos of the protagonists and the many angels. And perhaps the greatest radiance is displayed in the expression of the faces. In the *Resurrection of Christ*, when Mary Magdalene realises that the gardener is Christ, there is a wonderful human moment of longing and unfulfilled desire. Mary wants to touch her 'Master' and looks pleadingly with outstretched arms. But Jesus looks at her with a mixture of firmness and tender love that says that she must not touch him because he hasn't yet ascended. It is both powerfully beautiful and profoundly sad at the same moment.

After my contemplation of the frescoes, I walk to the *Piazza delle Erbe* and I saunter through the arcades of the *Palazzo della Ragione*. The *Palazzo* is a huge civic building bearing a resemblance to the Palladio building of the same name at Vicenza and with a roof that reminds me of an airship. The arcades at the base of this medieval building house shops specialising in various food delicacies. There are shops filled with various local cheeses and cold meats. There are butchers, bakers and wine merchants. There is a fishmonger, a fresh pasta shop and a butcher who specialises only in chicken. It is a paradise for food and drink connoisseurs.

Outside, the market stalls are heavily laden and artistically arranged with fruit and vegetables. The damp air conveys an intoxicating cocktail of smells. There are at least half a dozen different types of salad leaves, bulbs of fennel, carrots, cauliflower, spinach, apples, pears and oranges. The colours are so vivid and everything looks vibrant and fresh. The different fragrances mingle, sometimes vying with each other for attention, and always beckoning my undivided attention.

I make a shopping list in my head. I choose the most enticing vegetables and decide upon the supper that I would cook if I was staying in Padua tonight and I had a kitchen at my disposal. It would probably be roast fennel with fresh pasta and a wonderful salad, including rocket leaves and shavings of raw carrot. The meal would conclude with pear and some local cheese, all washed down by local wine. I am very sorry that I am not staying. I linger for a moment, hoping to distil the images and smells into my consciousness so that I can recall them at will when I return to England.

Now it is time for morning coffee and my visit to the famous *Caffè Pedrocchi*. I am enjoying my morning as a tourist and the luxury of being alone with only myself to please. I feel truly liberated in a way that I have rarely felt on my previous visits. In the past, there has often been some obligation, a deadline, or a worry, either real or imagined, which has interfered with my peace of mind and my ability to enjoy the moment. This morning, I gave myself permission to have a few hours off, undisturbed. For a short while, I am without restrictions. It is in this spirit that I decide to order a hot chocolate, without cream, instead of a cappuccino.

The *Caffè Pedrocchi* is an Italian version of the Pump Room at Bath, without the live music. A place to be seen in. A place to while away time in. A meeting place for mature female shoppers. A place of celebration and, above all, a place of luxury.

My *cioccolata in tazza* is exactly what it says, chocolate in a cup. It is not so much a drink, but rather a bar of the highest quality chocolate, which has been melted in my cup, or so it seems judging from the viscosity. It is thick, rich and creamy, but not too sweet, and I detect a hint of coconut in its flavour. It is moreish and extremely good. I place my chilled fingers gently around the cup and contemplate this most luxurious of beverages introduced in Baroque times.

As I sip my molten chocolate, I survey the surroundings. Classical marble columns trimmed with gold decoration, high ceilings, mirrors, chandelier lighting, marble floor, plum velvet upholstered chairs and white damask tablecloths. I try to absorb every detail and whilst I am doing this, chatter echoes around the vast space.

It is eleven o'clock. Half an hour has elapsed in what seems like just a few minutes. I return to the *Conservatorio* to collect my certificate. Everything is in order and I am content. I visit the ladies' room and collect my luggage from the porter.

As I am rearranging a few items in my bag, a voice says, "*Ciao*." I wasn't expecting to see anybody I know today. It is one of the mandolin students, the young man from Breganze. He is here today for a piano lesson. We have a chat. I tell him that I am about to depart on foot for the bus, which will take me directly to Venice airport. I will be back in England in a few hours. He asks when I will return. Soon, I tell him, probably for Giovanna's wedding.

"Until the next time then," he says, and we take our leave of each other.

"*Alla prosimma volta*," I murmur: until the next time then.

I have become inextricably linked with Italy. Whatever the frequency or duration of my future visits, I know that they will never cease. My commuting to the *Conservatorio*, the four years of formalised study, was just an intense phase in my continuing relationship with Italy. It will never let me go and I will never let it go.

Update

October 2008

> *'Attending the International Mandolin Symposium in Trossingen, Germany, is always a pleasure for a mandolin anorak like me.'*

I have just finished typing the first sentence of my article for a mandolin newsletter. I am quite pleased with my start. I continue to type.

> *'Mandolin talk starts casually over muesli and coffee first thing in the morning and then continues effortlessly until the small hours of the morning when you try to peel yourself away to bed having sampled a few glasses of the local wine or beer. The in-between time is punctuated by talks and concerts when there is a rest from talking, although not from thinking about the mandolin. The six hours left over and available for sleeping seem to pose no problem. Usually I need at least eight hours but during the symposium I am on a kind of mandolin high which gives my body more than enough energy to cope – well at least until I return home, collapsing and in need of some recovery time!'*

Quite a nice first paragraph! I'm on a roll now.

As I go on to outline the stories of the various teaching projects from around the globe that were presented, I can't help thinking how far the mandolin has come in such a short time. When I first started playing the mandolin, the novelty factor attracted a lot of my work. People were curious to see something different at a concert. Now I teach children in mainstream schools and just the other year one of my pupils passed GCSE music with an A★ using the mandolin for her performance. Even the way music education has changed is incredible. Not too long ago, music was treated like other academic subjects and involved loads of essay writing and theoretical study. Now, the practical element is an integral part of study and assessment. The same has happened in further education, so that most degrees are practical as well as academic. All of which brings me to the Bologna process.

Outside, the wind rustles in the pear tree at the bottom of the garden. It is really in my neighbour's garden, but it somehow feels as if it is in my garden. I notice how the leaves flash pomegranate and cranberry reds edged with gold foil. The colours are remarkable this year, just like the trees I saw last week in Germany. One of my pupils said that the weather has been perfect for good colours this autumn!

Mmm... the Bologna process. A few clicks of the mouse and I am at the official website.

Ironically, in a strange twist of fate, I learnt at the symposium that something called the Bologna process means that the mandolin diplomas are being changed to become degrees along the lines of British degrees. This is happening throughout Europe for all subjects, so there will be parity and transparency between the qualifications of different countries. In Italy and Germany, they are also introducing a new qualification for the mandolin, the Master's degree, again along the lines of the British model.

What this means is that I am already qualified with my Master's degree in mandolin performance, which I got sixteen years ago. Despite never finding quite the right moment to take the final exam in Italy, it seems, strangely, that I am already one of the most qualified people in Europe and I certainly possess a groundbreaking qualification which everyone now understands and values.

There are so many things I have learnt from the mandolin lesson, other than how to play the mandolin. And now, another lesson: I relinquished my attachment to obtaining the qualification, the piece of paper, only to find that it has come to me, and that, in fact, I had possessed it all along.

Glossary

Andantino: literally a small andante; andante meaning moving. Andante is usually a slow piece and andantino might be a touch faster or slower.

Appoggiatura: a leaning note which is written very small in comparison with the normal sized written note. It is a decoration which takes half the time of the big note next to it.

Arpeggios: chords in which the notes are played separately, one after another.

Broken thirds: notes that are three notes apart, or next door but one to each other, played separately. A really lovely pattern.

Cadence: punctuation in music, the full stops and commas etc.

Cadenza: a bit of solo improvisation often found in a concerto.

Chords: a group of two or more notes all played together at the same time.

Concerto: a kind of musical conversation between a solo instrument and a big group of orchestral instruments.

Dominant seventh: a type of chord with a seventh added and which gives you the feeling of moving on somewhere.

Fugato: in the style of a fugue where many voices or tunes all sound at once and yet seem to go together. A bit like different conversations at a party which somehow seem to blend together.

Fugue: see fugato.

Harmony: notes which when played at the same time sound sweet.

Largo: broad, slow piece.

Octaves: two notes played together, which are eight notes apart, counting the lower note as one.

Partitas: music for a single instrument, made up of a tune with variations and based on dances (sixteenth – seventeenth century).

Preludes: a beginning piece, historically church organ tuning pieces. The organist would play an improvisation using lots of scales and arpeggios, which were really to check whether the instrument was in tune.

Semiquavers: quite fast notes, four can be played during a single beat.

Sevenths: two notes played together, seven notes apart, counting the lower one as one.

Scales: a series of notes, which move by steps.

Sharp sign: looks a bit like the hash symbol on the telephone and used in music to raise a note by half a step.

Sixths: two notes played together, six notes apart, counting the lower one as one.

Tremolo: the trembling effect characteristic to the mandolin when a note is repeated very fast to sustain the sound.

Trill: two notes rapidly alternating.

Notes

[1] Charles Burney, *The Present State of Music in France and Italy*, Facsimile of 1773 London Edition, 1969, New York, Broude Brothers, P.120